EXORCISING DEVILS FROM THE THRONE

EXORCISING DEVILS FROM THE THRONE

SÃO TOMÉ AND PRÍNCIPE IN THE
CHAOS OF DEMOCRATIZATION

ALBERTINO FRANCISCO AND NUJOMA AGOSTINHO

Algora Publishing
New York

Library of Congress Cataloging-in-Publication Data —

Francisco, Albertino, 1976-
    Exorcising devils from the throne: São Tomé and Príncipe in the chaos of
democratization / Albertino Francisco and Nujoma Agostinho.
        p. cm.
    Includes bibliographical references and index.
    ISBN-13: 978-0-87586-846-2 (soft cover : alk. paper)
    ISBN-10: 0-87586-846-0 (soft cover : alk. paper)
    ISBN-13: 978-0-87586-847-9 (hard cover : alk. paper)
    ISBN-10: 0-87586-847-9 (hard cover : alk. paper)
    [etc.]
    1. São Tomé and Príncipe —Politics and government. 2. Democratization—
São Tomé and Príncipe . I. Agostinho, Nujoma, 1976- II. Title.
    JQ3685.A91F73 2011
    967.1502—dc22
                                    2011004661

Printed in the United States

Even if all other rights were denied to me, I would always remain free to think.

Prey is confronted by Predator, who is armed to the teeth, ready to attack. In order to fend off Predator, Prey sets a trap. At the right moment, Predator pounces, falls into the trap, and is caught.

"Oh, stop, why all the violence! Don't you think it's better to talk? Violence gets us nowhere!" exclaims Predator, who then begins to call for negotiations, as a democratic right.

Prey, a supporter of democracy, agrees in principle. Now, Prey has to decide whether to release Predator and initiate a dialogue. Yet, nowhere is it written that a predator should not eat its prey—so what happens if he frees Predator?

TABLE OF CONTENTS

INTRODUCTION

Exorcising Devils from the Throne: São Tomé and Príncipe in the Chaos of Democratization is an in-depth portrait of the island nation of São Tomé and Principe (STP). As a political treatise it examines the socio-political problems specific to STP, censures those who have caused or exacerbated those problems, proposes solutions, and calls for greater public awareness, discussing the policies and the individuals most responsible for an entire nation's despair and poverty. While bitterly honest, we aim to inspire enthusiasm in the readers for a beautiful, refined and vulnerable country which has slowly become lost in a battle of politics and private interests. Our main aims are to improve governance, promote development, and to protect human rights—and all of this through the promotion of civil society.

This Edition

The publication of the first edition of *Exorcising Devils from the Throne* brought us clear signs that there was real interest in such a book; in addition, it became possible to reorganize and enrich the work. Thus the 2nd Edition includes recent developments and trends in STP's socio-political situation and the amount of information has been increased significantly; the book has assumed a new analytical and political viewpoint, and has been rewritten with a more academic focus including endnotes, deeper analysis, authoritative references, and a bibliography.

The International Context

Today's major international challenges, whether social, economic, cultural, political, ecological, or scientific, frequently evolve into diplomatic and even military conflicts between the developed and "emerging" countries on the one hand and the developing world on the other. The so-called G-20—developed and "emerging" countries—together represent 90% of world GDP, 80% of world trade (including intra-EU) and two thirds of world population. The economic importance and representativeness of the G-20 gives it significant influence over the management of the financial system and global economy. Where does the African continent fit in? Africa remains, as always, a target of greed from the great international powers, representing both the largest source of raw materials and a vast market for selling the excess of products manufactured worldwide. Therefore, it is a matter of international concern that Africa remains in a state of social, economic and political backwardness.

Working with great cunning through the Bretton Woods institutions and the United Nations system, the international community and especially the developed nations have forced social, political and economic reforms in the black continent, aimed at forcing the adoption of multiparty democracy and the consequent decentralization of political power, which, in brief, has led the countries to the state of social chaos, internal divisions and tribal conflicts, as well as a rapid deterioration of the nascent economy. Any political power installed in the continent that is not shaped to the style of liberal multiparty democracy is quickly rebuked by the international community, which has always resulted in its overthrow. However, the results of democratization have left much to be desired.

This fact raises the question whether the current democratic system is indeed the best option for Africa. The answer is no. An analysis by Kataria (2010) of 150 countries, each with at least one million inhabitants, proves this thesis. Underdeveloped countries perform better when governed by centralist political regimes and perform chaotically when the system adopted is democratic. For example, DR Congo, Nigeria, Kenya, South Africa, Iraq, Iran, Pakistan, Bangladesh, Sri Lanka, Nepal, Thailand, Philippines, and India are countries where centralized political regimes have alternated with democratic regimes. All in all, democracy paved the way for an escalation of violence, destruction, rape, and weak economic and social development. In general, in the developing world, countries that are more successfully governed (for instance, in Africa, the Northern countries; in Asia, China) owe their performance to centralization of power, not to democracy. Democracy has been vector of civil wars and chaos; it has failed miserably in most of Africa, often leading to internal divisions and tragic humanitarian crises. Africa lacks stability and a political system suited to its socio-economic reality. Kataria further argues that it was not Africa that led democracy to bankruptcy, but democracy that has failed Africa.

Democracy performs well in developed countries but not in developing countries. Why? According to Kataria, what makes democracy unattractive for underdeveloped countries is their poverty and lack of education. She argues that democracy and poverty together lead to bankruptcy. Two or three centuries ago, Western Europe and the Americas were composed of countries with situations similar to those of underdeveloped countries today. In both cases, the progress of democracy followed the economic development, where possible, i.e., gradually, and it helped ensure stability and growth. The right to vote was expanded gradually as the economic power and education level of the populations increased. Thus, voting has been tied to economic emancipation. For this reason, democracy was established with great success in the United States and Western Europe. By contrast, when democracy was instituted in France in 1789, within a poor population with a very limited exposure to the larger world, the results were the same as those of underdeveloped countries today. In Spain, the democratic regime which preceded the dictatorship of Francisco Franco in the mid-1900s led the country to disastrous results, whereas his "dictatorship" led the country to rapid industrialization and relative stability. Similar results have been recorded around the globe.

What is relevant is that political power is only meaningful when it follows economic power. By itself, the right to vote is not a power.

In fact, when implemented prematurely, elections can lead to abuse and subversions. Society must follow certain procedures for social democracy to work. The mechanical juxtaposition of a formal constitution and elections by themselves—which many developing countries, including STP, have tried—does not generate progressive democracy. Additionally, as history has proven, science and reason rather than dogma and religion are key factors. Society must first follow a social and intellectual revolution to succeed with democracy. However, even so, if poor and semi-literate people constitute the majority, democracy does not work. Widespread poverty must be reduced first, perhaps through a decentralized market economy, but not decentralized political power or a democracy. Models of centralized powers and unitary states, despite their weaknesses, have been proposed as effective for developing countries. Wealth must be created and distributed, and there must be a strong middle class, prior to instituting democracy, because democracy of the poor is subversive and self-destructive.

The current division of the world into two blocs—the G20 vs. underdeveloped countries—creating economic dependency on the black continent, has been pushing the adoption of deep structural reforms and strengthening of democratic institutions in that continent. While for the wealthy, democracy can be understood as a blessing resulting in transparency, stability, economic and social progress, respect for human rights and other guarantees for people, in underdeveloped countries it has led to social backlash and economic decline. In many underdeveloped countries, such as the DRC, the process of democratization has opened social and economic wounds that will take time to be healed.

The Regional Context: The Gulf of Guinea

Speaking of Africa and its resources, a particular region has held the attention of the world owing to its large oil reserves and marine resources—the Gulf of Guinea. And it is precisely in this location that a small but nevertheless important country is located: São Tomé and Principe.

This country lies exactly at the point where the two main geographic references of the international location system cross: the Prime

Meridian (zero longitude) and the Equator (zero latitude). In other words, we are talking about a country which is geographically located in one of four central points of the Earth's hemispheres. The country has lush virgin rainforests which occupy approximately 30% of its territory and an enormous range of endemic plants and animals. It is extremely beautiful and can be suitable for development as a tourist destination. Thus based on geostrategic and economic considerations and due to its ecology, environment and natural reserves, STP has not escaped notice in the eyes of the world. Important development opportunities and resources exist but they have not been exploited; the country is now one of the most economically poor and underdeveloped in the world.

It is not the international context that is to blame for this sad condition. Due to its geographical location, its small size—both in terms of population and in terms of territorial extent—its climate, its pristine nature, and the enormous quantity and variety of natural resources, this country has been coveted by all. Even in the era of the Cold War, the country maintained relationships with both the Socialist Bloc and the Capitalist Bloc; it did not lack partners or opportunities to sign profitable economic agreements. What it lacked, indeed, was the sense of urgency, the knowledge and intelligence to make good on these opportunities—nothing more. However, there is someone we can blame—oh yes: the political leaders and the installed regime.

The Local Context

For over three decades, since its independence from Portugal in 1975, São Tomé has been a model of the worst possible economic and socio-political performance. Stories from STP have dominated headlines for bad reasons only: coups d'état, successive Government changes, poverty, corruption, poor economic and performance and Government scandal, and the like. The ambiguous provisions of the semi-presidential constitution with regard to the roles of the different state organs have provided fertile ground for conflict concerning areas of responsibilities and resource competition between the President and the Government, which have subsequently provoked various Government changes: thirteen different prime ministers and respective Government changes in fifteen years from 1991 to 2006. The consequent political instability has negatively affected the socio-economic development of this country, which has already been marked by poor institutional capacities and corruption among office holders.

Scholars agree that, as a result of STP's dependence on foreign aid and loans, STP has been what they term an "unviable state," even before the end of the Cold War, and ever since. There is also agreement concerning failures of public policy and weaknesses of the local economy.

The democratic process in STP has dived into a profound crisis. The country has been continuously shaken by a wave of scandals involving corruption (such as the recent scandals involving GGA, CGI, ENASA, STP-Trading and Oil negotiations, to name a few), and several high-ranking authorities have been summoned to appear in court. There has also been a long-running disagreement between the political parties in the country and the presidency and Government concerning allegations of corruption within the oil sector which have involved highly-ranked former and present Government officials.

The extraordinary close interconnections within the socio-political elite have facilitated the generalization of corruption and lack of accountability. This situation is even more extreme than those observed in other African countries because, due to the small size of the country, trafficking of influences can be kept within a small socio-political elite. Nevertheless, there is a whole dimension—a context—which acts behind the scenes, which is the socio-political performance in mainland Africa and the wide range of support that STP's political elite receive from the outside world—especially from various internationally-known corrupt governments.

Other nations have an interest in keeping the people of STP either under-educated or off-island. Those nations are giving the "leaders" money—or otherwise seducing them—in order to entice them into betraying their own people; at the same time, they are constantly seeking to benefit from oil-related contracts.

Recent corruption scandals connected with the signing of agreements with oil companies serve as excellent examples. Furthermore, successive governments—of which there are many—have admitted that their respective predecessors were involved in illegal agreements with such companies; however, neither the President nor the successive governments show the will to seriously prosecute those involved. This may be due to the fact that all have common interests; and quarrels can easily be resolved with the signing of new agreements. On a short-term basis, the removal of various individuals from the political landscape provides benefits to whomever is in power; nevertheless, in the long term, this can be harmful. Rather, for the underlying elite it is always better to leave the possibility open for future negotiations within their own ranks than to ever risk the emergence of a new movement, in opposition to the existing system, which would fundamentally represent the most marginalized social groups.

The lack of understanding of democratic ideals combined with the failure to adopt democratic institutions has caused the state to fail to conform with each of its four main purposes, which are: 1) to build a free, just and solitary society; 2) to guarantee national development; 3) to eradicate poverty and marginalization, as well as to reduce social and regional inequalities; and 4) to promote wellbeing for all, without discrimination on the basis of origin, race, sex, color, age, etc.

So far, the socio-political performance has been appalling, which leads to incompleteness and the fragility of the social, economic, political and institutional structures. There is not a consistent or even real sense of the concepts of state and nation. STP is a peculiar society in which one pretends to live in an established state, but the very idea of a nation and nationality is vague and diffused. The profound irresponsibility of politicians and Government officials has led the country to make fatal errors in international relationships which have restrained sovereignty and all other democratic principles. Furthermore, new generations have inherited an awful foreign debt, whilst Government officials have secured huge fortunes for themselves and their relatives, invested outside of the country. Consequently, for the majority of the population at least, the above-mentioned state goals still appear to be nothing more than a mirage.

The negligence and frivolous behavior on the part of the country's departments is another subject for discussion. There is a widespread feeling that professional service officials need not care about accountability; there are no moral or legal obligations to deontological norms. And because the São Toméan people no longer believe in improvement or better performance, they seem unable to strive for improvement. Furthermore, the state of human development in the country, or lack of it, is dramatic despite the economic opportunities in the archipelago.

All of this is a consequence of decades of deception carried out by state office holders.

STP does suffer a scarcity of basic resources—fresh water, salt, and the like—and the enormous economic vulnerability is accentuated by inadequate management. In addition, there is the glaring absence of policies, and of economic actors which, when they do exist, are feeble and ineffective. In the field of education, for instance, there is a decline in teaching quality due to the falling capacity—both physical and technical—with regard to school accommodation, such as the limited number of classrooms and consequent overcrowding, as well as the insufficient qualification and lack of interest amongst teachers.

Notably, some 50% of all teachers in the primary education field and more than 80% in the secondary education field lack appropriate qualifications. In a country with so many economic problems deriving from a lack of qualifications and training concerning economic agents, public officers and civil servants, the lack of attention given to the education sector is worsened still further by the lack of educational policies; moreover, less than 10% of the state budget is appointed to education, whilst a miniscule 0.4% of GNP is allocated for primary education.

In addition, given its unidirectional nature, the national educational system faces many more constraints at the end of the pre-university course; there is a stark lack of access to technical and vocational training. And where there are some embryonic training initiatives—whether technical, vocational or higher education—they lead nowhere, so that the youths of the current generation face serious fulfillment problems, both in terms of training and employment, which can only result in widespread frustration, discontentment, and revolt. As the situation seems to be worsening, the many occasional docents, forced by circumstances to annual recruitment, consequently manifest their rebellion through simple attitudes, words and actions.

The decline of the principal healthcare indicators is evident: food security and increasing poverty are real threats, all of which generate fear amongst the population, which is growing faster than the economy. The number of people living in extreme poverty is increasing alarmingly, whilst the number of poor people as a whole totals approximately 54% of the population. Even investments realized in the economic ground—some which are, without argument, considerably large scale—have not reaped the expected results. The degradation of the population's quality of life is all the more unsettling given the absence of a social security system.

With less than four decades as a sovereign state, the people of STP have little sense of nationhood. A kind of mental infantilism prevents the nation from defining appropriate state administration guidelines. To date, the nation has not been able to form a government of sufficiently responsible and qualified people to build suitable state organizations to govern and to steer the course toward sustainable development.

When discussing governance and human security, signs of a dogmatic lack of common sense are evident. Ultimately, governmental and institutional stability appear to be unattainable. Institutional weaknesses have hampered the process of confirming the citizen's liberal and democratic guarantees, showing up the inadequacies of the country's politico-administrative divisions, the insufficiencies of the constitution, the lack of stability and inadequate continuity of Government action. Juridical and institutional weaknesses are derived from inefficient political decision-making, the absence of clear sectored policies and the inefficiency of the public administration.

A sense of impunity reins, and a persistent lack of both obedience to and application of the law, which make it difficult to exercise civil and political rights and impede the effective protection of the citizens' legitimate interests. As well as in other domains, we observe here several forms of discrimination, where women, for example, are still prohibited from attending major decision centers (or are given minimal representation).

The nation is in a condition of widespread crisis. Many people now believe that the current situation is inescapable; this is a chronic cynicism which fundamentally erodes people's souls and minds, discouraging all attempts at finding solutions. It is urgent and vital that the São Toméan people begin to make up for lost time, acting in order to resurrect the country as a welfare, sovereign and transparent state which serves the legitimate interests of its citizens.

Is the current democratic system the best option for the country? The answer is no; the evidence proves otherwise. In the historical perspective, STP was better at times when it was ruled by centralized political regimes (Seibert 2001). Despite limitations in terms of individual rights such as freedom of speech and press, and certain civil rights recorded in centralized political systems, economic and social performance has been better than those recorded in the current democratic regime. This constitutes a factual proof that underdeveloped countries perform better when governed by centralist political regimes and have a chaotic performance when the system adopted is democratic (Kataria 2010).

The Contents of the Book

This edition is divided into three parts. In *Part One: Paradise and Hell on Earth*, as in the first edition, we present a complete picture of the country (the territory, people and its history) and provide a portrait of the political class, referring to the faith of people and the sins committed by the ruling government. In *Part Two: Performing So Badly*, we provide a description of the status and behaviors of the political class, and accordingly conduct an economic analysis of the country from a chronological perspective from the start of Independence in 1975 until the present day. We further give great prominence to the issue of oil exploration in the country, the fraudulent contracts signed with oil companies, and the strange partnerships with agencies and external entities. In *Part Three: Rising from the Dead*, we approach the national and international context in which the country and the people operate, and the character of political leaders.

Then we propose a new system of beliefs and values for the country, and we propose ways to rethink the current political system and to design a new one. Here, we suggest alternatives capable of reversing the situation by establishing a *New State System* (NSS) in an incitement to a socio-political revolution which would culminate with the displacement of the political class from power, and the establishment of a new regime, inspired by the people.

Methodology/Analytical Approach

This work is a result of intensive documentary research and direct observation. Both public and private data sources were consulted. The variety of sources together fulfilled all or at least some of the principles of authenticity, consistency, credibility, plausibility/representativeness, and were backed by facts. Sources included data centers such as the Biblioteca Nacional (STP's National Library), the Arquivo Histórico (STP's Historical Archive), the UN Library in São Tomé, and the Biblioteca da Assembleia (STP's Government Library), as well as numerous online information sources including local and foreign online newspapers, journals, and institutional web sites. However, consideration is also given to undocumented data or information which is observable even if otherwise not recorded, particularly signs and trends of the structural phenomena which impact socio-political performance. In order to gain knowledge and understanding of these socio-political factors, such data were accessed and/or gathered through the means of direct observation.

PART ONE: PARADISE AND HELL ON EARTH

CHAPTER I: THE PROMISED LAND

In a very real sense, the authors are personally convinced that a paradise on Earth does exist, and we will attempt to portray this to you: It resides in a country called São Tomé and Principe, a tiny archipelago of 1,001 square kilometers (386.5 square miles) of land and 206,178 (July 2008 est.) total inhabitants. It lies at the very heart of the world, located in the equatorial Atlantic just off the northwest coast of Gabon, and is crossed by the Equator Line and the meridian of Greenwich, which means that both its latitudinal and longitudinal coordinates measure 0 degrees. Whoever would have thought that the location of Heaven could be given with such precision?

The coast line of this beautiful country is 209 kilometers (130 miles). São Tomé is 50 kilometers (31 miles) long and 32 kilometers (20 miles) wide, and is the more mountainous of the two islands. Its peaks reach 2,024 meters (6,640 feet). There are sixteen other rocky islets, including Bombom, Caroço, Bjoné de Jockey, and Tinhosas off Principe Island, Santana, Sete Pedras, and Rolas off São Tomé Island. Principe is approximately 30 kilometers (19 miles) long and 6 kilometers (4 miles) wide, and the Equator lies immediately south of São Tomé Island, passing through the islet of Ilhéu das Rolas. Both islands are part of an extinct volcanic mountain range—the Cameroon volcanic mountain line—which also includes the islands of Annobón to the southwest, Bioko to the northeast (both parts of Equatorial Guinea), and Mount Cameroon on the African west coast. São Tomé, the sizable southern island, is situated just north of the Equator.

At sea level, the climate is tropical—hot and humid with average yearly temperatures of around 27°C (80°F) and little daily variation; temperatures rarely rise beyond 32°C. At the higher altitudes, the average yearly temperature still reaches 20°C (68°F), and nights are generally cool. Annual rainfall varies from 5 m (200 inches) on the southwestern slopes to 1 m (40 in) in the northern lowlands. The rainy season runs from October to May. For most of the São Tomé and Príncipe area, conditions are standard equatorial: unwavering heat and humidity. Several microclimates also exist, particularly on São Tomé Island, where the north has a drier, savannah-like climate, and the south receives much more rain, even during the dry season.

The driest and coolest months are from June to September, when temperatures hover at around 22°C. The rest of the year is muggy and hot, with residents and visitors swimming in rain and their own sweat. Temperatures rise to around 30°C (86°F) in March, which is also the wettest month.

There are only three seasons—*Chuvas* (the rainy season), *Gravana* (the long dry season), and *Gravanito* (the short dry season)—giving variations between 22–32°C during the year. The republic's climate is maritime equatorial tropical, which is hot and humid; the climate of the island of Príncipe is more humid than that of São Tomé. The real difference is made up by the several climatic zones, and the island of São Tomé is divided into several of these climatic zones; additionally, you will find various microclimates on both islands of São Tomé and Príncipe, which are thus home to a wide range of heavenly flora and fauna.

STP is the second smallest African country in terms of population (with the Seychelles having the smallest population). It is the smallest country in the world which was not previously an overseas territory of the British Empire or the United States, or one of the European powers. It is also the smallest Portuguese-speaking country in the world.

Wherever you live, you have a share in this place: It is a land where there is no God, no law, and no king capable of restricting you; the only condition to claiming your share is that you are a human being. This place and its people enjoy an untouched and fertile land, a delightful tropical climate, a pollution-free environment, and centuries of peace and harmony lining its history books. The atmosphere is imbued with a sense of bliss and harmony.

The men here used to talk with nature using a special language, and the sea, sky, land, and air, as well as the animals and plants, all lived together as one family. This is perhaps the only place on Earth where the nature of things inside you changes dramatically as soon as you go through it, to such an extent that you actually stop breathing with your lungs and instead start breathing with your heart.

One may question whether or not God and the Devil created this country together. It appears to be the result of an odd relation between an angel from the Heavens and a devil from Hell, who have seemingly given birth to three children: *The São Toméan Land, the São Toméan People,* and *the São Toméan Government.* It seems that God and the Devil then wondered where to place all three, regarding their instinctive principle of fighting for the best possible equilibrium of good over evil. First, it seems that their parents decided to settle them in the center of the globe. The Land was then sketched, creating a tiny twin-island archipelago, rich and fertile. Then the People were added—lovely and young, a mix of all human races. And finally, the Government was established, and was the worst possible example of human misfortune.

A huge amount of crude oil was discovered here[1], and it forms a powerful treasury hidden beneath the tiny archipelago; moreover, 30% of the country is covered by a protected Atlantic high altitude rainforest, called Obô[2], which is crossed by rivers and waterfalls. Since 1998, this natural reserve has been considered by scientists as the second most important among 75 forests of Africa in terms of the diversity of fauna and flora and the number of endemic species[3]. One may well won-

---

1   See, for instance, BBC News, 'Oil key to Sao Tome,' http://news.bbc.co.uk/2/hi/africa/3070813.stm (accessed 03 30, 2010).

2   The Obo National Park, 'National Parks,' http://www.obopark.com/en/saotomeprincipe/nationalparks.html (accessed 03 30, 2010).

3   The Obo National Park, 'Conservation History,' http://www.obopark.com/fr/saotomeprincipe/nationalparks/conservation.html (accessed 03 30, 2010).

der whether it is possible—and, more to the point, recommended—for human beings to live in such a tiny, remote and fragile place.

Two Pieces of Land, One National Unit

Separated by the sea, São Tomé Island (population 199,993 [July 2008 est.], area 859 km²) and Principe Island (population 6,185 inhabitants [July 2008 est.], area 142 km²,) are two gorgeous pieces of land that form one national unit: The Democratic Republic of São Tomé and Principe. It is administratively divided into seven districts: Água Grande, Cantagalo, Caué, Lembá, Lobata, and Mé-Zóchi in the São Tomé Island (where the capital is the city of São Tomé), and Pagué in Principe Island (whose capital is Santo Antonio). Since April 29, 1995, the last island became an autonomous region. It is enshrined in the constitution that both the districts and the autonomous region should be governed by elected municipal bodies. The governing councils in each district maintain a limited number of autonomous decision-making powers and, according to the constitution, should be re-elected every 3 years[4].

The political scene of São Tomé and Principe takes place within a framework of a semi-presidential republic representative democracy, whereby the President of the Republic is the head of state and the Prime Minister is the head of both Government and a multiparty system. The Executive power is exercised by the Government and the Legislative power is vested in both the Government and the National Assembly. The Judiciary is independent of the Executive and the Legislative. São Tomé and Principe has functioned under a multiparty system since 1990. After the promulgation of a new constitution in 1990, the country held multiparty elections for the first time since independence. Shortly after the constitution came into force, the National Assembly formally legalized opposition political parties. Independent candidates also were permitted to participate in legislative elections in January 1991.

---

4   However, although the constitution provided that the local and regional authorities should be governed by elected bodies at regular intervals, so far only two local and regional elections in STP have been carried out: The first one took place on 6 December 1992 and the second on 9 July 2006. The President of the Republic of STP, Fradique de Menezes, set the date for the forthcoming local and regional elections for 25 July 2010.

The President of the Republic is elected for a period of five years by direct universal suffrage and secret ballot, and can hold up to two consecutive terms. Candidates are chosen by their party's national conference (or individual can be run independently). A presidential candidate must obtain an outright majority of the popular vote in a first or second round of voting to be elected President. The Prime Minister is appointed by the President but must be ratified by the majority party and, thus, the appointed Prime Minister normally comes from a list of the majority party's choice. The Prime Minister, in turn, indicates the names of 14 members of the cabinet.

The National Assembly has 55 members elected for four years from seven multi-member constituencies by proportional representation. It is the supreme state organ and the highest legislative body, and meets every six months. Justice is administered at the highest level by the Supreme Court. Formerly responsible to the National Assembly, the Judiciary is now independent under the new constitution.

Since the constitutional reforms of 1990 and the elections of 1991, São Tomé and Príncipe has made great strides toward developing its democratic institutions and further guaranteeing the civil and human rights of its citizens. The São Toméans have freely changed their government through peaceful and transparent elections, and although there have been disagreements and political conflicts within the government agencies and the National Assembly, the quarrels were conducted and resolved in the open, "democratically" and under "legal proceedings," in accordance with the state's provisions—although not transparently, which calls into question the legitimacy of the final verdicts[5]. A number of political parties take part in the Government and express their views openly. Press freedom is (seemingly) respected, and there are several independent newspapers in addition to the Government bulletin.

After talking a bit about how the territory is divided and ruled by men, we can go back to talking about higher matters: the natural beauty. The small, friendly population inhabiting these comforting and restful islands ensures that visitors can experience heaven according to their own dreams in the microcosm of this unique island world. A significant percentage of this island paradise remains untouched by hu-

---

5 We'll talk about this issue in depth in later chapters.

man hands since it was shaped by nature; therefore, like the sea explorers of five centuries ago, all mankind still has the good fortune to taste a piece of virgin world far from the massive destruction humans are known for and to revel in the incomparable beauty of these nature-rich islands.

This is a unique place in the world where a person can escape the crowds and dive into tropical jungles with marvelous trees, flowers, extensive cocoa plantations, exotic birds found nowhere else in the world, dramatic landscapes of torrents and waterfalls, remote golden, black and white sand beaches, and sheer sea cliffs. You can climb ancient volcanic mountains in the rainforest, snorkel in crystalline waters, heighten the level of bliss with a strong, frosty drink next to a soft sunset, sip what is considered to be the best coffee in the world, and experience a culture which is a mix of those of Africa, Europe, America, and Asia.

Though all portrayals that are made regarding São Tomé Island are also true for Principe Island, this small oasis has far more to discuss. Fully 70% of its territory is covered by primary forest[6] that can be visited on foot, by all-terrain vehicle or boat. Just an hour from Gabon and Cameroon, only seven hours from Europe, the tropical island of Principe is a virtually undiscovered paradise in the Atlantic Ocean, north-east of São Tomé. Whales sport off unspoiled, deserted beaches, crystal-clear waterfalls cascade into the azure blue ocean, and the people are, above all, friendly and happy to meet newcomers. Principe is a sensational place to relax, dive, fish or turn adventurous. In this irregular scattering of soaring volcanic peaks, up to 20% of the trees, orchids and birds are said to be endemic. It has still been barely touched by the island's 6,000 inhabitants—or the damaging outside world.

A Heterogeneous People in Essence, One National Unit in Feeling

The population is a unique fusion of people from Africa, Europe, Asia, and America. The São Toméan culture of dance, music, art and food clearly shows how this perfect composition of elements from all

---

6   Africa's Eden, 'São Tomé & Príncipe,' 2010. http://www.africas-eden.com/Sao-Tome--Principe.asp (accessed 03 31, 2010).

four corners of the world merges together harmoniously and exquisite-ly. The population's growth rate is one of the highest in the world: 3.1%; the birth rate: 5.8 per one thousand; infant mortality rate: 37.12 per one thousand; life expectancy at birth: 68.2 years; density per square mile: 538. São Tomé and Principe is a country of young people with 46.9% of the population below the age of 15, and just 3.5% of the population older than 64 years[7].

Basically, there are five ethnic groups: the *Forros*[8], who are most-ly descents of ancient African slaves freed in the nineteenth century and Creole families who prominently featured in the history of the is-lands in the seventeenth to nineteenth centuries; the *Angolares*[9], who live in the south of the São Tomé Island; the *Monkos*[10], originals from the Principe Island; and the *Tongas*[11], descendants of plantation work-ers brought from Angola, Cape Verde and Mozambique in the first half of the twentieth century. Over 80% of the people claim to be Roman Catholic, with less than 3% Evangelical Christians and 1% Seventh Day Adventists. With these figures in mind, there are twelve Catholic par-ishes and a cathedral in the capital, with the roots of Catholicism dat-ing back to the fifteenth century.

That being said, as part of their African religious heritage, most São Toméans believe that the spirits of the dead are never disconnected from the world of the living. There remains a bond which requires the living to remember and propitiate the dead. Misfortune is often attrib-uted to spirits of the dead who may have been forgotten or not propiti-ated. And, whilst a spirit can reach a person who has emigrated and cause him or her illness and misfortune, it is believed that it remains bound to the island and to the place where he or she died. The most representative demonstration of this faith is the communal religious ritual called *Djamby*, in which an entire neighborhood or village gathers

---

7   Index Mundi, 'Sao Tome and Principe,' http://www.indexmundi.com/sao_tome_and_principe/ (accessed 04 1, 2010).

8   'Forro' means 'Free Men'.

9   'Angolares' comes from 'Ngola', meaning 'Angola' or 'who comes from Angola'.

10   'Monko' is for many people a pejorative name for the natives of the Island of Principe (*Monko* comes from the English word 'monkey' and means 'monkey'). Some people prefer the term 'Minu Iye', which means 'Son of the Island (of Principe).

11   The word 'Tonga' means 'a *mixed person*' or 'a person whose ancestors belong to different ethnic groups or races.'

to drum, dance, and witness spirit possession. Individuals can seek out a ritual specialist in order to obtain protection from rivals, restore their health, or gain the attention of a potential lover. On the *roças*[12], ritual specialists perform healing, divination, and spiritual protection.

There is a deep and widely held set of spiritist beliefs derived from the religions of African coastal societies. These beliefs are centered on the spirits of ancestors and spirits which reside in sacred places. Places containing the remains of hastily buried persons are considered dangerous, and people leave offerings to those spirits, permitting them to farm nearby. Spiritist rituals often center on healing and appeasing spirits who have been forgotten or wish to return to the world of the living.

Various people also belong to local religious brotherhoods, although there are few native priests, with most having emigrated from Europe. Religious festivals organized around the patron saints of towns and parishes are a feature of the annual religious calendar, and people tend to travel from other parts of the island to attend. Religious brotherhoods and sisterhoods play an important role in organizing these ceremonies and festivals. The most important Catholic rituals are baptism and the wake, followed by a funeral mass. Other sacraments are rarely observed.

On an archipelago with no locally produced consumer goods, travel and access to the outside world are symbols of high status. Educating one's children and shopping in Lisbon or Gabon are symbols of power and status. In addition, participation in traditional religious and dance societies is also a symbol of status which is being eclipsed by the adoption of the Western consumer culture.

A person who owns land in one of the small native holdings assures kin ties and the influence needed in order to secure state patronage. The old Forro families still control politics and resources. Achieved status through education is important but depends on patronage; for example, it is rare for poor people to advance through education alone. Thrift and hard work may advance the economic status of small farmers, traders and fishers, but their low status gives these people little

---

12   In STP, the term *'roça'* means *'rural village'* or *'rural community'*. It also means *'plantation'* or *'agricultural estate'*.

access to credit. Decades of economic stagnation and the fact that most resources are funneled through the state restrict people's opportunities to achieve social and economic mobility. Workers on the plantations are the most marginal citizens in social and economic terms.

Although separated by 150 miles of ocean, the people of the two islands of São Tomé and Principe keep intact the many ties that bind them. On both islands there are representations of all ethnic groups; there are groups speaking all national languages and expressing the same culture, values and symbols. However, recently, with the discovery of oil in the waters near the island of Principe, some opportunistic politicians have triggered the idea that these two peoples are not identical and that the island of Principe should seek independence to be able to follow its course as an independent country. For example, the online newspaper *Jornal de São Tomé (2003)* reported: "At the height of unrest that was experienced during the past week, one of the members of the Movement for the Liberation of São Tomé and Principe/Social Democratic Party (MLSTP/PSD), Simão Lavres, went so far as to admit possible independence for the smaller island, as pointed out yesterday in Lisbon's online newspaper Notícias Lusófonas (http://www.jornal. st/noticias.php?noticia=19)."[13] They do it with such conviction that they seem to have gained adherents among the natives of the island of Principe and their descendants, spread as they are across both islands and the Diaspora. Some people have even declared that the Island of Principe achieved independence in 1995 (see 29/04/1995: "The Island of Principe proclaimed its independence"[14] (http://fernandodeao55. spaces.live.com/).

Apart from this opportunistic idea fomented by short-sighted individuals without a vision or spirit of national cohesion, the islands of São Tomé and Príncipe are sisters; they form a single country by heart and are willing to walk together towards progress, overcoming all obstacles along the way.

---

13   Translated from Portuguese: 'No auge da agitação que se viveu durante a semana passada, um dos deputados do Movimento de Libertação de São Tomé e Príncipe/Partido Social Democrata, Simão Lavres, foi ao ponto de admitir uma eventual independência da ilha menor, conforme ontem recordava em Lisboa o jornal electrónico «Notícias Lusófonas»'.

14   Translated from Portuguese: '29/04/1995: A ilha do Príncipe proclamou a sua independência.'

One Nation, One History

There are several uncertainties regarding the discovery of the islands of STP. It is often assumed that the islands were uninhabited before the arrival of the Portuguese navigators João de Santarém and Pêro Escobar, sometime around 1470, but some authors argue that they were inhabited when the navigators arrived. The same uncertainty surrounds the dates of discovery, which are, at this point, assumed to be December 21 (St Thomas's Day) 1470 for São Tomé and January 17 (St Anthony's Day) 1471 for Principe. Other sources often give different dates, although they do not differ by much.

São Tomé was named by the Portuguese in honor of Saint Thomas, as they happened to arrive at this island on his feast day; for similar reasons, Principe was initially named *Santo Antão* (Saint Anthony), changed in 1502 to *Ilha do Principe* (Prince's Island) with reference and honor to the Prince of Portugal, to whom duties on this island's sugar crop were attributed. Portuguese navigators explored the islands and decided that these would be good locations for bases to trade with the mainland Africa.

After the Portuguese arrival, the islands were forsaken until 1485 when the first feudal lord, João de Paiva, tried by royal decree to settle São Tomé and cultivate sugarcane. However, the attempt failed due to tropical diseases and, despite it being exceptionally beautiful and fertile, Portuguese explorers found the archipelago to be inhospitable. Near giving up, their hopes raised again when the first successful settlement of São Tomé was established in 1493 by Álvaro Caminha, who received the island as a grant from the Portuguese crown. Under a similar deal—but years later—Principe was finally settled in 1500; however, attracting inhabitants proved to be difficult, and most of the earliest settlers were Jewish children, banished folks, and criminals sent from Portugal. Most of these settlers died early in childhood, but those who survived found the volcanic soil of the islands suitable for agriculture, especially for sugarcane.

The growing of sugarcane—a labor-intensive practice—could not be well achieved had Portuguese landlords not imported large numbers of slaves from mainland Africa. As the islands became Africa's chief sugar exporter, the Portuguese Crown took over in 1522 and 1573, respectively. However, attacks by superior sugar colonies in the Western hemisphere and the large slave population at that time, which was difficult to control, slowly but surely began to hurt the islands and required huge investments that the Portuguese crown was unable to maintain. As such, the following century meant decline of the sugar crop cultivation and the change of the archipelago's economic route by mid-17th century.

STP primarily became a transit point for ships engaged in the slave trade between the Congo Kingdom and the Americas. Portuguese settlers introduced coffee and cocoa in the early 19th century as two new cash crops in the rich volcanic soils. Extensive plantations, called *roças*, owned by Portuguese companies or absentee landlords, soon occupied almost all of the good farmland. By 1908, STP had become the world's largest producer of cocoa, which today remains the country's most important crop.

The practice of forced labor and abuse against the African farm workers continued in the *roças* system—a kind of feudal system—where the managers and landlords had a high degree of authority, despite the fact that slavery had been officially abolished by the Portuguese in 1876.

From the early 20th century and thereafter, the Portuguese were accused of subjecting contract workers in the *roças* to forced labor and poor working conditions. Labor unrest and dissatisfaction were constant issues, which continued to thrive and burn well into the 20th century. In order to avoid a rebellion, the Portuguese rulers carried out a cruel massacre in 1953, starting in a small village named Batepá and continuing through the island of São Tomé. Several hundred local inhabitants were killed. This Batepá Massacre remains a major event in the colonial history of the islands, and its anniversary is officially commemorated.

By the late 1950s, less than a decade after that regrettable episode, the Portuguese rulers received an adequate response from the population. A small group of São Toméans formed the Committee for the Liberation of STP (CLSTP) and established their base in nearby Gabon. They were not alone; other emerging nations across the African continent were demanding independence, too, and the Batepá Massacre was a perfect historical and contemporaneous argument used for claiming independence to the archipelago.

Soon after the overthrow of the Caetano dictatorship in Portugal in April 1974, the new Portuguese regime committed to dissolve its overseas colonies; consequently, in November 1974, a meeting with the Movement for Liberation of STP—the MLSTP (CLSTP had changed its name to MLSTP in 1972)—was held in Algiers, and an agreement was worked out for the transfer of sovereignty. A transitional government was put in charge until July 12, 1975, the date on which STP achieved independence (12th July). The MLSTP's Secretary General, Manuel Pinto da Costa, was chosen as the first President of the new state.

In 1990, fifteen years after Independence, the dictatorial regime ruled by Manuel Pinto da Costa ended when STP became one of the first African countries to adopt a democratic multiparty regime. Changes to the constitution were made, resulting in the legalization of opposing political parties. The first non-violent, free, and transparent elections took place in 1991, resulting in the election of Miguel Trovoada as president. Trovoada was a former prime minister who had been in exile for nine years before he returned as an independent candidate in 1990. In august 1995, a group of military officers attempted a coup d'état, killing one person and holding the President hostage for a week. The Angolan foreign minister mediated an agreement where the officers involved in the coup released President Trovoada and received a parliamentary amnesty, endorsed by presidential decree. As another condition of his return to power, the President agreed to give the military officers' council a greater voice in decisions affecting the army.

Trovoada was re-elected in the country's second multi-party presidential election in 1996. The Party of Democratic Convergence (PCD) won the majority of seats in the National Assembly, overtaking the MLSTP. The MLSTP became an important and vocal minority party. But, in the late 1992 municipal elections, the MLSTP won a majority of seats of five of seven regional councils, and, in October 1994, in early legislative elections, the MLSTP won again with a plurality of seats in the Assembly. It regained an absolute majority of seats in the November 1998 elections.

In the 2001 presidential elections, a new candidate backed by the Independent Democratic Action party, Fradique de Menezes, was elected on the first round and inaugurated on September 3.

Once again the army seized power for one week in July 2003. The reasons for this were the alleged widespread corruption in the governmental affairs and the illegal oil contracts bargaining by government officials and state agencies. An agreement was negotiated under which the Prime Minister was returned to office. President Fradique de Menezes was abroad, in Nigeria.

In the early elections of March 2006, a pro-presidential coalition won enough seats in National Assembly elections to form and head a new government. Since that time, there has been no dispute between the President and the Government. In the 30 July 2006 presidential elections, Fradique de Menezes again easily won a five-year term in office.

CHAPTER 2: THE SHRINE OF EVIL: IMPRESSIONS AT A GLANCE

The problem of this country lies in the character of the ruling class; its misery is a reflection of the political behavior which is a mix of greed and a desperate thirst for absolute power combined with a lack of love for the country. STP is very rich but São Toméans live in the most extreme poverty (poverty affects 54% of the population [2004 est.])[15].This chapter presents facts and scenes as displayed by the public figures—cruel stories indeed.

Many reasons have served as impetus for the "country's lethargy"; amongst them is the belief that foreign aid could solve all problems. In the 1960s, the preachers of the communist bloc of the Cold War alleged that independence followed by the then-socialist orientation for development would be the ultimate solution. Consequently, on July 12, 1975, Portugal was forced to hand the country over to "veterans" of the ML-STP to govern[16]. Seibert (1995) explains that, before April 25, 1974, the

15 AbsoluteAstronomy.com, 'List of countries by percentage of population living in poverty,' http://www.absoluteastronomy.com/topics/List_of_countries_by_percentage_of_population_living_in_poverty (accessed 04 03, 2010).

16 In 1964 the Organization of African Unity, OAU, recognized the Liberation Committee of STP, which transformed into the *Movimento de Libertação de São Tomé e Príncipe* (MLSTP, Liberation Movement of STP). After the military coup in Portugal in 1974, negotiations for independence commenced and on 12 July 1975 Manuel Pinto da Costa became the first president of the newly independent Democratic Republic of São Tomé and Príncipe.

MLSTP had not carried out any political activity in STP. The sub-delegation of the Portuguese General Directorate of Security (DGS) in São Tomé, the successor to the PIDE (International Police for the Defense of the State) from 1969, apparently not even aware of the foundation of the MLSTP party, noted in its quarterly report in December 1973 that, "Although there are no much information coming from abroad, we [the DGS] have the impression that the CLSTP is inactive or disorganized" (p. 242). Seibert stresses that, less than half a year before the beginning of the independence process in the islands, the same report says: "We do not think that the indigenous people [the São Toméan people], lazy by nature, have either the capacity or the cunning to take any initiative. Based on ancient prejudices, they blindly believe in the spell, calling it an effective weapon in the ruin or prosperity of any home. And so, they live their daily life, always suspicious, recognizing the talent of White man" (p. 242).

If the São Toméan people were indolent, so were their leaders; they were unable to fight for independence. Thus, the solution was to hand them the country for granted whilst the communists worldwide acted in the shadows, eating the best part of the cake. The country was turned into a "mother-in-law's house,"[17] a free haven for those who amused themselves by preaching Russian communism: Cubans, Bissau-Guineans, Angolans, Czechoslovakians, Chinese, Germans, and a myriad of others[18].

A few years after independence, the Portuguese returned[19]. They began by attacking the education sector, and then TV, radio and other media, the health sector, agriculture, tourism, banking, wholesale and retail sectors. For some years now, politicians have enriched their faith with the cultivation of new values: "neighborliness," "friendship be-

---

17   Translated from the local expression 'a casa da sogra' (the mother-in-law's house): At the "mother-in-law's house," a remarkable lack of discipline prevails, as the mother-in-law is easy-going when it comes to setting limits on behavior. Everything in her house is allowed, as opposed to "this house," where rules are there to be followed.

18   In 1980, the Sao Tomean Government asked about 2,000 Angolan troops and Soviet and Cuban advisers to enter the country. The collapse of the former Soviet Union in 1989 caused the end of international support for that regime.

19   IPAD - Instituto Português de Apoio ao Desenvolvimento, 'PIC e PAC,' http://www.ipad.mne.gov.pt/index.php?option=com_content&task=view&id=281&Itemid=251 (accessed 04 03, 2010).

tween the peoples of Africa," "closer ties with the East," etc., and this has brought new friends: Nigerians, Equatorial Guineans, Taiwanese, Brazilians, South Africans, Libyans, Moroccans, and a number of others, all of whom claim they only want to help STP in its difficult task of development—a case for thought!

Since 1997, there has been only one word uttered: oil. This fossil has represented the hope of a promising future for the São Toméan people; the rewards for those who always endeavored and dreamed of wealth and prosperity. Yet the country is in tears. At the outskirts of the capital city, children, youths and adults show clear signs of malnutrition and a lack of hygiene; people do not have or never had a decent salary. The terror launched against the nation is comparable to a bloody massacre, only no one talks about the victims. And we wonder: How long will this go on? Nobody seems to be doing anything about it. The Government acts like the guy who, instead of going to the store to buy poison to kill the rats infesting his house, spent his life trying to catch them alive to bring them to the store! These problems must be solved where they occur; the solution must go to meet the problems and not the opposite.

The thought that only a miracle could solve the problem is offensive. If any miracle ever happened, it was only once in history, when the universe was created. Change will only occur by the hands of man.

Crimes are echoed in countries where the courts are messy, police corruption has spread, there are serious social problems, the freedom of the press is limited, anarchy reigns along with the oligarchy, and the like. STP has already met these conditions. It is fertile ground for the proliferation of conflicts among marginal groups in society, or between them and the other part of society. Indeed, the numbers speak for themselves. In recent years crime has increased.

It is doubtful that STP can survive ten more years in this abyss; without wishing anything of the sort, one feels a terrible chill, a sense of the terrible cost of a revolution. It is like the drama of anti-personnel mines. It costs so little to buy them, even less to plant them; but it costs a fortune to remove them. It costs so little to find people willing to govern, and even less to install them on their thrones; but removing them seems about as hard as getting rid of a malignant cancer.

People are still afraid to publicly oppose the governing elite—they fear reprisals. If the state has no positive developments, if it does not apply the laws to the benefit of the population, if the population does not meet its obligation to the state, then the system is rotten beyond repair, and so a revolution must come. It is the only cure for this disease. The fears and uncertainties residing within people's hearts are irrational and are comparable to being afraid of ghosts. Ghosts are mere objects of human fantasy, reflecting their fears and their doubts about life after death and the "other" world. This explains the incredible capacity of humans to generate fears and submit themselves to them. The imaginary fears lying within the São Toméan people were fanned and enflamed to justify their doubts and limitations, and are dominating them. But a revolution cannot succeed as long as people's hearts are full of fear. For now, the São Toméan people see reality and truth passively, but with many questions, finally. When they realize that they must act, the doubts will disappear and will take with them the fear, which is, in this case, a conflict between man and his own senses.

As stated above, the political elite are like wild beasts and they believe that people are their prey. Therefore, one goal this book is to help people get rid of their predators. They must not allow themselves to be dominated by entities weaker than themselves, including that small group of corrupt politicians. A horse or a bull, if it knew its strength, would never allow a human to ride it. Most São Toméans still don't believe in their own ability to gather their forces, overthrow the installed power, and strategically plan for a better country for their children. But there is no reason to fear. It is imperative for them to kill the psychological fear they have inside them.

Even among social animals, the dominant males only remain in power whilst they are young and have strength. As soon as they begin to weaken, they lose their place to another, and they are killed or expelled from the community. Their subordinates do not hold a passive attitude towards the power; rather, all parties maintain a constant vigil. The animal world clearly has a society with standards, and power struggles are seen as important and necessary for the survival of the community. What is expected of humans, who themselves evolved from the animal world?

The São Toméan People, the country's government and the under-lying reality together constitute a war scenario that is as simple as this: People face Government, which seems to have the force of a thousand devils. Behind Government and its army is a cliff which it doesn't see. Government is within walking distance of the cliff and just needs to be forced to back up a bit; the war will be won by the people. The paradox is that not even the people know of the existence of that precipice, and therefore they don't try to push back the Government. In short, the arrogance and ignorance of Government wins out due to the sheer ignorance and lethargy of the people.

Thankfully, STP is peaceful by nature, and so bloodshed has not been part of the political quarrels and struggles for power. These people have always accorded value to the life of their opponents. But one must be careful. The society is changing.

Faiths Behind the Scenes

There is belief inside every human soul, and it deserves focused attention. Indeed, this book addresses beliefs, believers and belief makers, that is, politics, people and rulers. It is all about actions and perpetrators, and about good and evil. It is a journey through a remote place—both physical and metaphysical—around the frontier of the sphere of consciousness, the most distant place where the human mind can settle and create a reasonable human civilization, a place where people's actions are guided by an unshakable belief in the idea that nothing is possible except living, cheating, and obstructing other people's pathways to happiness.

It is not difficult to determine some of the reasons why so many "evil hearts" surround us, why their attitude seems to be contagious and, of course, why this country is one of the last places in the world where democracy can be a positive influence—or even survive at all. Here is a land that rose up as a paradise of freedom, the Promised Land for slave descendants after five centuries of suffering; whilst on the other side it serves as a sanctuary for "devils," ruling people as though guided by a malevolent compass set for self-destruction. The following chapters will describe some of the greatest crimes the rulers have committed.

The facts and analysis presented herein are based on the belief in the weakness of democracy and its ineffectiveness as a political ideal for STP at this moment. By calling for the country's rebirth and proposing a *New State System* (NSS) for the reborn country, the authors will contrast our vision with that of those who have been ruling STP, creating a complete human misfortune, a disaster of human development, where just a handful of men have so horrendously managed the resources and performed so poorly that the state has been led into bankruptcy.

By "democracy" the authors mean the entire basket of values that the most modern developed societies espouse, including liberty, equality, justice, and welfare for every sector of society, the struggle to balance the interests of individuals and the nation as a whole. By democracy we do not simply mean that public officials are elected on the basis of popular vote (whether purchased or freely given), enabling the rise to power of people with no training or skill or experience appropriate to the position. Democracy is not meant to open the way for corruption, anarchy, social inequality and socio-economic degradation of the country; even more, democracy need not mean political and administrative instability, lack of strategic planning, failure to initiate projects in the medium and long terms, or lack of a vision of national integration. Neither is the appropriation of public funds for private purposes and the distribution of power to members of one family and a small social elite equal democracy.

By contrast the politicians of this country have been labeling as "democracy" everything that is contrary to its very principles. Thus, the term has acquired another symbolic, and negative, meaning. If citizens in a democracy are all accountable for maintaining the country's state of affairs, it is our duty to denounce these shortcomings and do all we can to work toward a better future, to censure and to guide, and to secure appropriate leadership for the nation.

During the twentieth century all sorts of development and innovation was proposed and promoted. Yet STP remains inert, almost treading water, hovering in limbo. Ignorance and negligence seem to be the main characteristics of the rulers' councilors. Against all expectations and for more than three decades since Independence, almost nothing of value has been born in this most fertile land. Instead, on a large scale, men and women learn and perform to practice evil actions as a virtue.

Many people believe that the greatest sin São Toméans ever committed was to pretend to exist as a free nation, as a state, and even as a democratic system. But no! That is their right. The biggest sin was to have distorted the system and destroyed their most ambitious project, by creating a welfare state in the Democratic Republic of STP.

São Toméans express a lively desire for the occurrence of a national miracle that would bring immediate prosperity and easy wealth. The anticipation is so great that no one wants to work, and so, for a long time they have waited, effortlessly moving from bad to worse. At first glance, the discovery of oil appears to promise national salvation; but oil is not their only asset, nor even the most important. Their greatest wealth is not a commodity but Man: a compound of force, matter and spirit, which must be cultivated to produce resources or invent them where they do not exist.

In mid-1997, when the existence of oil in the country's Exclusive Economic Zone first came to light, the national environment was already a reflection of a decadent society. And, when they thought that all was lost and that they had to accept the humiliating conditions which come with being an underdeveloped country, new hopes were raised and, once again, dreams of wealth; however, that wealth still seems to be a mirage, out of reach as always.

Political influence remains the guiding force in all spheres of work and professional life of the citizens, and there is no respect for technical and professional competence, nor for individual experience and contributions. Evaluation procedures to assess, quantify and qualify services provided are lacking. People are judged not on the basis of their professional skills but their level of involvement and partisan affiliation. This discourages the elaboration of a state policy compatible with the acquisition of social welfare and the stability of the state apparatus.

These political trends favor a widespread state of lawlessness and unaccountability.

An Evil Creed

When the present authors were still little boys, we used to listen to our great-grandmothers' stories. They told us of certain monkeys that jumped around too much, from branch to branch and from tree to tree, as if seeking to be targeted by hunters' bullets. Though we could not fully understand the lesson at the time, it nevertheless shaped our thinking. We realized that monkeys were not the most intelligent beings and we thought they might not have a clear concept of life or adequate instincts for survival; the type of animals whose enjoyed the challenge of risking the most valuable thing they have—their own lives. This suggests that the essence of their creed was to endanger the most important attributes they possessed; it manifested in negligence, keen and ever-apparent irresponsibility towards their offspring, and disrespect and little care for life; and it was leading toward the extinction of their species.

But today we have a different viewpoint. Monkeys are just as fearful as us; they hate hunters and try to avoid them all the time; they love their children and own lives—and they try to avoid putting themselves at risk. That is, indeed, the monkeys believe in preserving life and in social interaction, as shown by the attention they give to hunters even whilst playfully jumping. The purpose of this belief is the preservation of species. What our great-grandmothers were trying to teach us was nothing related to monkeys at all. No doubt they wanted to show that we should always take care of our lives and avoid the ever-present dangers, and to know that when monkeys jump from branch to branch and tree to tree, they are choosing whether to play and gamble, being cautious, weighing up risks—and saving lives. Nevertheless, playing is part of social interaction—for both monkeys and human beings—and so they cannot stop playing altogether. It is always best to establish a balance between the two. And so, our great-grandmothers simply spoke of the need to live a vigilant life, to secure a balance between desires and exposure to dangers.

The Creed of the São Toméan political elite

Now, consider for a moment that the São Toméan politicians are monkeys, whose political ideas are the branches and political parties are the trees. Consider, for the sake of the example, that the word "change" is synonymous with "jump." Now, for instance, note the following:

Fradique de Menezes, who has held the office of President of the Republic since 2001, was politically born in MLSTP[20] and made his life and fortune on his links with this political party. When he decided to run for President, he joined the ADI[21]—the party of his predecessor, Miguel Trovoada. Noting that he could achieve greater income, if nothing else, he created his own party whilst on the throne—the MDFM/PL[22]. In short, he changed from "no affiliation" to MLSTP, from MLSTP to ADI, and subsequently progressed from ADI to MDFM/PL. Clearly, like those legendary monkeys, he jumped, jumped and jumped.

The President of the Republic from 1991 through to 2001, Miguel Trovoada, got his political start in CLSTP[23], a group that became MLSTP. He attempted to carry out a coup d'état in 1979 but failed; he was then arrested and exiled in France. He returned with the advent of political and institutional change which occurred in the late 1980s in STP, and ran for President as an independent candidate. Two parties supported him: CODO[24] and PCD-GR[25]. Whilst on the throne, he created his own party—the ADI. In short, he jumped from nothing to CLSTP to MLSTP, jumped from MLSTP to exile, from exile to the throne, and finally moved to the ADI: he jumped, jumped, jumped and jumped again.

DRSTP's [26] constitution states that the party or group that wins the elections is the one that should govern the country; yet, for the convenience of the national political elite, the country was ruled by the opposition from 22 June 2008 to 14 August 2010. After Prime Minister Patrice Trovoada was defeated in May 2008, a vote of no confidence

---

20 Movement for the Liberation of São Tome and Príncipe (MLSTP).
21 Independent Democratic Action (ADI).
22 Force for Change Democratic Movement-Liberal Party (MDFM/PL).
23 Committee for the Liberation of São Tome and Príncipe (CLSTP).
24 Opposition Democratic Coalition (CODO).
25 Democratic Convergence Party-Reflection Group (PCD-GR)
26 The Democratic Republic of STP (DRSTP)

was proposed by the MLSTP/PSD (which was then in opposition). President Fradique de Menezes asked the MLSTP/PSD to form a government in June, 2008; they chose Joaquim Rafael Branco[27] as Prime Minister. Trovoada's Independent Democratic Action (ADI) party denounced as unconstitutional de Menezes' designation of the MLSTP/PSD to form a government, but nothing was done. In short, initially all of them agreed with the constitution but at the midpoint some of them changed their minds, and then jumped!

Following an internal crisis in the MDFM/PL, Mr. de Menezes decided to publicly assume this party's leadership (the party he himself created). The parties with whom the MDFM/PL formed the coalition government disagreed with the President and, again, found that de Menezes was acting unconstitutionally. De Menezes disagreed with this censure and counter-attacked, deciding to withdraw all ministers of his party from Government. A new Government crisis was born. Amongst the four MDFM/PL ministers, two readily complied with the orders of the President and resigned; however, remained in their posts. But the status of these ministers in the Government lacked the final verdict of the President, who also was the leader of the MDFM/PL, i.e., he who had withdrawn them. Thus, they were forced to leave.

There are no precise statistics, but most of the political elite have no defined positions or firm convictions; they cannot even be faithful to their ideas. In other words, they spend their time changing—jumping!

We are then faced with a frantic and scary scenario: São Toméan politicians jumping from branch to branch, from tree to tree, changing ideas and political colors at the same rate which bank notes change, and for no reason other than to satisfy their ferocious yearning for a seat on the throne. They endanger the most important national resources— security, stability, credibility, economy, etc., leading to the destruction of the country.

Despite the little care they show for the socio-political environment, the São Toméan political elite is concerned with the perpetua-

---

27   Joaquim Rafael Branco is the President of the Movement for the Liberation of STP /Social Democratic Party (MLSTP/PSD), and the current Prime Minister of the country.

tion of their own privileges. Education for their children is guided by specific standards.

The principle tenets of São Toméan politicians seem to be:

1.1 Adore animals and not human beings. People are persona non grata and are not to be trusted.

By "animals" we mean a "race" of people that the leaders believe will neither betray nor conspire against them, and also will never claim any rights. These are humans who act like sheep, following their shepherds blindly and loyally, without questioning the direction or destination of the journey.

It follows from this tenet that the leaders need never create good jobs for poor people or those from inferior classes; they don't deserve to make a good living anyway. There is always a danger that people will revolt and claim their own rights or rights inherited from their ancestors; they ask too much, much more than they deserve.

Let's consider the facts. In this country, workers' strikes occur frequently, and people demand wage increases, improved working conditions and the like. The leaders say they lack means to satisfy such claims, but this is simply not true. Generally, governments are not motivated to ensure the welfare of people, and they instead arrange loopholes and excuses for not doing so. On November 22, 2004, the Union of Government Workers (STE)[28] promised to take to the streets thousands of workers if the Government did not increase the national minimum wage by 500% (which, at the time, stood at $30); however, only a few dozen workers attended the demonstration out of a universe of over 5,000 workers of the Civil Service. Aurelio Silva, the general secretary of the union, blamed the failure on alleged threats by the Damião Vaz d'Almeida's administration[29]. Silva stated:

> I too was intimidated. Both the General Police Inspector and the District Commander showed up at my house saying they would intervene if the demonstration went ahead. There was a lot of intimidation and misinformation.

---

28   Sindicato dos Trabalhadores do Estado (lit. Union of Government Workers)
29   Damião Vaz de Almeida was the Prime Minister of STP at that time (2004-2005).

Some analysts found that the poor attendance was due to the fact that the representative of the class had lost all credibility with public officials. However, the incident did happen—even if reluctantly. Nobody denied the serious allegations of Aurelio Silva; but no investigation was conducted and no prosecution was undertaken. Nonetheless, the popular demonstration in favor of improving wages and working conditions was classified by the Government as illegal since, according to the executive, it did not follow the legal procedures.

Common sense suggests that, in fact, intimidation was applied by the Government, for various reasons: first, the Government has not denied the accusations, which is tantamount to admitting the charge; second, no inquiry, consultation or anything else was conducted; third, if on the eve of the demonstration workers had agreed to demand wage increases in the order of 500%, then they surely felt they were being underpaid and were distressed by the situation. Why then did most of them not attend the rally? And fifth, some workers did show up, which means they were determined to fight for their cause despite the intimidation.

On November 4, 2009, the digital newspaper *Tela Non* reported that police tried in vain to stave off a rally of approximately 200 students, trained in Cuba, before the Government building (the prime minister's office) in São Tomé. Since they were unemployed upon their return from studying abroad, these students claimed their rights as citizens, saying that the Government should create conditions for their employment. Even before the students had come home, the Council of Ministers had announced that the country would define a strategy for their absorption into the economy, but apparently they were abandoned to their fate. More examples:

- On February 18, 2010, a five-day strike by employees of the Air Safety Corporation (ENASA) forced travel agencies to cancel their flights to STP. The workers demanded a wage increase.

- On November 25, 2008, the forty workers in the construction company *Mota Engil* went on indefinite strike, demanding better working conditions and wage increases.

- On February 4, 2004, the digital newspaper *Jornal de São Tomé* announced that the doctors of the emergency services of the country's main hospital, named for Dr. Ayres de Menezes, would strike in March, seeking increased subsidies and better working conditions.

- On February 8, 2005, the Criminal Investigation Police of STP (PIC) went on strike indefinitely, demanding improved working conditions.

- On May 2, 2008, hundreds of workers in STP protested against rising living costs in the archipelago. The Union of Government Workers (STE) organized a march of redundant workers, claiming they were entitled to compensation.

Strikes are constantly being waged to seek wage increases and better living conditions. But improving other people's living conditions is against the creed of the politicians, so the wages of workers are not raised to levels consistent with their living costs or needs.

A second tenet for the leadership is this:

1.2. Electricity was not made for the poor people; so you should make it available only for those who know how to make a good profit on it.

Generators should be installed in houses of landowners only. Don't bother improving public supply of this good. If you have the light you deserve, good! You are safe from the ghosts of the dark souls of the population.

In May, 2008, Prime Minister Patrice Trovoada was accused in the National Assembly of receiving 6,000 liters of free diesel per month from the state, estimated at a value of more than 96 million dobras ($5,242 US). The allegation was made by Mr. Carlos Tiny (Minister of Foreign Affairs and Cooperation from 22 June 2008 to 14 August 2010). The diesel fuel served to illuminate the residence of the head of Government. Responding to this accusation, Patrice Trovoada said that "The Prime Minister is entitled to electricity, and the state is fulfilling its obligations .... I'm not breaking the law."

The fortnightly magazine *O Parvo* conjectured that the "history of diesel" seemed to have been left untold. Most likely, it was not only Patrice Trovoada who enjoyed free fuel, but a whole list of others whose names were not disclosed.

For some years now, people have had to manage with constant power outages. The company holding the monopoly of the sector is unable to pull the country out of successive energy crises. The Ministry of Natural Resources and Energy estimated in 2009 that STP needs at least 30 megawatts of electricity to bridge the shortfall, though EMAE—the company with a monopoly to supply water and energy in the country—was producing just 13.7 megawatts (less than half the amount needed) up to October 9, 2009. From this date onwards, EMAE reduced that amount by another half, falling to just 5 megawatts of energy! With equipment and infrastructure dating back to colonial times, this company was to burst its seams several decades later. The power supply is streamlined so that supply to local public officials is permanent, whereas for the population, the supply is only a few hours every two or three days. Consider this: EMAE was never able to provide the country with even half the amount of energy it needs and, at the present moment, it can only provide one-sixth of the country's overall needs—or slightly more than 16.5%! However, the rulers insist on preserving this company's monopoly—with the state owning 51% of the shares.

1.3 Restrict people's ability to both think about politics and act against destructive political actions.

> Keep the people struggling to put food on their tables, and they will have no time or energy to explore, reflect and respond to political actions. Each one has the life he or she deserves, so let miserable people cry. Save yourself if you can. Don't cultivate piety or compassion. You are not God—He created the world, so let Him solve its problems.

By keeping wages extremely low, rulers and governmental officers limit the people's ability to buy books and journals. Although the minimum wage of civil servants is set at 650,000 dobras (STD)[30] per month, there is no stipulated national minimum wage, and most workers earn even less than that.

In terms of purchasing power, the 650,000 minimum monthly salary of a civil servant (May 2010 est.) would enable a person to:

- Buy 43kg of rice; or

---

30   Dobra is the national currency of the Democratic Republic of STP; STD is the symbol of this currency. Since January 2010 Dobra is anchored to Euro, with a fixed price of 24,500 Dobras per 1 Euro.

- Commute 65 times to and from his or her workplace, if the distance does not exceed 10km; or

- Buy a pair of jeans or a cheap mobile phone; or

- Buy 3-4kg of pork; or

- Buy 43 bottles of beer.

Clearly, the minimum wage in the civil service is far from meeting the minimum needs of a worker. Now imagine the lives of the thousands of families who earn less than that. As discussed above, in 2004, the Union of Government Workers (STE) called for increasing the minimum wage of around 500%. Essentially, for a worker to minimally meet his or her needs, he or she must earn at least 6 times what the Government pays him or her today.

The Government provides for the worst possible education for young people—as well as adults—and maintains a low quality of national media. Only one national and public television station exists, the TVS (São Toméan Television). It broadcasts for around 6 hours daily. Except for a few stories concerning the country, which are shown on the TV News, this television channel airs foreign soap operas, movies, music, and entertainment. People can also catch two television channels in Portuguese: RTP Africa (Portuguese Broadcasting for Africa) and International RTP (International Portuguese Broadcasting), which is shown on the TVS channel during the day. It is also possible to catch emissions in French on CFI/TV5 satellite, 24 hours a day. In contrast to the foreign television and radio channels, the national television and radio channels are of very poor quality: there are no editorial policies consistent with development strategies; disorganization prevails at all levels. Practically, there are no skilled staff—both programs and programming appear improvised and amateurish. Add to the limited technical and professional quality the fact that most of the issues and programs are foreign and do nothing to inform and advance the local populace.

As for the press, there are no daily publications. The media in STP are simply not significant and have very little social impact. Aside from a few regular weekly and fortnightly publications, there are poorly defined regulars linked to thematic areas.

There are various daily digital newspapers/magazines, although few people have access to them as the overwhelming majority of the population has no Internet access. Moreover, Internet connectivity is very limited and usage costs are exorbitant given the levels of local life. Even compared with prices offered internationally, the costs of Internet access in STP are very high. See table below:[31]

Internet Service	Set-up Fee	Monthly Fee
56kbps dial-up access (analogue)	420,000 STD (23 USD)	525 STD upload per minute (up to 1,300 USD per month) 1050 STD download per minute (up to 2,600 USD per month)
64kbps dial-up access (ISDN/ ISDN)	840,000 STD (47 USD)	Not available
128kbps dial-up access (ISDN/ ISDN)	840,000 STD (47 USD)	1050 STD upload per minute (up to 2,600 USD per month) 2100 STD download per minute (up to 5,200 USD per month)
Permanent Access 128kbps ISDN - Leased Line	63 EUR (84.3192 USD)	250 EUR (334.6000 USD)
ADSL 64/128kbps	84 EUR (112.4256 USD)	105 EUR (140.5320 USD)
ADSL 128/256kbps	84 EUR (112.4256 USD)	210 EUR (281.0640 USD)

Table 1: Internet Service Costs

In order to get a clear idea of what this means in terms of price and living costs, we conducted a comparison between the prices of an ADSL 128/256kbps package[32] (which is the best offer of such services provided by CST, the only telecommunications company in STP) with two standards, namely:

---

31   CST - Companhia Santomense de Telecomunicações, 'SERVIÇO INTERNET-Dial up e ADSL (Imposto s/ consumo de 5% incluido),' 2010. http://www.cstome.net/tarif/default_inter.htm (accessed 04 12, 2010).

32   As shown in the table above, this is the best offer Internet service in the country, both in terms of monthly cost and in terms of connectivity and quality.

- Standard 1: The minimum salary of the STP civil service;

- Standard 2: The prices for Internet ADSL service in other countries, considering two Internet service providers selected at
random.

According to Standard 1, the costs of set-up and monthly fees are, respectively, 3 and 8 times greater than the civil service minimum wage! Regarding Standard 2, one of two companies selected at random offers speeds of upload and download, respectively, 8 and 32 times higher than the highest speed offered in STP, and collects only 90% of the set-up costs and 9% of the monthly fees. The other company offers 8 and 47 times, respectively, the upload and download speeds offered by the CST, and collects only 10% of the price offered by the former. That company does not charge any set-up fee at all.

Hence, for citizens of STP, information is scarce and difficult to obtain, even relating to local news and events, and so the public are not aware of important issues affecting their lives. Thus, they rely on international media, which is generally inaccessible for most citizens. The officials of the country do, however, install parabolic aerials in their palaces in order to ensure they are connected with all important international communication channels, whilst the public may only have the opportunity and pleasure of watching Brazilian, Portuguese or French soap operas, American movies, Portuguese soccer games and championships, and the like.

With such low wages, high prices and poor services, how can people reflect on the politics of their country? It is much more likely that they spend most time thinking about what to eat, what to wear, and where to sleep. They will not have time to think about political action; and they will not have a well-formed political conscience which allows them to react properly to the harmful actions of politicians.

1.4. Do not improve health care. It is suicide.

Medicines should be expensive for the population, and health care services should be expensive and nearly nonexistent so that people think health care is only for those who deserve it. You can always get an appointment with a doctor in Portugal or Gabon, or elsewhere. It is up you.

Let's consider some examples. On July 17, 2008, President de Menezes returned from Belgium where, days before, he had been evacuated for emergency medical treatment. Speaking to the press, the surgeon Pascoal d'Apresentação, who accompanied the head of state, said that "[The president] stayed in Belgium for eight days primarily to treat a slight cardio-vascular attack" [note this]. Also according to this expert, "[T]he situation is under control; ... three months from now, the head of state shall return to Belgium just for a routine medical review." Importantly, however, on April 24, 2007, the Prime Minister at the time, Tomé Vera Cruz, was hospitalized in the University Hospitals of Coimbra, Portugal, having taken off from São Tome the day before, with a thrombo-embolism associated with a deep vein thrombosis. On March 6, 2010, the São Toméan news agency STP-Press reported that "the President of the National Assembly Francisco Silva[33], who was in Portugal for 'routine medical review' returned to the country."

These are just some examples, but are sufficient to make an interesting reading of the situation. In STP, everybody knows that public officials do not make use of the national hospitals because they lack the basic resources; instead, they spend large sums of public funds to travel to European countries for doctors' appointments and medical treatments which are, to use their own words, "routine." All of this is done with the money that should be spent improving the local hospitals.

2nd Commandment: Harass and chase as a means of personal defense.

> Don't tie their hands, but their throats. Fire everybody you don't know. If you don't so, soon or later they will judge us and set themselves up to compete with our business. Do not recognize the efforts of poor people striving to improve their lives, but persecute them, find them and give them what they deserve—humiliation. They are solely responsible for their miserable lives. Those who appear to be smart or intelligent should be eliminated. Never talk in public about those who may have advanced knowledge in politics or government, who bring new ideas. Avoid them; they may denigrate you. You are always the best, the example for the world.

---

33 Francisco Silva died on April 14, 2010.

São Toméan politicians have convinced themselves that families belonging to the political elite have the right to be famous or prosperous. They strive to keep their own children from mixing with those they consider to be parasites, who constantly importune them with complaints and claims of rights, even if they work hard.

Those who reach top management or secure command posts cheat without shame or pity, and this is, unfortunately, a vibrant and enthusiastic character trait of each of STP's politicians. By taking over their charges and tasks, sexually harassing females, and committing professional abuses, they find their way to perpetuation on the throne. They succeed.

3rd Commandment: Burn everything. Squander everything. Travel abroad and escape.

> Make this land a place utterly inhospitable to life while you can travel wherever you want and have your needs met elsewhere. Try, too, not to speak in the vernacular; it is a matter of status. You will be better able to impose your personality over those envious opponents by using words they don't understand... You are wise enough to be the king of this country. Don't rely on accountants. Keep those bastards out of your business; you don't need them. Call your cat "Hasdrúbàl," your little dog "Fubá," your favorite chicken "Jessica," and your children any foreign, extravagant, non-African and hard-to-pronounce name.

On Tuesday, 4 October 2008, a man named Hilário Garrido—who must have been very well-educated since he was Judge of the Supreme Constitutional Court and therefore part of the political elite—wrote an article, released in the digital newspaper *Tela Non*[34], to complain about the increasing fees in the Diocesan Training Institute John Paul II (IDF)[35], a high school belonging to the Catholic Church in STP, which entirely follows the Portuguese education system's curriculum. This man, like almost all elements of the São Toméan political elite, sent his children to study at the IDF institute because he thought that "Its importance stems from certain key factors.... IDF is guided by a curriculum that comes from the Portuguese education system, of course very

---

34 http://www.telanon.info/suplemento/analise/2008/10/14/473/ idf-%E2%80%93-stome-e-novas-propinas/
35 http://idf.fisicaequimica.com/index.php?lang=en_utf8

different from ours," and dispensing with any further explanation. In addition to drawing its technical, pedagogical and other qualities from the Portuguese education system, we understand that a key element is that students study *based on books*, i.e., all the pupils actually have books, which elsewhere in the country are basically unavailable, even in the Liceu Nacional (the Public High School) and maybe in the ISP[36] and other colleges in the country.

This man then characterized the school as having "those virtues which are to praise God." An individual who is a judge of the Supreme Constitutional Court should, one might suggest, have a different attitude and be capable of reasoning. This behavior is similar to all those belonging to the political elite. They are responsible for establishing and managing a quality education system, oriented towards the development of the country, but they do not meet these obligations; and then they speak as if they were not actors in the play.

The incompetent political elite act this way because, in their view, they are preparing a generation of people totally different from ordinary people. The former should be made to govern the latter, but to govern them with knowledge and experiences which are not useful to society, the economy, the culture or the local politics. The more they seem odd, the more they do not identify with the ordinary people. They have created the myth that those who speak with foreign accents are better educated than those who do not, and they use this to ensure the respect, admiration and power they need for their children to continue the saga of destruction of the country.

From the standpoint of sovereignty, what these gentlemen are doing is putting the interests of an entire nation at the mercy of foreign interests; in this case, Portugal. They are creating a free advertising campaign for a system that is inherently a competitor of their country whilst simultaneously creating negative propaganda against their own nation. At this rate the STP's education system will never be developed, whilst the Portuguese education system will become stronger and completely dominant. These gentlemen are the representatives of the national education system, and so they are responsible for its success.

---

36   Instituto Superior Politécnico (lit. Higher Polytechnic Institute)

Accordingly, they ought to convey a good image of the system wherever they go; it's their job to do so.

From the standpoint of international presence, the Portuguese education system is committed to instilling within its members the attributes of knowledge, ideas and experiences highlighting Portugal and publicizing a good image of Portugal. Students of this system will be ready to defend the interests of Portugal and to contribute to its development and good performance. Today, neo-colonialism is a national concern; therefore, to freely promote a foreign country and culture is to help the "invaders." And this is what has happened: the country is deeply dependent upon Portugal, at all levels, in all spheres of national life. This dependency extends to Brazil, Taiwan, Japan, Nigeria, Cuba and many other countries.

Although the relationship with international partners has created dependency and disadvantages for the country, it serves the interests of the political class. Indeed, Seibert states that,

> The input of foreign funds and creation, often uncoordinated, of projects within the economic and structural reforms increased and facilitated all forms of corruption by those responsible. It formed a small and relatively wealthy local elite, fully supported by resources guaranteed by foreign development aid and by a funding from private business interests. These resources have been largely directed towards private consumption and redistributed through networks of patronage instead of supporting productive investments in the country (2001, p. 346).

There is a cult of supremacy of foreign non-African cultures among STP politicians which must be carefully analyzed. They dislike everything which sounds local or national or African, and frequently travel to do their shopping in European, Asiatic and American cities. Even imports of commodities and materials available in the neighboring countries are made in Asia, Europe, and America, causing products to be extremely expensive for the local consumers. Vacations are spent in luxury locations, without concern for the expenditures, at the state's expense.

On March 8, 2008, the magazine *O Parvo*[37] reported that public officials had partaken in 2,016 official trips outside the country within a

---

37 "O Parvo" means "The Silly Guy".

six-year period. With these data and with many difficulties, this magazine estimated that the cost of those trips must have been $8 million!
This amount was one sixth of the annual Gross Domestic Product of
the country in 2002. Indeed, on March 31, 2008, the German researcher
Gerhard Seibert reacted to this disclosure as follows:

> The calculation of O Parvo is inadequate, because it does not dis-
> tinguish between trips paid by the state's treasury and trips paid
> by the hosts of a conference, meeting, etc. abroad. Moreover, the
> O Parvo calculation does not consider the Government spending
> in terms of the subsidies that the travelers on official business
> receive a day, including the per diem (ca. $ 200 per day; the fee
> varies by country) and entertainment allowance (approx. $ 20
> to $ 100 a day, dependent on the position of the traveler). Either
> way, the costs are considerable, especially for a country with
> few resources and many needs of the population. Ten years ago
> the World Bank reported that in 1996, until October, the Gov-
> ernment had spent more on travels abroad than in salaries for
> about 3600 civil servants .... These excessive trips abroad totaled
> $ 700,000 (an amount equivalent to 300 trips São Tomé–Lisbon
> in business class) and contributed to seriously worsening the
> state of public finances that year. In fact, trips abroad do not
> serve primarily to promote external relations of this microstate
> ... but often to increase [the traveler's] salary through the afore-
> mentioned subsidies, which can easily exceed a monthly salary of
> a senior and even a minister. Hence, it is important to any min-
> istry or Government agency to keep a keen eye on the distribu-
> tion of trips to try to balance these advantages. Any imbalance in
> the distribution of trips can create tensions and conflicts. I am
> convinced that our friend Custódio [another participant in the
> discussion] could tell many anecdotes about this, if he wants to.
> I heard that even the participation of ministers in the meetings of
> the Joint Ministerial Council [38] of the JDZ[39] in Abuja is constantly
> changing, as all [the ministers] want to benefit from the very high
> "per diems" that are paid to the participants of these meetings

---

38   The affairs of the Joint Development Zone are managed by a Joint Development
     Authority (JDA) that reports to a Joint Ministerial Council. The Council has
     overall responsibility for all matters relating to the exploration for and exploita-
     tion of the resources in the JDZ, and such other functions as the states Parties
     may entrust to it.
39   JDZ stands for 'The Nigeria São Tomé & Príncipe Joint Development Zone'
     created in February 2001; an area of overlapping maritime boundary claims that
     will be jointly developed by the two countries.

with the Nigerian ministerial colleagues. For a country as poor as STP, every dollar paid for less important travel is a loss for health, education, public investments, etc.[40]

Following the above comment, and for further clarification, on April 1, 2008, Gerhard Seibert further commented:

Excessive official travels do not only undermine the public accounts, but due to the resulting consecutive absences of directors and ministers, they also adversely affect the management of ministries and departments. One consequence of this mismanagement is that every year the Government violates the budget law, delivering the state budget (OGE) to the National Assembly with considerable delay. The late approval of OGE has become as habitual as the journeys [of public officials] abroad.[41]

4th Commandment: Keep yourself in the seat of power, and then, cheat, lie, steal and always say you are innocent.

4.1 Once upon the throne, make as much money as soon as possible, even if you have necessary to sell the entire country, including its population...

Take public properties for free; build extravagant palaces and import showy cars to enforce your status as an all-powerful man. Always borrow money, with no thought of paying it back; if anyone lends you money, it is because he or she wanted to do it; so you are not obliged to reimburse. The people exist to serve you, so they must work for you. The money is yours... Blame innocent people for your own faults; if you get caught, you can always appeal, using appropriate channels, networks and lobbies. If they find you guilty even so, don't forget: a little devil is always behind the door; he is guilty, not you. When required by the justice for you to respond for your crimes, always say you are innocent—a son of God could never commit a sin against his classmates. You should only be judged by God, not humans, not here, not now. Human courts are for stupid people, not you.

This is a frequent occurrence in the country. In fact, Seibert claims that,

---

40 Gerhard Seibert, 'saotome ● SÃO TOMÉ E PRÍNCIPE,' http://uk.groups.yahoo. com/group/saotome/message/20346 (accessed 04 13, 2010).

41 Gerhard Seibert, 'saotome ● SÃO TOMÉ E PRÍNCIPE,' http://uk.dir.groups. yahoo.com/group/saotome/message/20350 (accessed 04 13, 2010).

[D]ue to a weak judicial system and the lack of an effective auditing system, no individual acts of corruption entail the risk of large penalties. Rather, corrupt ministers were all too often promoted to very well-paid positions within local projects and international organizations abroad, often with the help of foreign governments and development agencies. Any disciplinary or legal action against suspects immediately triggers friends and family to use their influence to halt the measure. In these circumstances, the covenant between the members of the elite overrides partisan differences. (2001, 287)[42]

On October 31, 2008, the Court of First Instance began the trial of those implicated in what was classified as the country's greatest corruption scandal ever—the GGA Scandal. On March 27, 2009, a former director, Diogenes da França Moniz, and a former treasurer, Aurelio Aguiar, from the Office of External Aid Management (GGA) were sentenced to, respectively, nine and seven years of imprisonment for forgery, embezzlement and mismanagement in a fraud of approximately $4 million from the sale of food aid (rice) from Japan. Both men were also sentenced to pay damages to the state in the order of a billion dobras (approximately $54,673) and 650 million dobras (about $35,537), respectively. The Court files also stated that Filipe Bandeira—another of the defendants—was acquitted, and Leopoldino Matos—also accused—was permitted absence for health reasons for treatment in Portugal, and that, when he returned, he would be tried separately. This was the final swing of a huge process that took more than four consecutive years under instruction.

The GGA was created in 1993 with the intention of coordinating foreign aid from various parts of the world. In 2004, more than three million U.S. dollars were diverted from its coffers and, in 2006, another amount of more than two million U.S. dollars was reported as missing. After four years of judicial investigation, four employees of GGA were indicted and were presented to the Court. In just one day of hearings, these individuals helped the Court to produce a range of evidence of embezzlement and diversion of rice from Japan; on the second day, a judicial source confirmed that, for further clarification, the panel of judges would have to subpoena the former ministers and former prime

---

42 This is the first Portuguese language edition of the book; our translation.

ministers who ran the funds directly from GGA (then extinct). Some of the former ministers and prime ministers had diverted 3,000 bags of rice and several million dobras in cash for the refurbishment of private homes and gardens, the purchase of vehicles, etc., in a web of corruption unprecedented in the history of the country.

A report by the prosecutor, based on an audit of the GGA's accounts, provides the names of several national leaders, each of whom had been provided with large sums of money on the basis of false invoices. The scandal has been going on for years based on the rice offered by Japan, and allegedly it involved all the powers in STP since 1993! Furthermore, whilst on the one hand the GGA Scandal contributed to the economic degradation of the state, on the other hand it led to the downfall of the former Prime Minister Maria das Neves and her administration in mid-September 2004. It is stated in the record that Maria das Neves had also withdrawn from the coffers of GGA several million dobras in order to renovate her private residence. The same house had been rebuilt with support of Taiwan. According to the GGA's accountant, the former Prime Minister also seized another large sum of money in order to upgrade her agricultural enterprise, Vila Graciosa (literally, "Graceful Town"), located near the town of Madalena. A further million dobras were diverted by Maria das Neves to renovate her second private residence in the San Nguembú site. Reports by the defendants further indicate that during the lifetime of the Government of National Unity led by Maria das Neves the looting of public funds in the GGA was even more intense. Several other high officials in the archipelago were involved, including other former prime ministers, ministers and even the President Fradique de Menezes. The CGI—a private company owned by the president—also directly participated in the operations.

On November 5, 2004, the deputy of the National Assembly and vice president of the MLSTP/PSD Guilherme Posser da Costa confirmed his involvement in the GGA embezzlement scandal during the period of 1999 and 2001[43] as he left a court hearing in a criminal proceeding where he was indicted for attempted assault on the Attorney General's Office (PGR), Adelino Pereira, on November 3, 2004. Following this assault, Guilherme Posser da Costa was the target of an

---

43   He was Prime Minister at that time.

arrest warrant issued by the PGR. He justified the assault by an alleged breach of secrecy by the PGR, who eventually would have passed the GGA dossier to the media—even in judicial investigation. Posser da Costa accused the PGR of having circulated false information by calling him "the accused," damaging his dignity and honor that were under close scrutiny in the public sphere.

Asked by journalists whether or not he was involved in the GGA financial scandal, the former Prime Minister confirmed that he had given permission for various members of his administration and elements of his security guard to benefit from the GGA funds, which allegedly was used as a slush fund. "Some public spending was paid [by the GGA] under my order, such as payment of water and electricity bills for some Government members." Posser da Costa said that he authorized the regular provision of "some quantity of rice" for his personal guard.

In June 2007, the former minister of Commerce and Industry, Arzemiro dos Prazeres—one of the politicians charged with crimes of "abuse of trust" and embezzlement in the GGA financial scandal—said publicly that he had been unjustly treated. Arzemiro dos Prazeres had authorized the GGA to make a number of expenditures outside the law, but in a letter to the digital newspaper *Tela Non*, dos Prazeres argued that his involvement was so minor as to be of little relevance, because his name was linked only to some misspent 700 Euros (approximately $950): "If even the prosecutor accuses me of involvement in matters of no more than 700 Euros, then why do the media insist on associating my name with the misuse of millions of dollars?"

So a minister is caught stealing; he defends himself by saying he only stole a little bit (and apparently he does not feel any moral obligation to repair the damage), and then he sets the measure for how much one must steal to be considered criminal!

As per the meeting on January 5, 2009, the Court of First Instance heard four people, including Domingos Monteiro—who had previously been threatened with incarceration for refusing to appear before the Court—and Julio Silva, both of whom were deputies of the National Assembly. Domingos Monteiro, a dealer and member of the MLSTP/ PSD, and Julio Silva, a former Minister of Commerce in the executive of Maria das Neves (between October, 2002 and September, 2004) and current member of the Independent Democratic Action party (ADI), were summoned to explain the whereabouts of 3,000 bags of rice that had gone missing from the warehouses of the Aid Management Office (GGA) and subsequently turned up in the warehouses of the firm Irmãos Monteiro Lda (Monteiro Brothers Ltd.). The first statements concerning this matter established that the 3,000 bags of rice belonged to the former Minister, Julio Silva, but the deputy and owner of the firm revealed that Monteiro Brothers paid 360 million dobras (approximately $19,682) for the rice in four installments (of 90 million dobras each), which were received by the then-director of cabinet of Minister of commerce, whose name was not mentioned; however, the Court did not find the whereabouts of the money or proof of payment. Júlio Silva, who appeared before the Court as a witness, confirmed the request for credit, stating only that he did not know how things developed later. This witness was also confronted with evidence of $45,000 in imports considered "detrimental to the state." Júlio Silva allegedly spent that amount to import products to supply the market on the island of Príncipe, but the courts found no evidence that any product had actually been imported through this program. Additionally, he authorized the purchase of air conditioners worth approximately $12,000 for the Ministry of Commerce, and also the purchase and importation of two motorcycles to the island of Príncipe, for which no evidence of the amount spent was displayed.

In the second of many hearings, the Court heard the accountant of the extinct GGA, Aurelio Aguiar, describe how large sums of money were diverted for private purposes. His counsel Lucrécio Graça added that 3 million bags of rice had been diverted from GGA to a private warehouse, stating the following:

> We have here a case of 3000 bags of rice that have gone to a warehouse, according to the orders of the Minister [of Commerce] at the time. Payment for the bags did not appear in the box. Later, we came to know that 3000 bags were stranded at the warehouse of the Monteiro Brothers. And then we came to know that rice was not to be sold into the food supply, but to the Minister [of Commerce] that conducted the operation. Mr. Julio Silva was the Minister [of Commerce] at the time.

Basílio Diogo, the current director of Inspection of Economic Activities, was also associated with embezzlement at GGA. The GGA's accountant named the company CGI as one of the possible recipients of GGA funds, with no counterpart for the state. According to the accountant, the GGA was paying the entire costs associated with transporting this company's goods between the islands of São Tomé and Príncipe. Who owned CGI? The defendant replied that the owner was the President, de Menezes.

The Court seemed to have its hands tied, and consequently dismissed the case until it had heard the state rulers who ran these corrupt transactions. The former director of GGA—the defendant Diogenes Moniz—enumerated the events in chronological order:

"The administration of Prime Minister Armindo Vaz d'Almeida, in addition to allowing several distributions of goods, either for political reasons or for reasons of local parties, repeatedly asked various tranches of money without the right to restitution, arguing always to be a matter of the Government, and especially superior order, so that the subordinates, by 2004, in presence of the lack of rules in the civil service that allowed them to defend themselves from arbitrary actions of superiors, were obliged to comply with, or be dismissed for disobedience, relegating all a life and family into oblivion and hunger.

"In the office of Prime Minister Guilherme Posser da Costa—not forgetting the mandates of Norberto Costa Alegre and Raul Bragança (the latter in particular stood out the famous' Meeting of the Boards,' paid in full with money and property taken from the GGA by order of the Government)—the situation continued, with several recommendations and commitments for the benefit of cultural and political interests of parties in power, going to the point, both in Government and elsewhere, to recommend deliveries of various goods to Mrs. Poshy and Mr. Faruja for election campaigns, facts which I have always opposed to as Office Director.

"Another plus, even during the administration of Posser da Costa, under the recommendation of this man, all the bills of telephone numbers of officers and members of the Government were paid by the GGA without the likelihood of having a complaint by the directorate of the concerned Office. For this reason, in several meetings, I warned the rulers regarding financial losses and defaults that the GGA was to incur. But the rulers did nothing to resolve or find a compromise and accountability, impairing the GGA in several millions or even billions Dobras.

"In the government of Maria das Neves, the cases also remained then with shares of several ministers even more direct, although always at the beginning of several governments with the concerned ministers in charge, the meetings scheduled in GGA reported the actual situation in the Office, taking all the knowledge about the real situation of failure to meet commitments to donors.

"With regards to Mrs. Maria das Neves, in addition to the extensive responsibilities that I consider to be of the Government as a whole, the GGA's office made at her request several shipments of materials such as gravel, cement, sand and fuel, all paid by the GGA, to the Vila Graciosa farm, which belonged to her, and also provided—again at the request of this lady, as Government official—all materials for the completion of her house in San NGuembu, and proceeded to purchase of sinks and appliances for her home in the Bairro 3 de Fevereiro. Those parts were purchased at the store after the Casa Inglesa for remodeling her home after the coup d'état.

"I must stress, though, the delivery of sums of money to Mrs. Maria das Neves and the large sum paid by her order to Mr. Zé Neto for payment of dues to the Roça Monte Café and EMOLVE, as well as the use by public officials, and the state itself, of cement and asphalt without any input of money into the coffers of the GGA.

"In these same administrations, having Mr. Arzemiro dos Prazeres governing responsibilities, the following commitments and deliveries were made:

- Several cash payments and delivery of goods for celebrations in the villages;

- Payment by the GGA of rehabilitation of facilities of the Ministry of Commerce by both Mr. Assis Borges de Castro's and Mr. Amândio's companies;

- Instructions given to the GGA for payment of costs of election campaigns in the south of the country, and delivery of goods belonging to the GGA which were never paid by those responsible;

- Payment for transport of goods to the island of Principe, both at state and private level;

- Payment of rehabilitation of the [GGA's] warehouse on the island of Principe and the WFP's warehouse, run by a doctor who is a brother of the Minister Arzemiro dos Prazeres;

"In the presence of Mr. Júlio Silva as minister, there were also direct recommendations such as:

- Use of foreign currency to purchase various products to the Ministry [of Commerce];

- Acquisition of motor vehicles and three containers of various goods for delivery at the island of Principe;

- Delivery to one of the 'Monteiro Brothers' (Nino) of about 3,000 bags of rice without any financial compensation to the GGA;

- Payment with interest for the purchase of salt at the hands of Mrs. Tina;

- Purchase of two vehicles without reimbursement;

- Several payments to officials of the Ministry of Commerce;

- Several travel payments on behalf of country's leaders;

- All repairs of vehicles of the directorates of the Ministry, particularly the Department of Commerce, the Tourist Board and the Directorate of Economic Activities, going so far as [Julio Silva] had ordered at the time repairing the car belonging to Mr. Gustavo dos Anjos, his Advisor, and repair of the car of Mr. Carlos Quaresma, the husband of former Prime Minister [Maria das Neves].

"... I also declare that, by authorization of the various Government administrations, the GGA has made several deliveries of goods to the security guard of the National Assembly and the Government Palace, and to the Buffalos[44], during the coup[45]. Those goods also were never paid, [but were] always [delivered] alleging 'obeying orders.'

"I declare that, by order of the Government, the current State Security building were also rehabilitated and paid by the GGA."

Despite the evidence produced, all the senior leadership of the country, their advisers and staff directors, were considered exempt

---

44 "Buffalo" is a group formed by members of Battalion 32 of the former apartheid regime of South Africa. After a failed coup in the late 1980s, they were arrested. They were subsequently released as political prisoners after the fall of the Berlin Wall.

45 On July 16, 2003, there was a new coup, without bloodshed, in which elements of the Buffalo also participated.

from the trial by the Courts. The long list of names of those leading figures includes:

- The President Fradique de Menezes (and his private company CGI);

- Former prime ministers: Maria das Neves, Raul Wagner Bragança Neto, Armindo Vaz d'Almeida, Guilherme Posser da Costa, and Norberto Costa Alegre;

- Former ministers of commerce: Arzemiro dos Prazeres, Arlindo Carvalho, Júlio Silva, and Hélder Paquete;

- The former Minister of Foreign Affairs and Cooperation, Carlos Gustavo dos Anjos (the current ambassador of STP to Belgium);

- And more that we cannot mention for lack of space.

The Courts are ruled by individuals such as those who participated in the bribery scandal of the GGA, and so they opted to let the bosses out on the loose so that they could continue with the predatory actions against public goods. Corruption has therefore become an epidemic in this country, and is practiced by perpetrators unmasked for all to see. Since it is not possible to list them all, let's make an effort to mention a few cases that stand out.

The annual report of the Court of Auditors for the year 2008, made public on May 29, 2009, was considered by the digital newspaper *Tela Non* as "the most scandalous auditors' report ever issued" by a judicial body. Within this document, the Prime Minister Rafael Branco, and the entire executive team are accused of constituting a huge network of corruption. The report states that Rafael Branco is involved in the business of selling a public house, which is fundamentally considered by the Court as a serious violation and to be punishable by criminal proceedings. The National Assembly was also accused of being in collusion with the executive in order to "launder fraud and corruption and open the door to widespread appropriation of public assets and resources".

It seems that the former allies had begun to quarrel. The Courts, which had always given coverage to public leaders, were then "shooting" them. The President of the Court of Auditors, Francisco Fortunato Pires, said that he did not understand the Government's decision to abolish Court visas for the execution of public works through a bill that was approved by the National Assembly. He said:

"It is exactly on the completion of public works where the state spends more money, and more notes deviations occurs in many different ways. Interestingly, the Government decided to abolish the visa and is preparing to do the same with the sale of state property ....

"Through the cronyism, many state assets are going into the hands of private entities without any control, as has happened with the land and state enterprises. ... Even without giving the necessary visa, there were schemes to sell a farm house of the famous Vale dos Prazeres [lit. Valley of Pleasures], whose sale the Court was opposed and rejected by ruling, for there have been serious violations, punishable with criminal proceedings ....

"If the Government goes with the elimination of prior approval, [then] the question [remains], what will happen to the new generation?—for it is there for all to rush to the spoliation of all that is public: land, homes, vehicles, etc., etc, in addition to the deliverance of public companies, some of which are vital to the national economy, without complying with the criteria of transparency ....

"There are several episodes in which the coalition headed by Rafael Branco has made clear its determination to annihilate the Court of Auditors. Hence, the next episode is the process of reviewing the degree of recovery. The Government, in violation of constitutional and legal norms in force, used the occasion to introduce an article in a decree approving such a regulation of bids, by which it proposed removing the Court jurisdiction that determines in advance the documents and contracts in which the state engages to carry out its works, which is another absurd, because the route was left to the state not to avoid the wave of departures of its funds through various juggling that are made in contracts bidding and that, even with the prior examination, some are likely to escape detection ....

"The fact that the Court of Auditors... identified violations of existing legislation and the consequent commission of serious irregularities affecting the public interest did spark a wave of retaliation against itself—ranging from the reduction of its current budget to less than a third—which is a joint action of the Government and the National Assembly, which, without any previous study, initiated the review process of legal instruments which support the activities of the Court...."

Francisco Pires further stated that this was an absurd agreement between the Government and National Assembly; for him, there was only one objective within the partnership between these two Organs of Sovereignty, which was to whitewash fraud and corruption and open the way for widespread ownership of public assets and resources.

"Contrary to a practice of decades, even the state budget is now published only in abstract, not allowing ordinary citizens, as tax-payers, to exercise their right of control, since the pictures which explain the fate of the money are deliberately not published, giving thus room for manipulation of the money at the mercy of those engaged in fiscal management."

Foreign aid to STP—provided by countries such as Brazil, Japan and Italy—gave rise to at least three more public cases of alleged fraud involving the misappropriation of funds and foodstuffs. The latest involves a Japanese loan of 1.6 million dollars made available to the Chamber of Commerce, Industry, Agriculture and Services (CCIAS) of the archipelago for the trading of construction materials, which was diverted by the secretary-general of this institution, Cosme Rita—also a deputy and leader of the Party for Democratic Convergence (PCD). The allegation was made in October, 2009, by another member of CCIAS, António Quintas Aguiar, who believes that Cosme Rita made a "family- and party-owned management" of the Japanese credit, benefiting local entrepreneurs and politicians.

António Quintas Aguiar also leads a group of merchants who are stockholders of the STP-Trading, which is involved in another corruption case. STP-Trading is a company founded by local traders to manage products imported from Brazil. It comprises 14 members: D&D Produtos Alimentares Lda, Sogeco Lda, Hull Blyth Lda, Quintas e Quintas Lda, ADAC Lda, Arco—Íris Lda, Cuaco Lda, DFL Lda, Eduardo Luís—Lucumy Lda, Jacudi Lda, LL Bem Estar Lda, Martins e Azevedo Lda, Pereira Machado Lda, and Sousa e Filhos Lda. The company's capital is $ 15,000; its CEO is a police officer, the Quartermaster Armando Correia, the Chief Administrative and Financial Officer is Delfim Neves (from D&D Produtos Alimentares Lda), and the Chief Commercial Officer is Osvaldo Santana (from Hull Blyth Lda). STP-Trading took on the responsibility for negotiating with Brazilian traders the importation of food, which is the basis for a 5-million-USD-credit granted by the Brazilian government to STP. The criminal proceeding of which STP-Trading is a target concerns suspected corruption in the import of food unfit for consumption which was purchased with the above credit from the Brazilian government. After the Court had ordered that two of the defendants be "kept in custody" for 24 hours at the central prison, one of the suspects fled the police. The fugitive was the quartermaster Armando Correia (former police commissioner). At the moment they left the Court building, instead of getting into the prison guard car, Armando Correia ran towards another state car and stood on the run, heading for an uncertain location. The other suspect, Osvaldo Santana, went to prison.

The judge of the Court of First Instance, Silva Gomes Cravid, accused in the same evening the Minister of Interior, Raul Cravid, of "disrupting the democratic rule of law". In a press statement, Gomes Cravid stated that Armando Correia had fled under the protection of Raul Cravid of whom he was advisor. He stated that:

> "There is some protection from the minister with respect to Mr.
> Armando Correia. It is a very bad feeling because we are always
> vilified by the political discourse that the Courts do not work."

According to the judge, the defendant "fled in a state car, led by the private driver of the minister and protected by the police. Armando Correia used the state police, who are paid by taxpayers, to evade justice, which is at least the worst that can happen".

Armando Correia was later arrested. The financial director, Delfim Neves—who is also a deputy of the National Assembly and member of the PCD-GR party—is also one of the accused; however, he is protected by parliamentary immunity, and so he cannot be judged by the Courts. Hence, traders want parliamentary immunity to be lifted from Mr. Delfim Neves . Regardless, the National Assembly twice rejected the Courts" request for removing this man's parliamentary immunity. Parliamentary immunity is a shield that protects most São Toméan politicians from taking responsibilities from crimes committed. The São Toméan Parliament usually does not touch the immunity of its members. Since the advent of multiparty democracy in 1991, Justice has asked the National Assembly removal of parliamentary immunity of 37 deputies, but without success.

In recent years, most media coverage was concerning the diversion of approximately 3 million U. S. dollars resulting from food aid from Japan, known as "the GGA Scandal." In one stroke, about 6 deputies were implicated in the financial scandal. Despite damning evidence collected by the Courts, no deputy was accused in the case; no parliamentary immunity was removed. There is a heated confrontation between the Attorney General's Office and the National Assembly, which has always refused requests from Justice.

The country still recalls the case of the issuance of state treasury bonds, worth 500 million U.S. dollars. Some deputies were involved, and the National Assembly never removed their immunity. The Parliament has previously rejected an application from the Courts requesting removal of Adelino Isidro's parliamentary immunity. The persistent refusal of the parliament to deliver the deputies to Justice leaves the impression that the legislative body is a fortress—inaccessible for Justice.

In August, 2009, Prime Minister Rafael Branco and the District Boards were accused of assault on public health by the secretary-general of the MDFM-PL (the political party of President de Menezes), Raul Cravid[46], for distributing products unfit for human consumption to the population. Most of these goods have been declared unfit for human consumption by the competent bodies of the Ministry of Agriculture and Ministry of Commerce. Raul Cravid argued:

> "It is an attack on public health distributing products outside the limits of validity or expiration date. It damages the health of people. Please note that, recently, the Criminal Investigation Police withdrew from the shops all the products that were at the limit of validity. Why are both the Government and the district boards distributing these products?"

One week prior to these statements, the Board of Trade warned the population of the danger of consuming products imported by STP-Trading which had passed their expiration date. At the time, the Board of Trade promised action, stating that those who put such products on the market would be held criminally responsible. On August 21, 2009, the Ministry of Agriculture (MA) and the Ministry of Commerce (MC), through the Office for Agricultural Research and Technology

---

46 Raul Cravid was minister twice: He was first Minister of Public Finances and then Minister of Home Affairs.

(CIAT), and the Department of Commerce (DC) published the final results of bacteriological tests of various products imported from Brazil. The Government advised the population not to use butter imported from Brazil, as the water content did not follow normal parameters.

Already on August 24, through the Directorate of Health Care, the Ministry of Health (MS) came to challenge the analysis carried out by CIAT and the DC. In a statement signed by Eduardo Neto, the Director of Health Care, the Government said that the "MS challenges individuals of good will to analyze in credible and independent laboratories the same products as needed to help further reassure the population." MS further advocated the consumption of margarine imported by STP-Trading, stating that "the balance of the various components of margarine and products made from milk is fair and generally does not disturb the proper functioning of the body. However, it is common for persons to be surprised by such products because they are not accustomed to the consumption of them." Yet, STP-Trading issued a document of rejection and return of such margarine, as it recognized the fact that the product was not of a standard to be consumed by the population.

The Government also published the results of tests carried out on the milk compound that was imported instead of milk powder. Based on the examinations made by the Portuguese Authority for Food and Economic Security (ASAE), CIAT and DC announced that the identified milk compound was not part of the list of eligible assets, listed in Annex 2 of the memorandum of understanding between the governments of Brazil and STP, signed on December 12, 2007. They advised not to sell. However, in late August, 2009, the Prime Minister Rafael Branco—whose administration had ordered to withdraw the composite milk and margarine—advised the population to consume all goods imported by STP-Trading, saying that the analysis results proved that foodstuffs were safe for consumption—a contradiction.

In relation to the milk compound, there was another contradiction: it was soy milk. STP-Trading always maintained that it had ordered milk powder from the Brazilian suppliers, but they had sent the milk compound. The contradiction became even clearer when Brazil's ambassador, Arthur Meyer, in a letter dated August 24, 2009 sent to the São Toméan government, said that "the Ministry of Foreign Affairs of

Brazil has documentation that proves that São Toméan buyers knew that it was compound milk, and report that certifies the products were fit for human consumption and in perfect condition at the time of shipment.... According to Brazilian exporters, the compound has similar characteristics to milk powder, but is not classified as such, so it is much cheaper and thus preferred by importers."

A few days before this incident, prosecutors visited the warehouse in which all imported products were stored. They attested that all products imported in May, 2009, were on the verge of expiry. Most were due to expire before the end of the year. Beef and other foodstuffs imported from Brazil were at the limit of time, and should have been incinerated as soon as possible because the meat was not well preserved or was deteriorated. The visit of the Justice to the warehouse was deemed extremely important for the criminal proceeding that was in progress. Cooking oil—which was out-dated—was piled on the floor of the warehouse, and was considered too much exceeding the population's needs.

Ambassador Arthur Meyer hinted that the Rafael Branco's administration was implicated in the excessive import of oil foodstuffs. Due to the lack of cold storage and the fact that the shelf-life was on the verge of expiration, the product could not be consumed by the population.

> "There was a purchase of certain goods in quantity stipulated by the São Toméan government, well above the carrying capacity of the local market. For example, approximately 20 liters of oil per capita in the country" (extract from the letter of Arthur Meyer).

However, Prime Minister Rafael Branco, in his statement to the country, pledged that his administration had nothing to do with the import of such products, although the Government appeared to be involved in multiple contradictions within the commercial and financial scandal of the STP-Trading.

On August 28, 2009, the magazine *O Parvo* published on its website a curious news item:

> Rafael Branco and Mr. Nino [Domingos] Monteiro are in the Federative Republic of Brazil. Everything points to be a lightning trip to that country, concerning the latest developments of "STP-Trading," which describes the government of Rafael Branco as an important part of the scandal.

Rafael Branco left STP on the 17th of this month and said he was traveling for a private visit of a week. He would return home on the 24th, so the postponement of his arrival is a matter of several questions.

Incidentally, O Parvo knew, but without direct confirmation, that Delfim Neves' wife surprised Rafael Branco, Carlos Tiny and Nino Monteiro in Lisbon, at the latter's house, with vexatious messages to the "trio" that have purposeful led her husband to the scandal. The vexatious message was thus addressed: "... if my husband goes to jail, you'll go too, because it is you who put Delfim Neves in this ..."

On October 20, 2009, the digital newspaper *Vitrina* published another even more curious article:

The Attorney General Roberto Raposo is accused of allegedly hijacked the STP-Trading's process, which is still in pre-trial preparation in the prosecution. The complaint is from a group of defense lawyers involved in this process, which calls for the release of clients who are detained in the central prison for 2 months without charge. Fabio Pinto, spokesman for the lawyers, said that before this situation the magistrate's complaint cannot be deducted. According to Fabio Pinto, the Attorney General invaded the Office of the Deputy General Prosecutor broke open the drawer and took the case because he could not gather evidence adduced.

Another case relates to the diversion of more than a ton of pasta and cooking oil donated to the country by Italy in 2009. Food aid from Italy should be freely distributed to the neediest people. The Minister of Commerce at that time, Celestino Andrade, acknowledged that the Executive sold part of the cooking oil, and suspended the deal due to complaints received from the Italian government. However, after this decision, the former director of the Fund for Stabilization of Prices of Commodities (FEPPB), Demetrio Salvaterra, diverted and sold large quantities of these products. And although being investigated by the Justice and therefore forbidden to leave the country, he travelled to Portugal. In May of that year, the Government asked the Portuguese the extradition of this senior official as a fugitive from justice. In response, Demetrio Salvaterra told RDP Africa (the Portuguese Broadcaster for Africa) in Portugal that the Minister of Commerce, Celestino Andrade, had diverted approximately 70,000 Euros from the sale of part of the

Italian food aid. The Portuguese government did not allow the extradition and no-one was formally accused to date.

On March 22, 2010, a man—no less, a lawyer by profession, deputy of the National Assembly and member of the board of the MLSTP / PSD—known as Adelino Isidro, was suspended from "all [MLSTP/ PSD] organs and activities" by the political committee of this party, for having denounced "a corruption network with branches in Luanda," citing Prime Minister Rafael Branco, the Foreign Minister Carlos Tiny, the son of this one, N'Gunu Tiny, an Angolan official, Carlos Feijó, and a Portuguese lawyer from Sonangol, whose name was not mentioned, as part of this network. Adelino Isidro said that the concerned Government officials received bribes worth more than two million U.S. dollars in the sale of the state's shares in the National Company of Oil and Fuel (ENCO) to the Angolan oil company, Sonangol.

On February 17, 2010, a woman named Maria de Cristo Carvalho, the then Minister of Social Communication , resigned from office after being convicted by the Court of Auditors for mismanagement of funds of the Social Protection program between 2006 and 2008, when she served as Minister of Labor and Solidarity. Take heed: at that moment, she was condemned by the Court and was no longer Minister of Labour and Solidarity, but Minister of Social Communication. Despite the conviction, the Court did not demand her resignation. Her resignation was a personal decision.

4.2: Keep yourself in the throne to the eternity and please don't work! You are not so stupid.

> Think about power, not about your brother.
> Pay for votes; but don't pay too much. And take care of your looks.

Seibert states that, "The political and electoral dispute in STP has been peaceful, but the money has become an important component of the process. Many activists campaigning are not motivated by party loyalty or by personal convictions, but for the money, given that the campaigns create additional opportunities in a country where poverty is rampant. The wealthiest political parties do not restrict themselves to the disclosure of campaign programs, slogans and promises, committing themselves also in the distribution of bank notes and offerings beyond the usual range of advertising materials. Whilst these investments do not provide the votes in advance, because the ballot is secret, candidates must hold the purse strings before they know whether they were or not benefited. The strategy which focuses on personality over the content has been particularly marked at the local level, and in that context, patron-client relations have played an important role in partisan wrangling. The campaign allows both voters and candidates to create new patron-client relationships and continue to explore existing ones. The parties and candidates often make exaggerated promises which they cannot or do not wish to comply, but the voters, in turn, do not shy away from crossing at times partisan borders and haggling. We also often see political parties being addressed as patrons outside the election period by those who seek favors and financial support. However, at this point, not depending on voters, political parties tend to restrict the distribution of benefits and perks to their customers" (Seibert 2001, 391-392).[47] Seibert further states (2001, 435) that the absence of sharp ideological differences facilitates the formation of mutant coalitions between parties, which can be built against a common enemy, to defend common interests. However, the weight of personal conflicts—such as those which put, on the one hand, President Trovoada and ADI, and on the other hand, the PCD-GR—fundamentally prevent the formation of coalitions, although there are no significant programmatic differences.

The destructive belief of the political elite of this country has everything to do with corruption:

> In STP, the political system is not based on the presumption that the state machine is neutral; to the contrary, the Government is understood as an emanation of the ruling party and not as a neutral articulation of competing interests, reflecting the national plurality. Consequently, public officials do not feel obligated to the same loyalty to the governments of another party other than their own; neither is an ethic of administrative neutrality expected from them. In these circumstances, public institutions have been weak and disabled, whilst corruption, misuse of public funds, and other malpractices, blossom, fuelled by foreign development aid and foreign interests, with the complicity and tacit consent of the donor community. The corruption would not be

47   Our translation.

possible without the availability of funds and external financial temptations that they ferment. The conclusion for now is that, in STP, liberal democracy has introduced greater transparency in governance, but definitely had not led to greater accountability, and even less to decreasing levels of corruption (Seibert 2001, 292).

In a series of public scandals that occurred, the responsible persons are left innocent, with only defenseless subordinates being accused and prosecuted. Several public manifestations demanded justice for crimes against democracy and human rights rulers and Government officials have been committing. People require that punishments for corruption, harassment, and the like, carried out by state officials and rulers should basically observe two principles: First, there should not be amnesty, for it is never a good idea to assign amnesty to a person or association which one does not have a high regard for; and second, people should always realize that anything which destroys another is negative and unwanted.

After considering a number of cases from a chronological perspective, Gerhard Seibert found that cases of corruption were frequent and widespread during the fifteen years of single party regime which followed independence (203-205). However, in an age considered to be of transparency and democracy and, therefore, free from dictatorial pressure, the proliferation of corruption continues:

> The government of the PCD-GR was carried to power by popular demand of accountability from politicians, democracy and development. However, the new group of politicians began to show political attitudes and habits similar to those of their predecessors. The initial impetus against corruption was of short duration. So fast they got there [in the power], they found the fulfillment of election promises less easy and seductive than the struggle for wealth and personal aggrandizement. Political power was seen as a means of appropriation and distribution of wealth rather than a public service. These attitudes proved to be deeply rooted in local political culture, regardless of which party is in power or the political system. Democratic institutions simply absorbed the political attitudes and clientelistic modes of distribution of resources that had characterized the old regime. Moreover, due to a weak economy, in the new system, the São Toméan political

leaders remained financially dependent on the state, which encouraged rent-seeking and corruption (Seibert 2001, 291).

The political creed in this country seems to be a road, linking to a world hostile to national progress. When something bad occurs in the country, Government officials merely run away. The fact that there is no justice for the rulers and governmental officers is an everyday business. The courts have given full protection, priority, impunity and immunity to Government members and their partners. Government officers have become engaged in a kind publicly institutionalized corruption and, systematically, they do accuse and fire innocents.

One Thousand Prophets of Misfortune

From its independence on July 12, 1975 until the present day, the country's fate has been determined by several hundred senior civil servants, amongst them three presidents of the republic, eighteen prime ministers, and a huge legion of ministers, secretaries of state, legislators, managers, and so on. They are backed by a number of political parties and a destructive creed that can be spelled out in a few "commandments." In accordance with that creed, the projects they have undertaken have resulted in the destruction of the country. If they chose to profess another creed, they could have transformed this beautiful and diverse country into a viable state.

This section provides biographic details of some of the most important individuals who have shaped the nation's conscience since Independence. This group represents the leadership universe. They have been the inspiration of the political class and, therefore, are responsible for the acts and the choices made to date. The character traits observed in these individuals can be generalized to the entire political class.

President of Republic Pinto da Costa

Manuel Pinto da Costa, born on August 5, 1937 and educated in the German Democratic Republic, is an economist who was the first STP President. He instituted a one-party socialist state under the Movement for the Liberation of STP (MLSTP), and ruled for fifteen years from Independence in 1975 until 1991. For fifteen years, he ruled the country as an all-powerful, omnipresent and omnipotent supernatural power, teamed with a set of faithful followers who were all members of the MLSTP, the party they invented and managed. In 1978, three years after being assigned power, and willing to grow up and perpetuate on the throne, this man first stationed approximately 1,500 troops from Angola and Guinea-Bissau on the archipelago, following an alleged plot to overthrow the Government. He also brought Soviet, East European, and Cuban personnel as foreign supporters of his regime as a way of guaranteeing personal security and international visibility. In 1979, the Prime Minister at that time, Miguel Trovoada, was arrested and charged with attempting to seize power. His post was assumed by Pinto da Costa, and Trovoada was demoted to the position of Minister of Industry, Housing and Fisheries. After being arrested and detained for 21 months, Trovoada went into exile in France in 1981, and the MLSTP was reported to be seriously split. In the early 1980s, there was unrest in Principe, which was apparently provoked by separatists. Pinto da Costa became a totalitarian dictator: President of the Republic (and Prime Minister), Chief of State and Government, Commander-in-Chief, President of the ruling party, MLSTP, and so on.

Many people argue that Pinto da Costa was the mentor who brought democracy to the country, but actually the people's reaction against the despotism and the perpetuation of the plantation economy, as well as the centralization of power which turned the country into a bankrupt state, together with the international situation caused by the fall of the Berlin Wall, that brought democracy to the country. During the Cold War, the islands' geographic isolation and seeming lack of natural resources or even a deep-water port, made them of dubious value to either superpower.

During the first fifteen years after Independence, STP's economy, society, politics, security, etc., were handed by Soviets, Cubans, Chinese, etc. (the Soviet Bloc), who have focused heavily on support for governance, training of military cadres, equipping and advising of the armed forces, as well as espionage and counterespionage. For many years, the only radar system that existed in the country was supplied, installed and managed exclusively by the Soviets. This radar system was more in the interests of espionage and counterespionage of the Communist Bloc than of the people of STP, because it was used to control the entire maritime and coastal region of the Gulf of Guinea. After the fall of the Berlin Wall, which led to the departure of the communists, the radar was dismantled and taken back by the Soviets. After this, the country has known no radar system installed in its territory until the U.S. military expansion in the Gulf of Guinea in 2006, when a radar system was installed in STP by U.S. soldiers.

Assistance from the Communist Bloc had hegemonic character and was widespread, involving all sectors of national life. To be a little more specific, they provided massive training of local senior leaders in communist countries (Cuba, Russia, China, etc.); they had specific programs and schools for training of third world countries' personnel, for example, the Patrice Lumumba University in Russia[48] (it was renamed Peoples' Friendship University of Russia on February 5, 1992). Many students were sent to Cuba at an early age and remained there until they finished their higher education. Massive assistance was provided by Cuban staff: teachers, methodologists, counselors, researchers, etc. In the health sector, Chinese, Korean, Cubans and other communist doctors and nurses were sent en masse to provide health care to the population. STP also received massive military assistance from the Communist Bloc: There were Cuban, Russian, German (from the then Democratic Germany), and other communist troops entrenched in the country. The same was applied to all other areas of social, political and economic life of the country—the Communist Bloc took care of all the key tasks.

The strategy of the Communist Bloc was similar for all neighboring countries. They were focused both in North-South and South-South cooperation. All neighboring African countries received similar treatment from the Communist Bloc, and they were engaged in bilateral and multilateral cooperation relationships among themselves. Communists (Mainly Cubans and Russians) supported civil wars and independence wars in Angola, Nigeria, DRC, etc. For instance, STP received troops from Angola and Guinea Bissau, along with troops and military assistance from Cuba, Russia, Germany, Libya, Morocco, Egypt, etc.

In the straitened circumstances of the late 1980s, it became increasingly clear that the assistance from the Soviet Bloc would not be eco-

---

48   See website: http://www.rudn.ru/en/

nomically sustainable. The end of the Cold War represented not only the end of communism and the mass departure of the communist staff from the country, but also represented the disintegration of the USSR and a deep economic, social and political crisis in Russia. As a consequence, the development assistance STP received from the Soviet Bloc also ceased. Some steps towards democratic reform and a qualified repudiation of the socialist experiment were expected to open the doors to increased Western aid.

At the beginning of 1989, the Central Committee of the MLSTP, the single party, announced that a National Conference was to be held and that it would be open to "independents." Convened on 5-7 December that year, this conference called for the end of the single-party system and, on 10 December, the GR (Grupo de Reflexão) was founded—the embryo of an opposition party. Miguel Trovoada, who had been exiled in Paris, returned on 30 May 1990 after nine years abroad, and in August 1990, the Government organized a referendum in order to approve the change in the Constitution, abolishing the single-party regime (72% yes, despite a call from the opposition to boycott the vote). On 4 November, the GR transformed itself into the Democratic Convergence Party (PCD—Partido da Convergência Democrática) under the leadership of Leonel Mario d'Alva (President) and Daniel Daio (General Secretary). The MLSTP, in crisis, was reconstituted in mid-October 1990, and added the appellation Social Democratic Party (MLSTP/PSD—Partido Social-Democrata) led by Carlos Graça with the support of Pinto da Costa. In November, however, the latter mentioned decided not to stand for the presidential elections.

With the advent of democracy and after a few unsuccessful attempts to remain in power, Costa had managed his retirement in politics. He unsuccessfully ran for president in a democratic system in 1996, taking 47.26% of the vote in a second round against President Miguel Trovoada. In September 2000, Francisco Fortunato Pires—the President of the National Assembly of STP and a former Secretary General of the MLSTP-PSD—accused Manuel Pinto da Costa of being an anti-democrat. The rivalry between the two men is connected with the announcement by the former President of his intention to stand for the next presidential elections. And, again in 2001, da Costa ran for president, taking approximately 40% and losing to Fradique de Menezes, who won a majority in the first round. In an extraordinary Congress of the MLSTP held in May 1998, Manuel Pinto da Costa was elected unopposed as president of the party. And, in late February 2005, Guilherme Posser da Costa was elected to succeed him.

In 2002, his office was attacked by gunmen. The intention of this act still remains unclear. Manuel Pinto da Costa has been sent as Ambassador for life to the intergovernmental organization International Parliament for Safety and Peace in Palermo[49], Italy, and now heads their Department for Foreign Affairs.

A dictator can be born to live in a democracy, but someone accustomed to power can never live without it. Pinto da Costa could reawaken as a democrat but, purely because he was accustomed to power, could live in a system where he was not the ruler. But people seemed to have no reason to trust him again.

President of Republic Miguel Trovoada

Miguel dos Anjos da Cunha Lisboa Trovoada was the country's second president. He ruled for ten years, from 1991 to 2001. He was born in the city of São Tomé São Tomé and attended secondary school in Angola before studying law at the University of Lisbon (he did not graduate). In 1960, along with his classmates, he co-founded the Committee for the Liberation of STP (CLSTP), which was renamed the Movement for the Liberation of STP (MLSTP) in 1972. Operating out of its headquarters in Gabon, Trovoada served as the Movement's foreign affairs director from 1961 to 1975, and was instrumental in gaining recognition from the Organization of African Unity for the MLSTP in 1972. After independence, he became Prime Minister. But he was accused of treason and attempt to mount a coup. President Pinto da Costa fired him and sent him into exile.

After nine years in exile, he returned in May 1990 after a new constitution was officially adopted, ending one-party rule. He then campaigned for President. His return triggered a large-scale popular demonstration. Nevertheless, he had a bad performance as President. Despite occurrences which led Pinto da Costa to distrust and subse-

---

49   http://www.internationalparliament.org/en/index.htm

quently fire him and send him to exile, people could not expect him to perform so poorly as President.

Miguel Trovoada took advantage of a unique socio-political sce-nario at that time. In the general elections of 20 January 1991, the Dem-ocratic Convergence Party (PCD) beat the MLSTP, gaining 54.4% of the votes and 33 seats against 30.5% and 21 seats (with one seat going to the CODO party—Coligação Democrática da Oposição). In March, 1991, Miguel Trovoada, the only candidate standing, won 82% of the votes (40% abstention) and was invested in office on 3 April. It was the country's first multiparty presidential election. He was then re-elected in 1996. When he ran for president, he was not a member of any politi-cal party but, by the end of his first term, he had formed a new political party—the Independent Democratic Action (ADI). Daniel Daio from PCD-GR became the Prime Minister, but his relations with President Trovoada rapidly deteriorated, and the latter dismissed the former in April 1992 whilst supporting the emergence of the ADI which was led by his son Patrice Trovoada. A new PCD-GR Prime Minister, Norberto Costa Alegre, was appointed on 16 May 1992. Trovoada could not con-tain his thirst for absolute and authoritarian power. A president who comes from the hard line of Russian communism is not prepared to live in an environment of confrontation of ideas, and so the semi-presiden-tial democracy was a powder keg. Trovoada dismissed prime ministers at a rate of six prime ministers in five years. A curious fact is that his name, Trovoada, means Thunderstorm in English!

The early general elections of October 1994 punished the failures of both the PCD-GR government and President Trovoada: The MLSTP/ PSD won 27 seats in parliament against 14 for the PCD-GR, and 14 for ADI, with a low turnout (48% of the 56,000 registered voters did not vote). This was one of the first cases of a former single party return-ing to power in open elections—although it must be admitted that the party was now unrecognizable. Carlos da Graça became Prime Minis-ter. The social situation worsened, however, with the rise of a certain level of insecurity, something new in STP, and the political class went through bitter crises which did nothing for the reputation of the state.

From 15 to 21 August 1995, soldiers who had received no wages for several months, along with other politicians and the people, conspired against Trovoada, and then he was deposed in a bloodless coup, but was soon reinstated after agreeing to pardon the soldiers who participated in the coup. It was the first coup d'état of the democratization period in Africa. Second-Lieutenant Manuel Quintas de Almeida[50] announced the formation of a Junta of National Salvation with the sole aim of coming to an agreement with the political parties on the formation of an efficient government. The coup d'état was denounced unanimously by the international community and the African countries. The MLSTP/PSD, ADI and PCD-GR met the mutineers and agreed to negotiate in exchange for the re-establishment of the Constitution. The military demanded impunity and a reform of the powers of the Chief of State. On 21 August, the Assembly voted in favor of the amnesty and the coup d'état came to an end on the 22nd without having affected the day-to-day life of the population. International threats to cut off aid to the country hastened the Government's restoration.

President Miguel Trovoada came out of the crisis in a weaker position (his term of office was officially to come to an end on 3 April 1996). The MLSTP/PSD and the PDSTP-CODO signed a pact of national union on 29 December, but the PCD-GR refused to join them. Carlos Graça resigned on the 30th, allowing the creation of a government of national union until the presidential elections scheduled for 3 March 1996. This government took office on 5 January 1996 with Armindo Vaz d'Almeida (MLSTP/PSD) as Prime Minister, with a majority of MLSTP ministers but also four ministers from the ADI and one CODO.

Former President Pinto da Costa announced his candidacy as an independent citizen on 19 January with Miguel Trovoada initially waiting and then finally announcing his own. In the meantime, the electoral roll census was progressing with great difficulty due to a lack of means and great resistance from the population. In fact, 15 of the 60,000 voters were registered between the 5 and 22 February 1996. On 9 and 10 March, a strike by the police demanded a clearer definition of their role and that of the army, which was followed by a strike among the two staff from 11 to 17 March, all of which contributed to making the social atmosphere tense.

---

50   Manuel Quintas de Almeida died on 26 December 2006 during a stay in Portugal for unspecified health reasons.

On 3 March, the elections were postponed. Census operations re-started again on 22 March with assistance from France. Four other can-didates finally declared their intentions to stand, with the three main ones being former President Pinto da Costa, who won the support of a large majority of the congress of the MLSTP on 23-24 March, Carlos Graça as an independent candidate, and Alda Bandeira, designated by the PCD-GR, who called on the female population for support against the "inability of politicians."

The presidential elections were finally held on 30 June and 21 July 1996. In the second round, the outgoing President, Miguel Trovoada, won against ex-President Pinto da Costa with 52.74% of the votes. This narrow win opened the way to contestation of the fairness of the elec-tion, thus contributing to the aggravation of the political crisis which had previously started with the aborted coup d'état of 1995. The politi-cal scene thus became structured around two opposed poles: On the one hand, there was the MLSPT-PSD and the PCD-GR who governed with a majority and, on the other, the ADI, PDSTP-CODO, FDC-PSU and AP-PT, a coalition created in October 1996 in support of President Trovoada, but which held only a minority in parliament. The appoint-ment of the Prime Minister in 1996 set the tone of the confrontation between the two sides.

In search of a solution to the political crisis, President Trovoada put forward the idea of a Forum of National Unity and Reconstruc-tion. This forum was held from 27 to 30 March 1998 with some 600 delegates taking part—including the 55 members of parliament, the representatives of the political parties, the professional organizations, and the NGOs, etc. Although there were disagreements as to whether the decisions of the forum were binding or not, the participants did come to an agreement on the need to revise the constitution and to set up a government of national unity and to extend the term of office of the members of parliament until the end of the transition period. How-ever, these projects took time to implement, and the elections were fi-nally organized in November 1998. The MLSTP-PSD, the former single party, got an absolute majority with 31 of the 55 seats in the National Assembly. Its former ally—the PCD-GR—won 8 seats with the other 16 seats being attributed to the ADI, the party of President Trovoada.

He is, therefore, still obliged to work with a Prime Minister from the MLSPT-PSD.

There was a more positive note, however, when the presentation of the program of the new Prime Minister, Posser da Costa, was passed unanimously by Parliament. However, the two main parties in the parliamentary opposition—the PCD-GR and the ADI—have since announced that they will vote against approving the 2000 state budget, as it does not take the recommendations of the IMF and the World Bank into consideration. President Trovoada's term ended on 3 September 2001 when Fradique de Menezes was sworn-in as the new head of state.

President of Republic Fradique de Menezes

Fradique Bandeira Mello de Menezes was born in March 21, 1942, on the then-Portuguese colony of São Tomé, and was born to a Portuguese man and a local woman. He is the country's third president, and has been ruling from 2001 through to the present day. The São Toméan people simply call him Fradique. He first attended high school in Portugal and then studied Education and Psychology at the Free University of Brussels, although has not graduated.

He was foreign minister of STP from 1986 until 1987. He was elected President in July 2001 with about 55.2% of the vote, defeating Manuel Pinto da Costa, who received approximately 40%. Menezes took office on September 3, 2001 and, on July 16, 2003, whilst he was away in Nigeria, there was a military coup d'état led by Fernando Pereira, but the Government would be later restored back to power on July 23, 2003, following an agreement. There were rumors that it was Fradique himself who was the conspirator of the coup, and that his trip to Nigeria was nothing but mere production to divert people's attention. It should be noted that the coup was intended only to reach the Government and not the President. President and Government are two separate sovereign bodies (semi-presidential system) which have been rivals of each other. Thus, President was interested in a coup against the Government, as part of a plan to weaken all other political forces and gain absolute control of the country. Having directed public opinion in his favor, the President had assembled the foundations for the achievement of another mandate. He was re-elected on July 30, 2006, winning 60.58% of the votes and defeating Patrice Trovoada, the son of former President Miguel Trovoada.

In 2003, Fradique turned to Jeffrey Sachs of New York's Columbia University—the famous American expert on development aid—for advice and support. Sachs has vast experience and advised governments around the world. He has written a book called *The End of Poverty* and saw an opportunity to turn STP into a model case, taking his best team members to investigate the country from a first-hand point of view. Their goals were to help all São Toméans share in the new wealth whilst avoiding the error of depending entirely on oil. But, this seemed to be only a tactic to overcome people's intelligence. President Fradique de Menezes has renegotiated a number of oil contracts, but no one has seen the oil companies' contracts which should have been made public by law.

Like his ancestors Costa and Trovoada, Menezes has also met the São Toméan people in a frustrating socio-political and economic context, dreaming of prosperity. He promised give to the people the wealth they were dreaming of and vowed to keep this country free of corruption and instability. However, corruption and instability increased during his two mandates—as he officially supported them—by firing seven prime ministers in six years.

Prime Minister Posser da Costa

Guilherme Posser da Costa was born in 1953. He held important positions, both in the Government and within the Movement for the Liberation of São Tomé and Príncipe/Social Democratic Party (MLSTP/PSD). He served as Minister of Foreign Affairs on three different occasions: 1987-1988, 1990-1991, and 1994-1996; and later served as Prime Minister from January 5, 1999 through to September 26, 2001.

In early November, 2004, Posser da Costa allegedly damaged the office of Attorney General Adelino Pereira in an attack. Pereira said that this incident was due to an investigation regarding the embezzlement of aid funds, in which he ordered Posser da Costa's arrest. Due to the alleged attack, Posser da Costa resigned from parliament on February 15, 2005, just before his parliamentary immunity was to be removed.

On March 18, 2005, he received a two-year suspended sentence for damaging Pereira's office and "insulting public authority"; he was also required to pay compensation. Posser da Costa stated that Pereira had falsely accused him of being involved in the embezzlement of aid funds, and that he had only been a witness in that case—not a suspect. But Posser da Costa later confirmed his involvement in the GGA Scandal.

At its Fourth Congress, Posser da Costa was elected as President of MLSTP/PSD on February 27, 2005, succeeding party founder and former President Manuel Pinto da Costa. There were 708 votes in favor and three votes against him, who stood as the only candidate. Joaquim Rafael Branco succeeded him in this post in June 2008. Since then, he has been away from all posts and all important influences in this party.

Prime Minister Maria das Neves

Maria das Neves Ceita Baptista de Sousa was born in 1958. She is a former Prime Minister of São Tomé and Príncipe, and a member of the MLSTP-PSD. Before becoming head of Government, Maria das Neves worked as a civil servant in the Ministry of Finance and in the African Development Bank. She held major Government posts as Minister of Economics (1999-2001) and of Commerce, Industry, and Tourism (2002).

She held the post of Prime Minister from October 3, 2002, through to September 18, 2004, and was the nation's first female head of Government. President Fradique de Menezes appointed her as a Prime Minister after the previous three-party Government of National Unity led by Gabriel Costa collapsed following complaints from the army concerning recent promotions. Subsequently, on July 16, 2003 she was detained and briefly hospitalized after suffering a mild heart attack during a short-lived coup d'état. Other key Government officials were also detained. The democratically elected government was restored a week later. Maria das Neves resigned as Prime Minister on August 1, 2003; however, three days later, President Menezes reaffirmed his confidence in her, and she accordingly retained her post when a new cabinet was sworn in on August 9, 2003. President Menezes definitively dismissed her from the post on September 15, 2004, and asked her party to select a new Prime Minister following allegations of corruption, which were brought against her and members of her government. She denies ever participating in any corrupt practices. Three days after her dismissal, a new government led by Damião Vaz d'Almeida was sworn in.

Maria das Neves is a member of the Council of Women World Leaders, an International network of current and former women presidents and prime ministers, whose mission is to globally mobilize the highest-level women leaders for collective action on issues of critical importance to women and equitable development.

Prime Minister Tomé da Vera Cruz

Tomé Soares da Vera Cruz was born in 1955. He was Prime Minister of São Tomé and Príncipe from April 21, 2006 through to February 14, 2008. He was also Secretary-General of the Force for Change Democratic Movement-Liberal Party (MDFM-PL). Before becoming Prime Minister, he was Minister of Information and Regional Integration. A Romanian-trained electrical engineer, Vera Cruz served as Minister of Natural Resources in an MLSTP-led government from August 9, 2003 to March 5, 2004. His party, in a coalition with the Democratic Convergence Party (PCD), won the largest number of seats (23) in legislative elections held on March 26, 2006. Vera Cruz announced his resignation on February 7, 2008, and was succeeded by Patrice Trovoada on February 14, 2008.

During his term in office, STP slipped into severe economic crisis. The price of a kilogram of rice jumped five-fold. The fact that food is mostly imported was not a novelty, but its supply at that time became shorter than ever, with yogurt coming from Libreville in Gabon and pasta from Lisbon. Although electricity was only available for 12 hours a day, EMAE—the state-owned electric monopoly—raised its prices by 68%.

Prime Minister Patrice Trovoada

Patrice Emery Trovoada is son of the Former President Miguel Trovoada; he was born on March 18, 1962, in Libreville, Gabon, and was named after Patrice Emery Lumumba, the first Prime Minister of Congo (Leopoldville). He was Prime Minister of STP from February, 2008 through to June, 2008 (only three months). He served as the Minister of Foreign Affairs from September, 2001, to February, 2002. He was also the Oil Adviser to President Fradique de Menezes, until Menezes fired him in May, 2005, alleging that Trovoada had used his position to advance his business interests. Trovoada is Secretary-General of the Independent Democratic Action (ADI) party. He ran for President in the July, 2006, presidential election, but was defeated by Menezes— the incumbent president. Trovoada received 38.82% of the votes. On February 14, 2008, he became Prime Minister after being appointed by Menezes following the resignation of Tomé Vera Cruz, but his term lasted only three months, when he was defeated in a censure motion in the National Assembly on May 20, 2008. The motion—introduced by MLSTP/PSD—received 30 votes in favor, 23 opposed, and two abstaining. In June, 2008, President de Menezes asked the MLSTP/PSD to form a government—and accordingly this party chose its leader Joaquin Rafael Branco as Prime Minister.

The negative impact of Patrice Trovoada's short term in office was to be highlighted. He took many trips abroad at the expense of public money and made excessive use of public resources. For example, he spent seven-thousand liters of diesel per month to feed his power generator, which amounts to 90 million STD (5,242 US dollars) per month.

Prime Minister Rafael Branco

Joaquim Rafael Branco was born in 1953. He is the President of the Movement for the Liberation of São Tomé and Príncipe/Social Democratic Party (MLSTP/PSD), and Prime Minister of the country from 22 June 2008 to 14 August 2010. He was Minister of Public Works in July, 2003, when he was detained by the military during a briefly successful coup d'état led by Major Fernando Pereira.

This man requires no introduction; his name is commonly associated with corruption scandals.

The Greatest Sins

Within this section some of the most negative contributions given to the nation by the political elite will be depicted. Although the international community always describes these individuals as "national heroes," they are accountable for the country's current state of affairs. They are at the roots of the problems the nation faces today, through their greed, corruption, laziness, political ignorance, social negligence and frivolity, useless emigration and human capital flight, cheating, ideological infantilism and pseudo-heroism, despotism, dogmatic stupidity, and the like. Due to their relevance, following are brief explanations regarding each of them.

Greed

Greed is the instinctive desire to possess everything without satisfaction and always wanting more. It does not reflect the need to purchase only that which is necessary to meet the desires of the body and soul of an individual, but is a feeling instilled in the individual making him or her want everything in excess and without limits. On the one hand, manifested greed means a paradise for the subject to take, and on the other hand, it can symbolize the beginning of the ordeal for those who are used as a means for the purposes targeted by the greedy impulses.

Every day fierce fights erupt between members of the political class for the possession of disproportionate amounts of land. Blind and greedy, they cannot even measure the value of the objects of their struggles; even after having acquired some more land in the Quinta da Favorita[51], for example, they continue fighting for a yard near the Praia das Conchas[52]. With unbalanced envy and a lack of sight, they fight each other, even in the parliamentary sessions, because their neighbor has had a few meters of land more than them. They trigger heated arguments which begin in the streets, passing by parliament and often finishing in houses of drunkenness. And finally, when they take posses-

---

51 Quinta da Favorita is a private farm of President de Menezes, where he owns a luxury home, which has been the most popular site for him to take rest, leisure and vacation. It is said that Fradique spends more time at Quinta da Favorita than at the official residence of the Head of state. It is a popular spot, used as a symbol of quality standard or leisure. Many political actors have an interest in land in the vicinity of the farm.

52 Praia das Conchas is one of the places where the President de Menezes has a private residence. It is a vast expanse of land, forest, sea, sand and plant and animal species, very sensible and coveted for tourist exploration. This site has been disputed by several local political players.

sion of their desired land, they build giant walls as a demonstration of strength. Not satisfied with that acquisition, they get so uncontrollably drunk in order to forget that unmistakable lump growing in their chest because one of them, say, have built a house overlooking the sea—a place that the other wanted.

We once saw a fight—which actually went on to make the head-lines!—and was between a minister and a deputy in the area of the Campo de Milho[53]. The minister was Delfim Neves[54], and the deputy was Adelino Isidro. These two young politicians have clashed several times. The fiercest fighting between the two happened in 2007 because of a piece of land located in the Campo de Milho, which both compet-ed. The deputy was said to have dropped his trousers and showed his buttocks to the minister—an obscene and rude gesture which, in our culture, is the most extreme way of insulting or showing contempt for someone. The minister, humiliated, decided to take his gun and fired shots at the deputy, but the latter was not targeted. The two men con-tinued to shoot each other bullets of shotgun and AK-47, tormenting the whole neighborhood[55]. The deputy ended up being arrested by the police and the scene ended in the bar of the Court, where the deputy was forced to compensate the damage caused to the minister.

The two had already been faced in the Santa Margarita estate dur-ing the campaign for the parliamentary elections of 2006. Once in full parliamentary session, Adelino Isidro rebelled against Delfim Neves. The former asserted that he had met the latter in a situation not fitting for someone who was then a minister: Delfim Neves had defrauded a foreign man and fled to the island of Príncipe to escape the police. PCD and MLSTP/PSD were part of the coalition government that was ruling at that time under the command of Rafael Branco, but Delfim Neves (from PCD) and Adelino Isidro (from MLSTP) could not coexist. The rivalry between the two men could even put at risk the relationship between the two parties.

---

53 Campo de Milho is a residential neighborhood located on the outskirts of the Sao Tome City. It is a new development consisting of luxury villas and inhabited by people of high society.

54 Delfim Neves was Minister of Infrastructure in the government of Tomé Vera Cruz, from April 2006 to February 2008.

55 AK-47 is a semiautomatic machine gun of Russian manufacture, which is wide-ly used in conflicts in Africa.

In September, 2009, Augério Amado Vaz, a Judge of the Court of First Instance, issued an arrest warrant against Adelino Isidro, claiming that the latter had taken possession of a judicial matter. The warrant was only detailed on paper, as the bailiffs did not execute the order of the Judge. Adelino Isidro sought himself to appear before the Court on September 17, 2009, volunteering to be arrested, which ultimately did not occur. One day later, on September 18, 2009, at the door of the Court, Adelino Isidro accused Delfim Neves of having orchestrated the arrest warrant in collusion with the Judge Augério Vaz. Adelino Isidro said his recent public statements regarding the STP-Trading Scandal had stoked Delfim Neves to prepare his arrest in a partnership with the Judge.

Adelino Isidro was positioned as a major campaigner against the process of importing food products considered to be unfit for human consumption from Brazil (the STP-Trading Scandal). He even stated that Delfim Neves, sought by justice in the process, was leading a gang of corruption with many tentacles in other political parties—including the MLSTP/PSD. Adelino Isidro passionately argued that Delfim Neves should be sent to the central prison, where there were two other directors of the STP-Trading[56].

Adelino Isidro vowed that the arrest warrant made against him issued by Judge Augério Vaz had the hands of his rival, because of the fierce fighting he has conducted against Delfim Neves—who was involved in the STP-Trading Scandal:

> "I assume this is the product of a certain function in the orchestration of my speech not to accept a whole avalanche of corruption that goes in this country, having taken a stand against the STP-Trading because ... there is a group of individuals, led by Mr. Delfim Neves, diverting funds that should be made available to the society. This is a persecution against me."

In response, Delfim Neves stated that,

> "Mr. Adelino Isidro elected me as a target, and is not today. When a question appears surrounding my name, he appears to confront me. When you see something against him, he thinks I'm behind

---

56   On Thursday, 29 October 2009, the Director General of the STP-Trading, Armando Correia, and Commercial Director, Osvaldo Santana, who were in custody since August, were freed by the Court of First Instance.

---

it. Adelino Isidro is blindly looking to see that Delfim Neves goes to jail at any cost, even if [I'm] innocent."

In turn, Adelino Isidro presented the reasons:

"... before yesterday [September 15, 2009], Mr. Judge Augério Amado Vaz was having dinner with Mr. Delfim Neves in the house of Mr. Delfim Neves. This is duly acknowledged. Yesterday, we saw the car of Mr. Augério in the backyard of Mr. Delfim Neves. It is public knowledge that Mr. Judge Augério is partnered with a company that is involved in the case of STP-Trading, the D&D, and this is the reason why Mr. Judge Augério took a measure of this kind".

Delfim Neves adamantly denied everything:

"First, I must stress that Mr. Adelino Isidro is nothing but a liar. Again, he is the biggest liar of this republic. Mr. Judge Augério never has been to my house. Moreover, he is not my friend, and much less dines with me and spends time at my house. Moreover, in my house, I have security and electronic surveillance system. I evaluated the records and found that neither Mr. Adelino Isidro nor his cronies passed on the perimeter of my house, at least in recent days".

On September 18, 2009, Judge Augério Vaz stated that it was not the first time that Adelino Isidro—who is also a member of the Higher Judicial Council, appointed by the President de Menezes—was indicted in "theft" cases. The Judge added that the warrant was successful because Adelino Isidro returned the documents he had illegally removed from office to the Court, and that Adelino Isidro tried to corrupt him in order to facilitate the final process for one of Adelino Isidro's clients:

"...on several occasions I talked to him personally. I spoke to the clerk to try to contact him, but Mr. Adelino Isidro told the clerk that he had agreed with me. Although he is my friend, I never go into this kind of schemes.

"... it is not the first time that Mr. Adelino Isidro is indicted in the commission of theft cases. Recently, I had to redesign a process that appeared as performers the bank BISTP (that Mr. Adelino Isidro is Attorney) and Mr. Noronha. This process has mysteriously disappeared from the Court."

The evidence shows conflicts between senior parties in the nation—deputies, judges, ministers, etc.—and private interests: a man was, at the same time, a minister and a senior officer of a company, which was involved in corruption cases; another man—his rival—was both a deputy in the National Assembly and "private" lawyer, defending private interests; both men were involved in a fight over the buying and selling of a piece of land—and they were engaged in unlawful agreements, indicted for corruption. Will there be compatibility between the exercises of public office and the exercise of private activities?

The workplace also seems to be an arena for colleagues to behave as gladiators. For example, one wants to court the new female employee, and so they complain and compete and ultimately bicker when finding out she has been staged with another. They do not feel pleased with the wives and numerous lovers they have, but always look for "fresh meat" to seize. Seibert (2001450-452) states that:

> It is expected of a wealthy and influential man that he offers to his lover(s) housing, money and favors, such as a job, a scholarship abroad, a car or a trip. Corresponding to these expectations, a man flaunts his wealth, spending it with women who, for him, are an indicator of social status such as a good house or a car off-campus. The fact that a minister or an officer of superior rank holds intercourse with the secretary or other employees in his department fits more the rule than the exception. In parallel, he can be seen walking the roads of the [main] island in his official car on weekends, seeking a new relationship or an occasional adventure. From the standpoint of women, the relationship may represent a personal advantage or forms of family support, so that for a young girl from low social class, being sexually attractive usually becomes a valuable element, managed with some calculation. The expectations and substantive requirements of the lovers fall in the redistributive logic of accumulation that De Sardan (1996;1999) considers being a fertile ground for corruption (452).

In order to sustain and maintain a whole army of lovers, wives or girlfriends, one needs money—lots of money. Hence, in parallel, the struggle for the possession, control and seizure of public assets to satisfy their addictions become necessary for social existence. This instinctive and uncontrolled desire leads them to grab and to sell everything that they consider to have any commercial value. They seized all the assets of the state, registering them in their names or names of their relatives. They sold the old colonial gardens, historic homes, public bathhouses, state cars, beaches, lands, agricultural estates, buildings, and artifacts. These people are like Tasmanian devils, which scientists consider the most unsavory animals in the world. Tasmanian devils, in addition to their unbearable odor, are extremely selfish and greedy; they spend their time eating and fighting for scraps of food whilst making an unbearable noise. They are ugly with big eyes, sharp teeth and claws.

Corruption

The drama of corruption in this country remounts the fifteen years of Pinto da Costa's one-party regime, when, concentrating on all economic, political and military powers in his hands, this ruler usurped large amounts of the country's income, later being considered as the country's richest man—and even one of Africa's richest men!

Costa also engaged in dishonest business with foreign private individuals, such as Christian Hellinger, the multinational (São Toméan, South African, German, Philippine, Angolan, and other nationalities) who has had many oil and non-oil business interests in STP. Being one of Pinto da Costa's closest friends and business partners, Hellinger has been greatly benefited from these scandalous contracts and assignments and has been a key player in the STP life for two decades. He has enjoyed top-level political connections in STP, Gabon, and Angola, and has allegedly been said to have strong links with individuals closely associated with the South African Military Intelligence and French intelligence. In STP, Hellinger owned and operated a charter air service, the exclusive Marlin Beach Hotel in São Tomé, the Bombom resort in Príncipe, a fleet of boats, and the company Solar Construction[57].

Trovoada and de Menezes succeeded da Costa in the presidential business. Trovoada attracted friends and made enemies, but always in a square of personal earnings. In 1997, he chose to diplomatically recognize the Republic of China in Taiwan (ROC), against the wishes of the Government and the National Assembly. The People's Republic of China (PRC) retaliated by cutting off the diplomatic relations with STP and forcing STP to immediately pay a debt of 17 million U.S. dollars. The unilateral decision of Miguel Trovoada seemed illogical, but

---

57   Frynas, Jdrzej George, Geoffrey Wood, and Ricardo M. S. Soares de Oliveira, 'Business and politics in São Tomé e Príncipe: from cocoa monoculture to petro-state,' *African Affairs*, 2003: 51-80 .

there were rumors that the President had received a bribe of 30 million U.S. dollars from the Taiwanese government to sign the papers. This caused quite a stir but, as always, everything remained under wraps: STP does not enjoy absolute freedom of the press; there is much that is stifled, and there is a great deal of political persecution of individuals who consider opening their mouths.

After ten years filled with nifty diplomatic tricks and political pitfalls, Miguel Trovoada had to leave the throne by virtue of law. Subsequently, he "appointed" de Menezes to succeed him in the throne throughout a secret pact in which de Menezes would keep Trovoada's wealthy son—Patrice Trovoada—as his partner. Patrice Trovoada was de Menezes' Foreign Affairs Minister and Oil Advisor. Corruption was the only language these individuals could fluently speak—until the time at which both men disagreed; and then, Fradique de Menezes fired Patrice Trovoada, complaining that the Trovoadas were treating the state as their private property. Patrice subsequently became his rival, stating that, "My father and I chose Fradique as President, but one can always make mistakes." When asked about corruption, Patrice Trovoada answered: "...corruption is part of the islands' tradition, and buying votes is part of the course. I do it and so does Fradique." He insisted that all he ever did was strive to save what others had ruined.

In fact, de Menezes helped to plant in people's minds a seed which blossomed into the idea whereby, in order to become rich, all one has to do is to become a Government official for 24 hours. He was the mentor of one of the most profound political crises ever witnessed in the country—he fired nine prime ministers during a seven-year period!

There has been a long-running disagreement between the political parties, the President and the Government concerning allegations of corruption within the oil sector. This essentially involves highly-ranked former and present Government officials. The year 2005 was one of the hottest years of de Menezes' two terms. The exchanges of insults between President de Menezes and the MLSTP/PSD had raised tones in a shameful way. The press secretary of the President, Adelino Lucas, had read statement in which de Menezes criticized MLSTP/PSD and the head of the parliamentary wing of this party, Jorge Amado. De Menezes had questioned the professional capacities of Jorge Amado and considered him to be a corrupt individual who "should look at himself in the mirror to see other party mates who were also undoubtedly corrupt." The day after the statement was issued, Jorge Amado said he had spent all night and morning looking in the mirror, but found no corruption. However, he stated that he had found "two pigs with African swine fever, which the President de Menezes had imported and transported on a private plane and that, despite the efforts of relevant departments of the Ministry of Agriculture, nothing could be done to prevent the entry of two such sick pigs being present in the country." Jorge Amado said further that he had seen in the mirror a series of abuses of power of de Menezes, such as the properties of the state which President usurped, and the continual violations of the constitution of the country which the latter was committing. De Menezes was accused of criminally having occupied large acres of land on the Praia das Conchas and also other land—also in Praia das Conchas—which he surrounded entirely with a wall of more than two meters tall, and built a huge mansion, complete with swimming pool inside. Similarly, Jorge Amado said the President usurped the Quinta da Favorita (his famous private residence) and embedded within it sophisticated facilities and telecommunications security. It is said that this was done at the expense of stolen public money.

It remains important to mention a huge ground located in Villa Maria that President de Menezes traded to the Pestana Group[58]. He had to overthrow the historic residence of Nuno Xavier[59] to build a car park for hotel Pestana Equador. The demolition of that residence was an illegal and provocative act of disobedience to the order of the Courts. The authors of the demolition claimed that they had it run by "superior orders," without specifying who had given such orders. Fradique

---

58   The Pestana Group is a Portuguese group in the tourism sector, with interests in industry and in services. It manages hotel properties in three continents: in Portugal, Brazil, Argentina, Mozambique, South Africa, Cape Verde and STP.

59   Nuno Xavier was the first Minister of the Government of STP, a national hero, born on September 13, 1940, at Roça Margão in the town of Trindade. He is a charismatic figure of the people of STP, who signed the treaty which gave this territory the status of independence and sovereignty on July 12, 1975. He died in a helicopter crash on June 8, 1976, when he was on an official visit to Portugal. Nuno Xavier encompasses the fundamental representation of the ideals that motivated the original and collective will of independence. It was decreed by the 2nd Civil Judge of the District Court of São Tomé an injunction that prevented demolition of the house of the National Hero Nuno Xavier.

de Menezes held and abused the surrounding area in which the Fort João Jerónimo (historic heritage) was built, and gave it to the Pestana Group to build the hotel Pestana Equador. De Menezes also intended to close a public road—the road of Pantufo—to leave free the access to the hotel and the casino, which were built with his permission.

One of de Menezes' former ministers of Natural Resources, Manuel de Deus Lima, made a deal with a company in Liechtenstein when working for the country's Central Bank; the deal was to create a São Toméan commemorative millennium coin. The only catch was that a portion of the profits would go directly to him. Lima was sentenced to two years' probation—which didn't prevent him from being named minister.

Several high-ranking authorities have been summoned to appear in court on charges of corruption. Corruption is omnipresent in the national life. Nowadays, it is considered smart to be corrupt. Corruption is sometimes bewildered by the immensity of the opportunities. The generalized poverty and related social problems provide fertile ground. Due to the fact that it is widely accepted and legitimated by the dominant class in this society, corruption generates and sustains a number of other social problems.

Corruption is widespread among the country's best-educated citizens, those who hold all the information regarding state's businesses and performance. Corruption further restricts access to knowledge and learning by deviating people's senses from correct information sources. It is a kind of knowledge which is seen as an easy route to individual gains. This anti-pedagogic attribute has unpredictable consequences, for the agent of corruption is unable to prevent his or her future behavior or fit the accepted norms.

Laziness

Does working and striving for improvement not give the individual self-empowerment, a greater sense of self, a reason to be proud? Since Independence, laziness has become the characteristic of this country. The fifteen years of Manuel Pinto da Costa's one-party regime was marked by the lack of a social order which could educate citizens in the value of hard work; instead, the regime promoted absenteeism, dilapidation of public property, free lunches, no taxes, and so on. It managed to rely on foreign aid rather than domestic production of goods and services. Directing the country's economy exclusivity towards agriculture based on large farms and only a few crops, they led STP astray. Industry was marginalized, the creation of a local market proportional to the country's wealth was obstructed, science was abandoned and a system of social inequality was fostered.

All of this came as a result of laziness, the refusal to partake in any form of labor. Refusing labor, the regime established alliances, international cooperation relationships, and thus, assured foreign aid, paying back the free-ride with all existing natural resources and opportunities. To date, politicians avoid thinking, hard work, long-term planning, and the like—and all of this is due to their ideological laziness. They rely on straightforward contract biddings, immediate earnings, trading important natural resources and opportunities for their own gain.

Laziness seems to be a major obstacle in the country's development—there is a reduced amount of people's laborious activities. People's resistance to labor doesn't only affect production of tangible goods, but also generates decrease of intellectual activity, straightforward wealth seeking, and degradation of citizenship.

Political Ignorance

The existing lack of understanding of democratic ideals and the failure to adopt democratic institutions has led the state to fail to achieve each of its four main purposes, which are: 1) To build a free, just and solitary society; 2) to foster and guarantee national development; 3) to eradicate poverty and marginalization, as well as reduce social and regional inequalities; and 4) to promote wellbeing for all, without discrimination of origin, race, sex, color, age, and other forms of discrimination. A lack of knowledge is incompatible with a desirable level of democratic performance within a society. For a society to be considered democratic, it is required that its citizens have overcome political unawareness and political illiteracy. Political unawareness is one's inability to be conscious of or perceive a political condition or event. It is the quality of anyone who is unfamiliar with the established political environment.

Since independence, STP has been governed in the way a flock of sheep would be guided by negligent shepherds—lacking orientation. In such conditions, the sheep graze wherever they want, and the shepherds cannot gather the animals in an orderly flock. For the flock to graze in an orderly and convenient fashion, and in order to ensure they feel protected from wild beasts, furtive hunters and/or thieves, it is necessary that shepherds are competent, skilled and experienced. Competence of a shepherd is related with an accurate understanding of the flock, the grazing fields, imminent dangers, etc. It is not enough that shepherds have mere ideas in their minds—it is fundamental that they know how to implement those ideas, how to apply the knowledge they possess in the correct orientation of the flock, keeping them within their sights, never leaving or allowing them to graze outside of the ideal order. Precision, skill and experience are required attributes.

São Toméan rulers (shepherds) have never been able to carry out the tasks to which they have been appointed: they do not know the people they rule (the flock); they don't understand the country, its resources and values, etc. (rich pastures, wolves' dens, etc.), and are themselves "lost in the wilderness." The orientation of a state is its ideology. To its detriment, STP has never had a suitable ideology in place. All the state has done to date is to imitate ideologies—communism, multiparty democracy, semi-presidentialism, etc.—without even understanding to what extent they suit the country's reality.

So far, the socio-political performance has lead to incompleteness and fragility of the country's structures. There is not a consistent and real sense of the concepts of state and nation. STP is a peculiar society in which one pretends to live in an established state, but the very idea of a nation and nationality sounds vague and diffused. The huge political irresponsibility of politicians and Government officials at large has led the country into critical international relationships, which have restrained sovereignty and other democratic principles. New generations have inherited an awful foreign debt, whilst Government officers have obtained huge fortunes.

Social Negligence and Frivolity

There is a widespread feeling that people don't care about accountability in professional services in STP and don't meet moral obligations to deontological norms. People seem to assume any task they want. If decided to be a lawyer, so the individual is a lawyer; the same is true if he or she decides to be an economist, accountant, journalist, policeman, singer, and so on. There is neither a sense of responsibility nor obligation to comply with contracts. Everyone feels free to undertake any unwholesome acts to enjoy the life he or she wants. People are usually disfigured, even in the way they think or express an idea: It seems they don't reflect on things.

In September 2006, the first female incorporations in the São Toméan army occurred. It seemed that the country had too great a need for soldiers that it was necessary to call for female incorporation. This is not to suggest that female incorporation in the army should not be enforced, but it is necessary to create proper conditions first. In the STP army, soldiers starve and live in poor conditions. Was the army able to offer conditions which are suitable for the incorporation of females? Female incorporation in the army was not planned to meet any specific goal. One army officer admitted to having sex with several female soldiers, and said that other colleagues did same act on a regular basis. Some girls became pregnant and were passed to availability. Some female soldiers prematurely ended their pregnancies in order to continue the military service. Thus, incorporating females into the army only satisfied uncommon whims of officials. How is this useful?

The commercial exploitation of child sex, headed by Government officials, has increased in STP. This is usually presented as a "tourist attraction," while the real opportunities for tourism development are not exploited. Instead of increasing tourism revenue in the country, this kind of business has increased the number of people affected by sexually transmitted diseases and illegal sex with minors.

In 2007, the first university was created in STP—the Universidade Lusíada de STP (UL-STP). This was seen as an original event which deserved endorsements from most national voices. STP was then the first country in the world where a university had been created in just a few short months. The quality and utility of that university was questionable, since a variety of resources which STP does not have on offer are required to equip a real institution of learning. But it looked good on the surface.

The persons behind that achievement declared that they had established higher education in STP, which was not true, because two other similar institutions—the Instituto Superior Politécnico (lit. Higher Polytechnic Institute, ISP) and the Instituto Universitário de Contabilidade, Administração e Informática (lit. University Institute of Accounting, Administration and Informatics, IUCAI)—were in the country more than a decade before.

UL-STP functions like a lobby, offering a team for a few Government officials, their children, wives and husbands to play. One thing was sure: the individuals who rule STP seem not to have adequate knowledge about education or policies. Foreign organizations and governments have understood this for a long time and classify this country as "a set of accumulated and unordered tents, with neither a king nor law, with neither order nor orientation." They don't recognize state institutions or accept publicly issued documents, saying they are not reliable.

In the existing political lobbies, marriage is a kind of trading business. A man picks up woman who is viable candidate for being his partner. The selection process seems to be, "Okay, you put me in charge of certain state business, and then I will marry you," and quickly they are married. After a few years, these "anomalous" marriages give birth to kids. When they grow up—but before getting scholarships for studying abroad—their parents give them occupations in "humanitarian actions," "civic works," or some other likely "philanthropic business"; and this is just the tip of the iceberg. Behind these actions they transfer public funds to the bank accounts of their families. Gradually, as any cub, they grow up learning hunting techniques their parents teach them. When they are adults, the saga of their ancestors is repeated down the generations.

The above listed facts show evidence of widespread social negligence and frivolity in this society. Several social studies conclude that the São Toméan people don't believe in further performance, so they appear to be unable to strive for improvement. This is a consequence of almost four decades of deception carried out by state office holders. The status of human development in the country can help to make a vast and dramatic analysis of the situation, given the uncertainties about the economy and opportunities for production in the archipelago.

Useless Emigration and the Flight of Human Capital

So far, this nation's mind has been shaped by a disproportionate venture on emigration. This has been one of the nation's major concerns, which comes in the form of relying on emigration in order to reap any level of success. As a social phenomenon, emigration is the act of leaving one's native country or region in order to settle in another, seeking better opportunities or means to improving one's actual economic or social conditions, such as an improved level security, employment, and the like. Emigration usually occurs as consequence of wars, hunger, climate change, natural disasters, persecution, and so on. However, emigration for the São Toméan people does not fit into any of the above-mentioned criterion. Why do São Toméans emigrate? There is no good answer to this question, but psychological causes may be behind people's behavior rather than any other motive.

São Toméans seem to emigrate by instinct; it appears that they are biologically conditioned to emigration. Irrespective of whether one is wealthy or poor, the dream is nevertheless intact, and that is to emigrate. Often, as an immigrant in a foreign country, they live in inferior conditions than those they were accustomed to in their homeland. Emigration begins with a dream, which crosses with "confrontation with the reality," flows into "frustration" and damages the whole economy, due to frequent human capital and money flights.

Major emigrants are the elements of the ruling class, who emigrate in search of a safe place—a sink—where they can deposit the result of misappropriation of public assets. Emigration of the ruling class occurs both whilst exercising public office and when they are deprived of these positions. In the Diaspora, most see their fortunes diminish and ruined before their eyes. Many ex-ministers and ex-directors work in Europe in jobs which are unfitting with the social status they were supposed to occupy. They travel on public transport and do their shopping in fairs. After a beggar life in the Diaspora, these "unemployed politicians" return home completely bankrupt. Most parts of the national income and mental efforts have been spent in emigration of senior state officers, who maintain bank accounts in foreign countries and frequently travel abroad.

Travelling outside of this archipelago is almost an impossible attainment for most people due to their financial limitations, difficulties in obtaining visas, and so on. Paying for travelling outside this archipelago occurs as the result of a lifetime of money savings as, for instance, the average plane ticket to and from Portugal costs about forty times the average monthly wage. Therefore, emigration task is mostly accomplished by high-class families. Government officials only stay in the country whilst they are in charge of state business and, after these short periods, they go back to emigration. Thus, they promote both financial and human capital flights, which put the country's economy at risk and foster dependence on foreign aids.

Emigration is a kind of not-for-profit enterprise for most people who subscribe to it, mainly because of its high investment and low or null return. Because only wealthy people can emigrate, migration in STP is not a matter of poverty—it is regarded as a moral duty and symbol of high status.

Cheating

In the first week of July, 2004, the Criminal Investigation Police (PIC) arrested more than a dozen people on suspicion of belonging to a network of "money laundering and counterfeiting," a phenomenon that is known in STP as "laundering." In less than a month, the number of people involved in this case amounted to more than forty, including civil servants, businessmen, a police officer belonging to the PIC itself and several deputies of the National Assembly. It was all over a "network of qualified fraud" as opposed to a "network of counterfeiting and money laundering," since there are no technical and technological conditions in the country for the purpose of making counterfeit notes. Let's see how this type of fraud or "laundering" works.

Con artists, commonly known as "measurerers" or "scrubbers," began to approach the target of fraud—their potential prey—claiming that they have some "black notes." In the lexicon of these individuals, "black notes" are notes issued by the U.S. Federal Reserve to finance conflicts in several African countries, including Liberia. They claim that these notes are true notes but, for the sake of safety, they are blackened and sent with a "special liquid" to the destination. At the destination, the notes are "washed" with the aforementioned liquid to become able to go into circulation in any market. However, according to the scammers, there are situations where transport (particularly air transport) is hit by bullets from warring factions, and the "black notes" which are packaged into packets or small boxes consequently disperse. These (true) notes are caught by certain individuals, especially the military, who then negotiate with anyone able to get such "special liquids" to wash them. However, all this was a ruse to extort money from people. Furthermore, the scammers said the "special liquid" was very expensive and rare, so the targets of the fraud are enticed to pay for it and, in return, he or she receives half of the notes after washing. In some cases, people were persuaded to buy the notes at a price considered to be two or three times lower than the assumed total value of the notes after washing. The truth is that the "black notes" were simply plain papers or thin cardboards which could be discarded in the water.

The rubbish started with the following quote: con artists brought a bunch of "black notes" (hundreds), and the first five notes on top of the bunch were genuine banknotes, comprising 1, 5, 10 and 20 U.S. dollars, which were also coated black with a product, like the rest of the packet. They wash or clean these genuine banknotes and subsequently present them to the client and, after drying, the former deliver them to the latter for him or her to bring them to the bank for testing. Indeed, because the first notes were true, after received by the banks, con artists claim this fact as irrefutable proof that the remaining notes are also true. With this technique, a network of senior state officers—including deputies of the National Assembly—engineered a qualified swindling operation in the country, affecting an undetermined number of people. Most of them were completely ruined; having invested everything they had and even mortgaged all their assets. Once more, the involved parties escaped punishment of justice, having been protected by the Courts.

Ideological Infantilism and Pseudo-Heroism

During the past three and a half decades, STP has honored symbols that have not contributed to national progress. The political class has accustomed the people to think they make up a fragile nation, and that any other people can easily torment, humiliate and oppress them. Also implicit in people's memories is the idea that STP cannot win, because no one in the country ever won in the past. There have only been examples of failures—and people usually lament and cry instead of facing and overcoming. They don't believe, for example, that it is possible to develop quality science, medicine, and technology in STP worthy of international recognition.

The overwhelming majority of those considered heroes were martyrs and were defeated by the colonialists. To cite just a few examples, Yon Gato, Giovani, Paulo Ferreira, and "February 3, 1953" are associated with acts of martyrdom of the São Toméan people at the hands of Portuguese colonialists. Therefore, STP is seen as a country of martyrs and defeated people.

It is essential to distinguish a martyr from a hero, and to separate and treat them accordingly. The younger generations should preserve the memory of the martyrs in order to be clear about the violent environment in which their ancestors lived, to know and understand that people were harassed, wronged, humiliated and insulted. Heroes are to be remembered by the new generations in order to know that they are capable of winning; heroes are to be emulated, and one should take patriotic actions oriented towards victory.

Besides the martyrs, the remaining "national heroes" were poets. The political class instilled in the minds of people the idea that poetry was a "weapon of struggle," that poetry was used in the fight against colonialism, and that it was with thanks to poetry that the people became independent. This is like making someone believe that a group of individuals, armed with their poetry, stood in front of an army of settlers and managed to defeat them just by declaiming their "magic" poems! The truth is that these poets have done nothing for the people; they have not even inspired them to action. The independence of STP was granted by determination of the United Nations and as a result of armed struggles that were undertaken in other African countries.

The following section discusses the case of two men who have been held up as our most important national heroes—Francisco Tenreiro and King Amador.

Signs of a Fake Ideology

The National Hero Francisco Tenreiro

Francisco José de Vasques Tenreiro—alias *"Francisco Tenreiro"*—is officially considered a national hero of STP. There are several public tributes made to Tenreiro, including topographical references, names of establishments, including the fact that his bust is stamped on the 100,000-dobras bank note—the most valuable bank note in the country. However, elevation of this man to the rank of national hero resulted from ignorance of the country's political class.

Francisco Tenreiro was born on the island of Sao Tomé on January 20, 1921, in the Rio do Ouro estate, son of Emílio Vasques Tenreiro, a Portuguese farm manager, and Maria Carlota Amália, an African woman working in the countryside of Diogo Nunes. He was taken to Lisbon whilst still fairly young—when he was only two years old—at a time when the United States and France had heard the new voices of black intellectuals claiming rights and proclaiming the identity of African peoples. He distinguished himself as poet and essayist; there are several Tenreiro's essays in the fields of geography, sociology and history scattered across various magazines and newspapers. In life, he published an essay, "The Island of Sao Tomé" (1962)[60], and further published several poetic works, namely, "The Island of Holy Name" (1942)[61] and "Poems" (1967)[62], which was reissued in 1982 under the title "Heart in Africa"[63]. Francisco Tenreiro grew up and lived in Portugal where he studied at the Higher Colonial School and became a full professor at the Faculty of Letters of Lisbon. He died in 1963.

---

60 Lit. "A Ilha de São Tomé."
61 Lit. "A Ilha de Nome Santo."
62 Lit. "Obra Poética."
63 Lit. "Coração em África."

Citing various sources, Seibert (2008) states that Tenreiro was one of the leading figures amongst the young African students in Lisbon, all exiles geographically, psychologically and culturally; however, citing Fernando Macedo[64], Seibert states that Tenreiro was not involved in political activities that the group had gradually developed so as not to endanger his family life and academic career. Moreover, Tenreiro was a moderate man who was more connected to the cultural protest. Unlike his colleagues in the African Studies Centre (CEA), he did not militate in the political opposition against the regime; in fact, Tenreiro not only left the ranks of African nationalists, but was also committed to the Estado Novo (1933-1974)[65]. In 1958—the year that Agostinho[66] Neto and Amílcar Cabral[67] founded the anti-colonial movement (MAC)—Tenreiro, after a conversation with Marcelo Caetano[68], became a member of the National Union (then the only legal party in Portugal) by the circle of São Tomé in the Salazar's National Assembly, where he remained during the term of 1958-1961 and the following until his death.

Tenreiro was seduced by promises of liberalization from Marcelo Caetano, in a moment when he was solidifying his academic career

---

64　Fernando de Macedo Ferreira da Costa (1928-2006) born in Lisbon, descent of São Toméans, was one of the greatest Portuguese thinkers of the twentieth century and founded, following the Revolution of April 25, 1974, along with Henry de Barros, an institute with his name, devoted to cooperatives. He was also professor in the Faculty of Economics, Lisbon.

65　Estado Novo (lit. "New State") was a dictatorial regime in force in Portugal in the period 1933 to 1974, led by Antonio de Oliveira Salazar.

66　António Agostinho Neto (1922 - 1979) was an Angolan doctor, trained at the University of Coimbra, who in 1975 became the first president of Angola until 1979. In 1975-1976 he was awarded the "Lenin Peace Prize." He was part of the generation of African students who came to play a decisive role in the independence of their countries in what became known as the Portuguese Colonial War. He was arrested by the PIDE and deported to Tarrafal (Cape Verde), and then convicted to fixed residence in Portugal, where he fled into exile. Then assumed the leadership of the Popular Movement for the Liberation of Angola (MPLA), of which he was already honorary president since 1962.

67　Amílcar Lopes da Costa Cabral (1924-1973) was a Guinea-Bissaunian agronomic engineer, writer, Marxist and nationalist guerrilla and politician. Also known by his nom de guerre Abel Djassi, Cabral led African nationalist movements in Guinea-Bissau and the Cape Verde Islands. He was assassinated in 1973 by Guinea-native agents of the Portuguese colonial authorities, just months before Guinea-Bissau declared unilateral independence.

68　Marcelo José das Neves Alves Caetano (Lisbon, August 17, 1906 - Rio de Janeiro, 26 October 1980) was a lawyer, university professor of law, a historian and politician, and the last President of the Council of the Estado Novo.

which was flickering. He was the only Black man amongst the 120 deputies, with all deputies for Angola, Cape Verde, Guinea and Mozambique being White men. For the Salazar's regime, the presence of Tenreiro in the parliament served to show that Portugal was a multiracial society where a Black African could be a congressman. Tenreiro's political path reveals that he was neither "a convinced patriot" nor a "hero of Independence" as he is officially celebrated in STP. In fact, Tenreiro did devote many speeches to his homeland and he called for the improvement of conditions of the native population of STP; however, he never questioned the right of Portugal to maintain its colonial empire; even less did he support the independence of STP. Reacting to the UN pressure in favor of decolonization, in October 1958, Tenreiro defended the position of the Salazar's regime, apparently inspired by the theories of the Brazilian *Lusotropicalist*[69], Gilberto Freyre[70] (1900-1987), in a speech at the Portuguese National Assembly, stating:

> It is thus understandable that the Portuguese people do not get tired of talking about the strong unity between all land parcels, and that they consider both the overseas provinces and the most remote nations as belonging to Portugal or being Portuguese folks, and that they remain staunch supporters of assimilation

---

69 *Lusotropicalism* is a belief and movement especially strong during the António de Oliveira Salazar dictatorship in Portugal (the Estado Novo regime), proposing that the Portuguese were better colonizers than other European nations. It was believed that because of Portugal's warmer climate, being geographically close to Africa, and having been inhabited by Romans, Visigoths, Moors, and several other peoples in pre-modern times, the Portuguese were more humane, friendly, and adaptable to other climates and cultures. In addition, by the early 20th century, Portugal was by far the European colonial power with the oldest territorial presence overseas; in some cases its territories had been continuously settled and ruled by the Portuguese throughout five centuries. It celebrated both actual and mythological elements of racial democracy and civilizing mission in the Portuguese Empire, and was a pro-miscegenation attitude toward the colonies/overseas territories.

70 Gilberto de Mello Freyre (March 15, 1900-July 18, 1987) was a Brazilian sociologist, cultural anthropologist, historian, journalist and congressman. In the 1930s, Freyre introduced the controversial idea of a 'Brazilian racial democracy', in which he argued that the racial mixing that was looked down upon in Brazil was enriching the culture. In particular, he believed that the Iberian-Catholic tradition would play a prominent role within the hybrid culture, but also that miscegenation among all the races would produce a more unified and robust racial and social mix and enable everyone to attain opportunities within Brazilian society. Within this paradigm, he coined the term *Lusotropicalism*, which refers to the propensity of Portugal to have adapted and lived in an environment that was able to harmoniously mix the various cultures and races of Brazil.

within a community of feeling and spirit. No other colonizing country can adopt a similar position, and herein lays the originality of the national case (Seibert, 2008, p. 7).

Seibert (2008) further argues that, if Tenreiro was a convinced patriot, his country was Portugal, and STP was part of the Portuguese colonial empire. Quoting an article published in 1961, Seibert states that Mario Pinto de Andrade[71] criticized Tenreiro as one who "unfortunately today cooperates in the defense of Portuguese colonial policy."

The São Toméan politicians—whom declared Francisco Tenreiro as national hero—probably did not carry out a critical analysis on the life and work of this man. They were limited to superficial examination of the texts of his poetry, which were beautiful and related mainly to the island of São Tomé; however, from here to the point where this man can be considered a national hero, there is a long way to go. For example, Mobutu could be considered one of "the greatest" Africanists and nationalists of all times, for having established a regime in his country, deeply rooted in the exaltation of African culture and identity; at the same time, however, he was one of the most bloody men and oppressors of his own people, maintaining a special relationship with people inherently hostile to the then-Zairians and Africans at large. As Mobutu cannot be considered a hero for the Congolese people, Tenreiro also can't for the São Toméan people.

Tenreiro was a great scholar of his time—but how much worth did his immense skills, qualifications and experiences for the São Toméan people? His personality cannot be disassociated from the fact that he had collaborated with a bloody racist and colonial regime that decimated millions of innocent lives. No matter how beautiful his words were, no matter how inspiring were his works and studies, they were words that did not correspond to practice. Indeed, Seibert says:

> There was a change of ideas from the young poet of Negritude[72] to the geographer and later deputy. Possibly the turning of Tenreiro occurred at the time of the end of the CEA, around 1954. Already

---

71   Mário Pinto de Andrade (August 21, 1928-1990) was an Angolan essayist and political activist.

72   Negritude (Négritude in French) was the name given to a stream of literature that has grouped French-speaking black writers; it is also an ideology for exploitation of black culture in African countries or populations with significant African descent, who were victims of colonial oppression.

as a deputy, Tenreiro saw Negritude only as a cultural movement for the emancipation of blacks, but did not accept its political impact. Unlike his African counterparts of the CEA, Tenreiro did not politically radicalize and did not opt for an armed struggle against Portuguese colonial domination. The fact that he lived all his life in Portugal, along with personal reasons—such as family life and his career he wanted to preserve—also played a role in the Tenreiro's pathway. His book on São Tomé reflects the commitment to the Salazar's regime and the ideology of the time. The book contains no direct reference to the theory of Gilberto Freyre's Lusotropicalism, which has been appropriated by the Estado Novo in the years 1960/1970 to justify scientifically the Portuguese colonial policy, though apparently guided by this theory. Claiming that there had not been pure slavery in STP, but a kind of servitude, Tenreiro supported the dominant view of the Salazar's regime that there was an alleged leniency in the history of Portuguese relations with Africans to defend the Portuguese presence in Africa at a time of independence of most European colonies in the 1960s. Due to the alleged absence of slavery in STP, Tenreiro reinvented history, transforming the slave revolt of 1595 in an assault of the Angolares. He also was guided by the ideological postulates of the [Salazar's] system, when he stressed the [positive] impact of Portuguese influence, minimizing the presence of African concepts in the culture of STP. As Tenreiro shared the views of the regime, he did not discuss the massacre of February 1953 (Seibert 2008, pp. 12, 13).

How can an enemy of a people be considered a hero of that people? Tenreiro was an educated man and, indeed, had developed the philosophical side of human consciousness, which appends to knowledge about the world an extreme ability to manage feelings. At this level, a person can weep before a cruel reality, shocking to most people, whilst in his heart, he laughs heartily at the ruin of another. Evidence shows that Tenreiro had already developed this side by publicly supporting a regime that had attempted to exterminate his own people. Tenreiro could argue that he was no supporter of the extermination of his own people, and the fact that he had not commented on the February 3, 1953 massacre was an omission due to ignorance. If he was not aware of such a blatant incident, he was therefore not as smart as was portrayed, and his work therefore cannot be taken as a reliable description of reality. It is not possible to be a supporter of an ideology or political system whilst at the same time disagreeing with the result of that ideology or political system.

Tenreiro cannot be considered a hero of a people who in no way took advantage of his capabilities, actions, ideas, options, affiliations, and so forth. If Tenreiro's geographic studies had some utility, they served the Portuguese colonial administration and not the people of STP. The Salazar regime was oppressive and hostile to the people of STP, and so Tenreiro's statements in defense of that regime were oppressive and hostile to these people.

The Inconsistency and Disappointment of an Ideological Symbol and Myth Called King Amador

The legacy of Amador Vieira, who was later named "King Amador," is an important raw material for the construction of an ideological symbol, which is necessary for the cohesion of the people of STP. However, in the treatment that was given to the story of Amador Vieira, there are great inconsistencies and incoherence. For over three decades—since Independence on July 12, 1975—despite being declared as the greatest of the STP's heroes, there was not a national holiday to honor this symbol.

The story of King Amador ended the day he died, tortured by the Portuguese colonial authorities. He was defeated that day, victim of betrayal of one of his countrymen; however, the day devoted to the memory of King Amador, a recently established national holiday, is precisely the day of defeat. Thus, the symbolism of King Amador has not inspired a sense of patriotism and duty to contribute to national development as it should. That failure has to do with the way the story was compiled. If they had included in the plot of King Amador elements which could characterize him as clever or genius, this symbolism would have produced better effects.

The way the history of King Amador was plotted is sufficient to consider the political class as having lied to the nation, in collaboration with Russian communism. The history told so far was reshaped to match the ideals of this ideology. Communism is based on the presupposition that the power belongs to the people, who are seen in categories: the working masses, young people, women, and so forth. Any nation that promotes this ideology generally uses a legend of representing a mass revolution, which opposes an established colonial or imperialist regime and wins. It is important that that victory seems to be achieved through bloodshed, say, heroic blood. It is necessary, too, that there are heroes (people's heroes—anonymous people who were killed for the sake of the revolution), and that, at least apparently, the territory under colonial or imperialist domain had been occupied by a foreign power (in STP's case, Portugal) and that the revolution was aimed only at recovering the land and entrusting it to its ancient lords (in our example, the people). It is necessary to give the idea that there was a power in place before the occupation (a kingdom, an empire) in order to prove that all the fights fought were fair and also to demonstrate that the bloodshed was unavoidable.

In the impossibility of proving the existence of an organized local community before the Portuguese settlement—which should immediately imply presentation of a ruling personality who had been seized by the occupants, and because it is inconsistent talking about foreign occupation without showing evidences of an autochthonous power before occupation, it was necessary to create a king's image, a communist style epic figure. The São Toméan historic personality who most adequately illustrates such an image was as a fugitive slave who, in the sixteenth century, led a slaves' rebellion, invading the main city of the archipelago. That rebellion was considered to be the greatest amongst them all, involving approximately five thousand fugitive slaves, and lasting about one week. Hundreds of rebels and settlers and the slaves' leader (who was later named King Amador Vieira) were killed. In fact, King Amador never existed; there is no record of such a person having existed within an autochthonous kingdom in STP. The character of King Amador was created to stimulate São Toméan patriotism only. It was said that King Amador was not a slave, but an autochthonous king—a descendent from a dynasty which lasted with Simão Andreza, considered being the last king of the Angolares.

The Angolares have been understood as being the true owners of the São Toméan land, having inhabited the southern part of the São Tomé Island before the Portuguese settlement. The national-communist imagination understood that these people had already had in place a social organization compared to a kingdom, called the Kingdom of the Angolares. Angolares were characterized as being warriors and fearless people (with historic achievements such as never having been subjected to colonial ruling), and, thus, the idea that they had battled for centuries to recover their space was born. This history culminates with the most important achievement of the Angolares people: The revolt of King Amador.

This image of patriotism, together with the Massacre of Batepá of 3 February 1953, alimented the creation of the most important state's symbols. Despite being compiled, they were based on a mixture of rumors, hear-say, and true facts. As the history was false and the arguments were not valid, the Independence based in these presuppositions was not well achieved, and even less achieved was the instituted power and the fake heroes and national leaders as created by the Russian, Cubans, Chinese and other communists of that epoch. The 4th January (King Amador's Day), 6th September, 19th September, 30th September and all other national holidays created under the false STP's history were connected to the fifteen years of the communist inspired one-party regime. Thus, upon instauration of multiparty democracy in the archipelago, all of these symbols were forgotten. In the fifteen years immediately following Independence, there was a cult of the above-mentioned symbols, which involved the entire society; in the schools, they were studied seriously. The end of communism implied trivialization of all these things.

Remarks

One ought to realize the need for cultivating collective self-esteem and patriotism throughout identification, creation, institution, veneration and cultivation of national heroes. What is worth considering is what kind of heroes stimulates the search for national progress and self-fulfillment? What heroes represent and enforce the national values? How must they be created (where must we take them from)? How must they be instituted, venerated, transmitted, and cultivated? These questions can be answered after gathering the following requisites:

- A national ideology, thought through and optimized for the progress of the specific nation

- An optimized strategy for the prosecution of the objectives envisioned by the ideology

- People properly educated and trained, able to understand, interpret and successfully execute the underlying strategy.

It is evident that, in the context of São Toméan communism, none of the above requirements were observed. The figure of King Amador (and other borrowings from Russian communism) did not contribute to the affirmation of the São Toméan identity and the visibility of the country in the world, nor did it contribute to the achievement of national progress; rather, it contributed to the success of communism in STP and the economic and social progress of the country where this ideology came from.

Every ideology has, let us say, a *center of convergence* (center of the ideology) to where all its successes converge. The heroes (real or imaginary) are simply symbols or stereotypes of that ideology, representing the ideological ideals. In the case of religious ideologies, the heroes are the saints. The ideological center of Catholicism, for example, is the Vatican. The Vatican is the wealthiest state in the world, holding an immeasurable fortune in gold. In the case of Islam, the center is Saudi Arabia (the cities of Mecca and Medina). It is not a novelty that Saudi Arabia is the most prosperous state in the Arabic world. In the case of communism, the center was the USSR, now extinct but once one of the most powerful countries in the world. As for the free market and democracy, the center today is the USA... no comment!

The fall of communist regimes around much of the world led to the decline of Russian power; similarly, if all Catholics lose their faith in Catholicism, a crisis would hit the Vatican and Europe; the same would happen to Saudi Arabia if Muslims lost their faith. If the entire world rejects democracy, then the USA will face an unimaginable crisis.

This means STP is in need of an ideology setting itself as the *center of convergence*, and its national values and aspirations as the values to be respected; the ideological objectives must envision the achievement of national progress; the heroes to be cultivated must come from such an ideology.

Despotism

Despotism was fully effective during the first fifteen years of independence, under Manuel Pinto da Costa, the totalitarian leader of the time. Even with the establishment of democracy in the country, the vestiges of this "sin" remain. Experience taught the people that the only safe place to be in STP is in the halls of power. Consequently, numerous attempts at usurpation of power have taken place in the country, and several failed coups have resulted in a profound sense of political instability. Absolute power and the idea that it is up for grabs has led politicians to commit "political atrocities and to destroy the Government machine, leading the country to ruin.

Dogmatic Stupidity

Stupidity is the lack of intelligence; *dogmatism* is the attitude of someone who is so sure that his or her ideas are right that he or she expects other people to accept them at face value. *Dogmatic stupidity*, then, is the quality of someone who is not intelligent, and whose stupid, misguided course is predestined, unchangeable, permanent, and imperative. This describes people who do not even stop to consider changing his or her often actions and thoughts, even when they are not rational and do not produce positive results. A *dogmatic stupid* person commits the same mistakes over and over and, rather than seeking to correct them, insists on their perpetuation. An example would be a Government official who has run many state projects and led each of them to bankruptcy, yet nevertheless insists on creating new, similar projects, whilst applying the same methods and techniques, and evincing surprise that the projects never come to fruition; this is a *dogmatic stupid* person.

After Independence in 1975, President Pinto da Costa led the country to a ruinous economic performance. He was helped in this by the volatility of cocoa prices, other officials' policy failures and, most crucially, the result of collapse of the colonial apparatus of the coercive labor force. He nationalized the *roças* and later regrouped them into 15 Empresas Estatais Agro-pecuárias (State Agriculture and Livestock Enterprises, called "empresas" for short), a move which was defended as necessary in response to the flight of the Portuguese. Despite the immense national potential of exporting non-cocoa products and raw materials, he insisted in not diversifying production of local resources, and, in collaboration with his foreign partners and national team members, he disastrously implemented foreign-assisted projects, from the reintroduction of cattle by the Dutch to the establishment of a poultry farm by the Cubans. The decline in cocoa production was not matched by the development of other exports of goods and services. Instead, the accent on cocoa's role as central to the economy was repeatedly underscored.

The same techniques have been applied in the country, with the same results being reaped: the same teaching methods, almost always the same infrastructure, the same methodologies, the same curriculum, the same building construction techniques, and so on.

The failure to generate hard currency has been particularly severe, as the São Toméan economy has always been highly import-dependent since colonial times. When discussing governance and human security, signs of *dogmatic stupidity* are evident. Governmental and institutional stability appears to be an unattainable goal; the level of wellbeing and the fulfillment of the citizens are poor. Persistently, series of institutional weaknesses have hampered the process of confirming the citizen's liberal and democratic guarantees, making clear the evidence in support of the inadequacy of the country's politico-administrative divisions, the insufficiencies of the Constitution, the lack of stability and enough continuity of the Government action, the persistence of imperfections and inefficacity at the jurisdictional apparel. The political class has dogmatic stupidly enforced the lack of institutional performance, based on the inefficient ability of political decision-making, the absence of clear sectored policies and the inefficiency of the public administration. It has dogmatic stupidly reigned an environment of corruption, complete impunity and a persistent lack of both obedience and application of the law, which makes it difficult to exercise the civil and political rights, as well as the effective protection of the citizen's legitimate interests.

Dogmatic stupidity makes a person arrogant, aggressive and sometimes ill-educated. The dogmatic stupid individual is unable to recognize his or her own mental inability, errors of reasoning, or ignorance and never looks at a difference between opinions as being a difference between what is right and what is wrong, but as merely a difference of positions between rivals, based on hostility between oneself and another. A dogmatic stupid individual will always face a divergence of views on a particular concept as a personal affront. This is a peculiar feature of the political class of STP.

Part Two: Performing So Badly

In Part Two, we will discuss how politicians work as a team and how their behavior led the country into complete bankruptcy. We will address the internal and external links of the ruling class, as well as their behaviors, the economic and geostrategic interests of some international powers, and the oil business.

Chapter 3: The Clown's Party

Thanks to its political class, each passing day in STP is worse than the day before—increasingly dirty, with remnants of lavish political affairs, in a routine they call Government. On 12 July, 1975, a bunch of political clowns ascended to the throne led by a legion of prophets of misfortune, whose inspiration comes from a few commandments they follow blindly, and the result of their actions has been a range of "sins," among which corruption is the most common. The state machine ended up disorganized and ruined, while, the living conditions degraded, and development opportunities were wasted.

In this bizarre scenario, the governing power and opportunities are experienced intensely like a big party, the clowns' *party*. State powers are shared by four organs of sovereignty: the President of the Republic (representative and deliberative), the Government (the executive), the National Assembly (the legislative) and the Courts (the judiciary). It's that semi-presidential system, something that people speak about everywhere. If a person is not in, he or she cannot understand what is going on. The semi-presidential system is akin to a great banquet, where the President holds an itinerant nightclub—"Shake-the-Dust"—and the other three organs of sovereignty are guests of honor. People comprise the audience, who only can clap and do other less important things. President de Menezes owns Shake-the-Dust since 2001.

Recently, the entourage of the President has gone far in this world; he has barely stayed in the country. The President is very ambitious, but not in the usual sense. His ambition is to break as many dishes as he can, throw stones at the neighbors' windows, trample the flowers in the garden, and not do his homework. Got it? Not pleased with the enormous success he achieved in the country, he decided to make a long tour to as many countries as he could. Along with the huge 'royal family', he moved several times to Taiwan, Equatorial Guinea, Nigeria, Portugal, United States, Brazil, Belgium, Angola, Cape Verde, Libya, Morocco, Mali, Ethiopia, and many other places.

After a long tour abroad, Shake-the-Dust returned home to play in allusion to the typical Government's Tumble Festival! In the style 'take your foot off the floor' of the traditional fundões[73], Shake-the-Dust has played in dancing matinee for everyone. There has been no music for all tastes, but the hot rhythms of rumba and the sokope[74] has shaken ... all the country's dust, particularly, when they released the classic "Take your hands off my teats"[75].

Three years ago, de Menezes overthrew the government of Patrice Trovoada[76]; recently, he took his ministers from the government of Rafael Branco[77], and this had to be refurbished; the Government did not fall down but it was shaken. President de Menezes took too long to make that decision, but in March 2010, he scheduled the regional and municipal elections for July 25 and general elections for August 1 of that year. This was strongly opposed by political parties other than the President's own party, the MDFM/PL. Political parties alleged that the

---

73   The fundões were generally open spaces, used for dances and parties at night, like nightclubs, and were very prevalent in STP in the past. With the introduction of nightclubs from the 1990s, fundões have disappeared.

74   Sokope is a folk dance of STP, which is danced with just the feet. They say that the word 'sokope' derives from the phrase 'só com os pés', which means 'only with your feet.'

75   This is the title of a popular song of the 1980s translated into English. This is a very comical and sarcastic song, which was highly appreciated both in STP and in Angola and other Portuguese-speaking countries.

76   Patrice was Prime Minister of STP from February 2008 to June 2008, when he was fired; but he returned to the post two years later, in 14 August 2010.

77   Rafael Branco was the Prime Minister, the Head of Government, at that time.

interval between the two elections, only one week, was very tight and de Menezes was accused of arming a personal plan for his party to win the elections so that he could became Prime Minister after his term[78]. But MDFM-PL did not win any autarchy in the municipal elections of July 25, 2010. In the Legislative elections of 1 August of that year, it secured only one place among the 55 deputies in the National Assembly—only 4,932 of the 78,000 voters chose MDFM-PL, which dropped from the first to the fourth place among the major political parties. This fact represents a hard defeat, since MDFM-PL had won the 2006 elections and became the Government, winning 12 of the 55 places in the National Assembly.

There are fools and clowns without masks, waving heads to all sides to flit between unconfident, undetermined, insecure yes and no answers, and then back to maybe. This is the scenario the politicians have secured for the people, who were born already convicted and so long have been misruled. And now, we are watching from the balconies the peak of a festival of exotic rituals which has lasted for years—a game with no rules, and not just a spirited contest but a hard game, not dissimilar to the struggle between bulls. In the final analysis, those who come down are the poor grasses, which have nothing to do with the demand. Preparations for the climax of the party are being finalized, and the flurry of activity is complete, with only the whirring of excitement. On the one hand, disorganized juries meet to decide on the organization of the event; on the other hand, worried people are quick to pick a good place to accommodate. As always, there will be votes for sale, and political sellers are finalizing their outlets. It is time to put an end to that.

In the game of life, sooner or later everyone has to get involved, and so here we are voicing our humble musings. People do not know how to have their voices heard by confused politicians. The political course of the country has deeply annoyed the society which is clearly on the brink of going mad. It only needs one voice; a wise and confident force to remove the clowns from the throne, once and forever.

---

78   According to the Constitution, the President of Republic cannot hold more than two consecutive terms; thus, de Menezes can no more re-apply for the post of President.

But first, how to change such backward mentalities, which were hoaxed for years by corruption and ignorance? With so many questions and mutterings, it is no wonder that people are in such a state of disorientation, with a clear lack of knowledge concerning the reality of those who rule them.

Here is a reflection on the tormented arrangements of the public affairs in STP, which helps to understand how cunning it is for a head of Government choosing between unknown folks and his close friends. Whilst the latter are less suspicious of his maneuvers of political manipulation, the former are concerned with not falling into the political abyss, doing the dirty work. The Prime Minister is the one who holds "the knife and cheese" in his hands, so he never allows another person to "cut the cheese." For instance, some calls made initially by the Prime Minister Rafael Branco were premeditated, allowing him to gain time to better eliminate threats. The candidates who endorsed the controversial charge of the Oil Department, which caused Carlos Marques psychological problems[79], when this man was trying to hold that "hot potato" with bare hands, rejected Branco's invitation to participate in the new government; they had already predicted what awaited them in the party hall. In mid-October 2008, Prime Minister Rafael Branco requested the resignation of the Minister of Natural Resources and Energy, Agostinho Rita, for alleged involvement in "unlawful act." Agostinho Rita, who was also general secretary of the MDFM-PL[80] at that time, was allegedly involved in a small financial scandal involving the Company of Water and Electricity (EMAE) and his own University Institute of Accounting, Business Administration and Computing (IUCAI). A few days after joining the Government, Agostinho Rita has ordered EMAE to pay in advance the scholarships of three employees of this company who studied at IUCAI, amounting to little more than

---

79   15 days after being invested as Minister of Natural Resources, Energy and Environment, Carlos Fernandes Marques resigned, claiming that his health had deteriorated to the point he could no longer drive the office.

80   MDFM-PL was part of the coalition government that was ruling the country at that time, formed by three parties: MDFM-PL, PCD-GR, and ADI. After the fall of Prime Minister Patrice Trovoada (from ADI), Branco (from MLSTP/PSD, opposition party) was appointed as Prime Minister. This government was unconstitutional, according to the constitution, for the Prime Minister must be a member of the party that won the elections, the MDFM-PL.

three thousand dollars. The matter was the subject of controversy and the Council of Ministers reviewed the issue. Agostinho Rita was forced to "restore the truth" through the media. Thereafter, Branco, as Prime Minister, decided to terminate the term of Rita in Government, and shouted from the rooftops that he would fire him. MDFM-PL rejected the resignation of Agostinho Rita, whom this party reiterated the "political trust" to continue to serve as Minister of Natural Resources and Energy. However, Branco quickly dismissed Rita. The Presidential Decree number 22, published Thursday, 16 October 2008, named the "business manager" Carlos Marques to replace Rita. Carlos Marques had been Chief Financial Officer of the Empresa Monte Café, a Board member of Airports Management Company (ENASA) and, more recently, the Chief Financial Officer of the Center for Professional Training in Budo-Budo. He was Member of MDFM-PL National Council.

Fifteen days after being appointed minister, Carlos Marques was forced to seek his resignation, citing health problems. The fact was that Marques had set out fake diplomas of both bachelor's and master's degrees in business management. The name of the university where the degrees came from is Pacific Western University (PWU), from the United States. PWU was charged with "selling degrees" and is considered what the U.S. would call a "diploma-mill." PWU, which the government of the state of Texas, for example, does not recognize or deem lawful, was not included in any list of the U.S. Federal Government as an accredited institution.

The former Minister Carlos Marques was not alone in this batch of graduates from PWU. Also former Foreign Minister Ovídio Pequeno obtained his academic degree from PWU. These revelations were also extensive to Prime Minister Rafael Branco—very good people question the veracity of his qualifications. Carlos Marques "has gone wrong in the picture," felt ashamed and tendered his resignation. Branco tried to stop him, but in vain. When candidates who play a particular role of theatre are permanently replaced, it is certain that things are slipping. Bear in mind that this is what has happened to the posts of ministers in charge of Oil, Water and Energy, along with their heads of Government, who have often been dismissed since the fall of the Berlin

Wall[81]. This is a kind of Government's ritual dance in which the President of Republic—also being the Honorary President of the MDFM-PL[82]—controls the pace. Although the Prime Minister is proposed by the party that wins elections, and Government members are proposed by the Prime Minister, it is the President of Republic who promulgates. Every time a proposed Prime Minister does not please the President, or whenever the latter is not in sympathy with a minister proposed by the Prime Minister, he simply does not promulgate. At first, everything is seemingly beautiful, awash with splendor and happiness, with the ministers invited to come and dance, but, in the end, even the strongest men cry—and this is not merely a joke but a serious statement: They look at public office as being insignificant, unimposing child's play or roles in the theatre.

There is a story of "a gang of thieves" which does not allow us to sleep quietly. They robbed the GGA (Aids Management Office) for years and were finally caught. Former prime ministers, ministers and directors, were said to also have been in place. Indeed, if they were in place at that time, then surely they also were robbers and should be arrested. But the ringleaders of the gang have been deliberately left on the loose ... and as a result, they have participated in very many other scandals, injuring all the people.

Allocation of Government positions has caused political instabilities and quarrels among members of different groups. It is often the case that when someone feels threatened, he or she tries to escape, using poor excuses and disclosing hidden scandals housed within il-

---

81 Fradique dismissed prime ministers at a rate of seven prime ministers and governments in six years.

82 In late 2009, de Menezes was elected president of the MDFM-PL party at an Extraordinary Congress. He announced that his name would be in the list of deputies from the legislative elections of 2010. If the MDFM-PL won the legislative elections of 2010 he would become Prime Minister. At that time, de Menezes said he planned to return to the parliamentary home as a deputy as soon as he finishes his presidential term, i.e., in September 2011. But the constitution does not allow the President of the Republic to perform other functions, either private or public, during his term. After much controversy and political turmoil, de Menezes announced that he suspended his mandate as President of the MDFM-PL. De Menezes also said he had delegated all powers to the vice president of the party, Joao Costa Alegre, and stressed that he will return to the leadership of the political movement he founded as soon as he finishes his term as President of Republic in 2011.

licit Government business. For example, in Chapter 2, we addressed the fact that the deputy of the National Assembly, Adelino Isidro, was dismissed from all functions held in MLSTP/PSD after denouncing a corruption scheme involving the Prime Minister Rafael Branco, the Minister of Foreign Affairs and Cooperation, Carlos Tiny, the son of the latter, N'gunu Tiny, and a number of other senior personalities in the nation. However, Adelino Isidro himself found his tail caught in scandals of corruption, and only escaped jail because he is protected by the National Assembly and the Courts. Adelino Isidro only denounced that corruption case because, in the sharing of cake, they gave him no bite. He threatened to report other cases of corruption that he had knowledge.

On 12 November 12, 2008, Branco appointed Cristina Dias to the post of Minister of Natural Resources, Energy and Environment, replacing Carlos Marques. But some time ago, when he was opposition leader, Branco made a statement regarding her, when she was in her "first courtship" with the Government as Minister of the Economy, describing her as an "incompetent professional"! Surely this statement speaks volumes, and raises the question as to why he chose her.

The "ballroom" continued on in the heat of the power music and dance—a crazy thing! It's an in and out, hell of a run, like beans competing against each other, and, in the end, everything ends up mixed together in a saucepan. As was expected, Cristina Dias did not spend much time in the Government. She was fired in January 2010, when the last Government reshuffle—sparked by de Menezes and complied with by Branco—has happened. In February 2010, the High Court of Auditors tried Cristina Dias and convicted her with misuse of public money and with having charged accrued interest in granting credits to third parties. According to the Court, these crimes were committed when Cristina Dias was director of the Micondó Association. The Court has forced the lady along with the accountant of the Association, Ezequiel Fernandez—who also was charged for the same crimes—to restore 262,107,780.00 dobras to the state's coffers[83].

---

83   The Minister of Social Communication, Youth and Sports, Maria de Cristo Carvalho, was also caught. The Court tried and condemned her for mismanagement and misappropriation of funds from the Directorate of Social Protection,

Cristina Dias did not even want to take responsibility at such a high, but some gentlemen held the lady tightly in the dark, and tested her before she surrendered completely; others, however, fled from Branco's call, knowing beforehand who they would probably be forced to endure for a long time. After Carlos Marques was fired, it was very difficult to find within the MDFM-PL someone to replace him. Almost all party members rejected the position. Cristina Dias was the exception and, thus, was considered to be very courageous. This has left some bizarre dance partners standing with their nerves rattling skin-deep; others have experienced psychological malaise. Nothing was better than a lady who already knew the track well to do the Branco's will. The dance of power is simple to start, but easily one person falls and is kicked out of the room, being replaced immediately. Those who were initially rejected in the "sharing of the cake" had some reservations about the future of Branco in the Government[84], and feared to get close to him, feeling that soon they would be forced into leaving because the house of Government is a hell—a place where isn't able to sit long enough; the cave of the Devil.

The all-powerful President de Menezes was doing whatever he wanted, whilst Branco did not want to fall behind and was attempting to show that he, too, was an excellent power dancer. Now is Trovoada the Son, who continues the course. People, as good followers—and who actively play the role of clowns of the court—cannot do justice to the performance of their bosses. Thus, there at the top, President and Government are free and happy to dance...

---

and forced her to replenish around 30,000 Euros. Following this, she decided to leave Government, calling for her resignation.

84   Rafael Branco was sacked in August 2010, two years after being appointed Prime Minister.

Chapter 4: State Bankruptcy

In this chapter we examine the failure of the São Toméan state. This process has two phases: one in which it was supposed that the country had no resources or development alternative, and another in which it was blindly believed that the country is one of the most gifted of the world in terms of natural resources and development opportunities. The state went bankrupt in both phases.

Geographically, STP is an archipelago located in the Gulf of Guinea and is composed of two islands. It has an area of only 1001 square kilometers, a population of about 200,000 inhabitants, and is considered to be the second smallest country in Africa in terms of population. STP is considered to be situated in the center of the world (a cross between the Equator and Prime Meridian; latitude 0°, longitude 0°), where one of the world's largest reserves of crude is located; yet, it is surrounded by oil-producing countries such as Nigeria, Cameroon, Equatorial Guinea, Congo, DR Congo, Gabon and Angola, which grants it a strategic point in the world, internationally coveted. STP is believed to be at the epicenter of a giant oil field, with up to 11 billion barrels of oil lying under its territorial waters.

Politically, the country is governed by an allegedly democratic semi-presidential regime, which grants it the status of "geopolitical island," since no country in the sub region has this type of system. All other countries in the region are democratic presidential. This makes the political issues of this tiny country complicated to address. STP is also a linguistic island, because it has the Portuguese as official language and, except for Angola, no country in the Gulf of Guinea speaks this language. In religious terms, it is almost exclusively Christian, with some influences of traditional African religions, which increasingly are losing importance in everyday life. Thus, there is some insularity in the country's religious domain.

Economically, STP's most significant defining trait is its classification as a small island developing state (SIDS). SIDS include low-lying coastal countries which share similar development challenges such as having a small population, limited resources, remoteness, susceptibility to natural disasters, and vulnerability to external shocks, as well as excessive dependence on international trade and foreign resources, and with little or no market or price influence. Their growth and development are often further thwarted by high transportation and communication costs, disproportionately expensive public administration and infrastructure due to their small size, and little to no opportunity to create economies of scale. In addition, these states face challenges caused by insularity, whether being an archipelago or not, tropical climate, and whether being mountainous or landlocked.

Historically, it is a very young state with less than four decades of existence as an independent country. But its rich 5-century colonial history has episodes of successful use of resources and opportunities available to it, which greatly encourages reflection on its economic status and possible solutions. At various historical moments, these minuscule islands have assumed chief importance and significant achievements within the global economic system:

- In the 16th century, the islands were the world's greatest sugar producer;
- By the mid-17th century, they were a major transit point for ships engaged in the slave trade between the West and continental Africa, with the islands becoming a post for the slave trade between the Congo Kingdom and the Americas;

- In the nineteenth and early twentieth century, they were a major source of cocoa and coffee;

- Its strategic location in the center of the Gulf of Guinea has been an important factor in the island's history and culture, and was noticed by both sides during the Cold War.

Nevertheless, since its independence from Portugal in 1975, STP has been a model of the worst possible economic and public administration performances.

The Road to Bankruptcy

STP's first adopted development strategy was founded on a model of centralized management of the economy. That policy put attributed evidence to the central role of the state in the economy, which, throughout systematic recurrence to issues of inconvertible paper currency and rigid mechanisms of control of the financial policy, guaranteed financing of the cyclical state's budgetary deficit. As a consequence, the state lost its financial independence, which resulted in an increasing need for external aid for acquisition of equipment and commodities to satisfy the population's basic needs. From 1985 onwards, the regime gradually shifted away from the socialist model and subsequently established accords with institutions of Breton Woods and the African Development Bank concerning a Program of Structural Adjustment (PSA), which was aimed at the macroeconomic stabilization, structural reforms, improvement of public sector management, the reform of the financial system, and the protection of the most vulnerable social groups. But this policy failed miserably.

Seibert (2001) argues that the economic objective of the socialist regime to increase production of cocoa and finance the diversification of the economy with revenues from the export of cocoa was not very different from guidelines of the Breton Woods institutions in the late 1980s. However, the regime attempted to run its program under a centralized economy and maintained the plantation economy under the state ownership. In a short time, it became clear that neither the ruling party nor the state had the ability or the means to realize their hegemonic ambitions. In fact, the policy of the socialist one-party regime amounted to an attempt to sustain a bureaucracy manned by the *Forros*, burdened by political patronage of the work of former contract plantation workers. Factors such as lack of qualified personnel, the widespread incompetence, weak institutional and organizational capacity at all levels, the prevalence of clientelist and personalist criteria in making political and economic decisions, and predatory attitudes of public office owners and managers, which diverted resources of state-owned companies to their advantage, contributed to the global downturn of the economy. The failure in the creation of a modern work ethics in a society deeply marked by slavery and the forced labor helped to reinforce this crisis. Closely associated with this debacle is the maintenance of the plantation system under state ownership and consequent blocking of the emergence of agriculture of smallholders.

Despite the large amounts made available by foreign aid, there has been virtually no real economic growth, whilst income per capita has declined and poverty levels have risen dramatically since the projects with foreign funding have served primarily to support small local elite without having a significant impact on the overall economy. The institutionalization of liberal democracy has proved incapable of transforming the inefficient and slow-moving state bureaucracy from the status of a center for distribution of jobs and favors and privatization of public funds into an efficient administration, able to guarantee the conditions necessary for a functional market economy. All the Government has been plagued by competition for resources, with negative effects on cooperation and coordination among various industries, which, thus, could not execute projects and implement policies. Holders of public office manage to personally monopolize relevant information and contacts, as this facilitates the misappropriation of funds. The resulting non-application of solid institutional rules and persistence of personalistic criteria in decision making have contributed to the lack of efficiency.

Approximately two decades after Independence, in 1994, a UNDP document on the poverty line collected some data on the poverty situation in STP; its findings indicated that 40% of the population lived below the poverty line and close to 30% lived in extreme poverty. STP's external debts evolved on an increasing rate between 1992 and 1999, from $US 172 million to $US 294 million. These facts steered the state towards the adoption of sustainable development and poverty—reducing strategies, which were considered national priorities. The adoption of the Poverty Reduction Strategies began in November, 1999, with the World Bank and IMF's assistance. The authorities prepared a preliminary draft of the Interim Poverty Reduction Strategy Paper (I-PRSP) and a policy matrix, which were submitted for review by the civil society (including labor unions, the chamber of commerce, religious leaders, and non-governmental organizations—NGOs) and donors, in order to launch the participatory process for the preparation of a full-fledged I-PRSP, which happened in December 2002. Based on this I-PRSP, the Poverty Reduction Strategy Paper was prepared in 2003, and a reviewed version was presented in 2004. The Strategy, whose implementation is still in course, provides an analysis of poverty and describes a set of measures which have been designed with the objective to achieve sustainable growth in per capita income, and to improve the living conditions of the population, which are both equal priorities. The document addresses sustainable development issues in three main areas of economic sustainability, socio-political sustainability, and environment sustainability. However, no positive results were recorded to date.

In September 2003, at the request of the former Prime Minister Maria das Neves, the government of Taiwan established a five-member advisory group in order to formulate a Comprehensive Economic Development plan for STP. In January 2004, the Taiwanese Advisory Group, led by the council for economic planning and development, Dr Jing-Seng Chang, presented a document which provided for and recommended an integrated long-term development plan for the country. Still, in July 2003, by request of President de Menezes, an advisory project on sustainable development as led by Professor Jeffrey Sachs, who is Director of the Earth Institute at Columbia University in the City of New York, was created. This project had three key focus areas: 1) The development of Oil Revenue Management Law; 2) the design and execution of a National Forum; and 3) the formulation of a Plan of Action in order to achieve sustainable economic development. No positive results were recorded to date: Despite the efforts made, the Taiwanese development plan was not successful and the strategy of Prof. Jeffrey

Sachs was frustrated by the inability of São Toméan public administrators. Prof. Jeffrey Sachs and his team returned to the United States disappointed, having relations with President de Menezes and the Government deteriorated, with no apparent possibilities of recovery.

Several development strategies, plans, and projects have been implemented, but few or none have achieved the expected results. Despite their consistency in terms of economic concepts, policies and practices, they did not meet the country's expectations, in part due to the existing lack of supervision and inadequacy to or incompatibility with the existing infrastructure, human resources, and legislation. Most development solutions were based on, proposed and developed by external entities such as international organizations (the African Development Bank — AfDB, UN, IMF, the World Bank, etc.) and foreign governments such as Taiwan, Portugal, Brazil, EU, USA, Japan, China, etc., through mechanisms of cooperation and development frameworks. Some happened concurrently to the same goal, having similar strategic methodologies. For example, both the Taiwan's Comprehensive Development Plan and the Columbia University's Advisory Project on Sustainable Development were initiated in 2003, almost simultaneously. Each of them individually proposed a development plan for STP, working independently and funded by their respective sponsors, with little or no Government supervision.

In 1991, STP introduced a multiparty democracy. Since then, elections have been regularly and peacefully held, despite two failed military coups in 1995 and 2003, respectively. The ambiguous provisions of the semi-presidential constitution with regard to the roles of the different state organs have been fertile ground for conflicts concerning areas of responsibility and resource competition between the President and the Government, which have provoked various Government changes—15 different Prime Ministers and respective Government changes have occurred in 19 years during the period of 1991 to 2010. The consequent political instability has negatively affected the social-economic development of a country which has already been marked by poor institutional capacities and corruption by office holders. Stories from STP have dominated headlines for only negative reasons: coups d'état, successive Government changes, poverty, corruption, poor economic performance, and the like.

STP remains a potential world strategic point, but it is currently an unviable state. The cocoa sector, which represents 95% of exports by value, is still a very important and thriving provider of local employment, but, irrespective of this, it is of little importance to the country's balance of payments and the state treasury. STP's agricultural exports did not even suffice enough to cover the country's own food needs, let alone generate a surplus. The country's ratio of debt to exports of goods and services remained high at 337% in 2007, but was vastly improved from a figure of 1,736% (one thousand seven hundred thirty-six %) in 2006[85]. The basis of STP's political economy has firmly shifted towards overwhelming dependence on external resources: In mid-November 2003 the Government submitted an annual budget for 2010 worth about $65 million, of which capital investment accounted for $42 million. The budget was $10 million higher than the previous year's, and included $13 million stemming from the expected payment of signature bonuses by oil companies. Foreign donors financed about 80% of the budget. The state's budget for 2007 was estimated to be a total amount of $US 96 million. On the revenues side, this budget benefited from the annual budget of $US 23 million out of the National Petroleum Account. Some 70% of this tiny budget was externally supported. The state budget for 2009 was estimated at 150 million U.S. dollars and 90% dependent on foreign aid! At the end of 2009, not even 70% of this budget was implemented. Nevertheless, Prime Minister Branco has publicly said he was pleased with its implementation and that that was evidence of success and ability to implement public policies. In November 2009, the National Assembly approved the state budget (OGE) for 2010, which was estimated at $US 153 million. Again, this value is sustained at about 80% by foreign funds. The value of the state budget for 2011 is again $US 153 million; however, the proportion of external funds is 13% higher—93%. These figures give us an indication that perhaps the state budget for 2012 will be 100% financed externally!

---

85   United Nations Statistics Division, 'Sao Tome and Principe,' http://data.un.org/CountryProfile.aspx?crName=Sao%20Tome%20and%20Principe (accessed 05 01 2010).

The country is the recipient of one of the highest per capita amounts of development assistance in the world. The IMF, the World Bank, and foreign or international donors have used this leverage to encourage economic reform. There is an agreement among authors that as a result of STP's dependence on foreign aid and loans, STP became what they termed as a nonviable state even before the end of the Cold War and has remained unviable ever since. There is also the agreement that failures of public policy and the weakness of the local economy are the key reasons as to why the country remains amongst the poorest states in terms of GDP per capita. By early 2000, the country had the highest debt to GDP ratio amongst heavily indebted poor countries. Even after official aid transfers, the current account deficit for that year was approximately 50% of GDP! In late 2006, the country had a debt estimated at 300 million U.S. dollars (about $ 2,500 per capita). This debt was equivalent to 640% of Gross National Product! In September of that year, a joint mission of the International Monetary Fund (IMF) and World Bank (WB) travelled to the islands to make the assessment of the macroeconomic policies of the country and its financial stringency. Finally, the external debt was forgiven, but at what cost? The country has deteriorated more quickly from 2006 than in previous years.

Oil—Where's the Money?

It's still expected that STP will soon become a major crude oil-producing country, but there is every reason to think that the coming oil wealth will weaken the Government's pursuit of good economic governance. STP is optimistic that substantial petroleum discoveries are forthcoming in its territorial waters—the oil-rich waters of the Gulf of Guinea. This optimism has paved the way for an endless series of shady episodes which culminated with the signing of agreements and deals highly damaging to the country.

Rumors of the existence of oil in STP—both at sea and underground—date back to colonial times. There are visible signs on the surface in Uba Budo and elsewhere. In the late 1980s, Christopher Hellinger, an alien from the troubled past[86], in collusion with the then-

---

86 Hellinger is a man of multiple nationalities (German, Swiss, Sao Tome, South Africa, etc.), who made his living selling diamonds in Angola. He served as

President Manuel Pinto da Costa, made the first oil prospection in the area of Uba Budo. He was leading the Island Oil Exploration, a company registered in the Bahamas. Due to the lack of Government transparency at that time—the country being ruled by a totalitarian one-party regime—this business was never clarified. Nevertheless, there were many rumors circulating that the pursuit in the business of Hellinger with Pinto da Costa was not really oil exploration, but the exploration of something more profitable than oil: mercury. They say much mercury was extracted and exported secretly, at the convenience of the political elite. Then, they mysteriously ended farms, claiming have been a breakdown in the exploration machinery.

In 1995, it was discovered that STP is located on a huge oil reserve, and the whole world said that the country would become an El Dorado—this could turn every inhabitant of the country into a millionaire! In 1997, the Environmental Remediation Holding Corporation (ERHC), a U.S. company, signed with the Government of STP a 5-million-US-dollar monopoly oil-exploration agreement for 25 years—a highly damaging business for the country. The contract was soon described by some outside experts as extremely lopsided. Since then, despite renegotiations and doubts which still hang over the feasibility of this undertaking, the company has been engaged in state affairs, surpassing the technical and ethical frameworks and, above all, culminating with "pious" hopes for transparency advocated by the Nigerian-São Toméan bilateral committee managing the Joint Development Zone. ERHC finally got most of the exploration concessions.

Associated with small companies and already implicated in the exploration of deposits of the Equatorial Guinea, ERHC now has the exploration rights for five out of nine blocks, which were auctioned in 2004 and granted in 2005, being the majority shareholder of the two more promising blocks. ERHC was purchased in 2001 by Chrome Energy, which belongs to the Nigerian billionaire Emeka Offor—the "Godfather" of Anambra state policy in Nigeria. He is also chairman of a board where Howard F. Jeter, a former U.S. ambassador in Lagos,

honorary ambassador of the Philippines in several countries, including STP and South Africa; he had close links with the secret police of South Africa and France. He had many business interests and in STP and Africa; his current business interests remain unclear.

is a member. Offor, incidentally, is one of the main financiers of the re-election of President Olusegun Obasanjo in 2003.

A scathing editorial in the Washington Post, published on June 1, 2005, made clear that the granting of exploration rights looked bad[87]. Shaxson (2008) estimated that Americans and Nigerians cheated STP using ERHC. Prime Minister Patrice Trovoada, former executive of ERHC said that, when negotiating to establish the Joint Development Zone (JDZ), members of the Nigerian delegation were not willing to accept anything. The discussion began with the distribution of 90% for Nigeria and 10% for STP; however, the Nigerian shares were reduced by one-third, subsequently amounting to 60% for the Nigerians and 40% for the islands.

In their overwhelming success both in ERHC and in the manage-ment of the JDZ (the Joint Development Authority, JDA, which is headquartered in Abuja), the appetite of neighboring Nigeria could not be more telling. Once, a São Toméan journalist said that Nigeria looked increasingly likely to treat STP the way Saddam in Iraq had treated Ku-wait. The population does not understand why the oil money is slow in coming. Before being subjected to the dictates of ERHC, President de Menezes was unceasing in his denouncements of the contracts signed with this company. At that time the President appeared to be toler-ant of U.S. companies, which are today highly critical of his adminis-tration. The situation reached such a point that a U.S. advisory was installed in the country, who wrote a historic speech delivered before President George W. Bush in 2003 in Washington. At that time, the islands seemed about to receive a U.S. Navy base in order to "secure" he deposits in the Gulf Guinea, from which Washington planned to import 25% of the crude oil by 2015.

Another case of highly damaging relationship with oil companies involves the Norwegian Petroleum Geo-Services (PGS). Political con-tacts all the way inside STP's presidential family enabled this Norwe-gian seismic services company to obtain two lucrative agreements in 2001. Many wondered how that could be, because it could never have happened anywhere else in the world. Today, STP is the loser in the game. The country signed a production agreement with PGS but ended

---

87   *The Washington Post*, 'Corruption in Nigeria,' 06 01 2005: A.18.

up with a new business start-up it had never requested. The companies transferred the rights amongst themselves, and STP became a mere pawn.

PGS utilized a Canadian intermediary, Wade Cherwayko, as a bridgehead on the island. The Canadian had close contacts inside the country's presidential family; Wade Cherwayko is a close friend and business partner of Prime Minister Patrice Trovoada, who is son of then President Miguel Trovoada. The President's son was called in on behalf of the authorities in the middle of the negotiations with PGS, and this is how PGS succeeded in landing its contracts—without having been through a bidding round.

When PGS was criticized by the Norwegian press in 2003, the company explained that it wanted to get out of one of the two criticized contracts—the production agreement. However, the newly established Caribbean-registered Equator Exploration company which had bought the production agreement that PGS had in STP was run by the same man who negotiated the contract on behalf of PGS, the oil adventurer Wade Cherwayko. The transfer of the rights from PGS to the Canadian intermediary was even carried out without the authorities being able to intervene. Consequently, STP is saddled with a partner it did not want. Now the new company is expecting to become an operator in the most promising areas on the country's shelf.

The two agreements PGS signed in 2001 were criticized as being unreasonable. A World Bank-supported report prepared by an American law firm considered them "extremely one-sided," much to STP's disadvantage[88]. One of the agreements concerned seismic surveys in which PGS received the right to map the sea floor of the country's territorial waters, and to accordingly sell the data to the international oil industry. The second agreement gave PGS exploration rights to three oil blocks in the country's territorial waters, in areas that PGS could freely choose. Moreover, the Equator Exploration has thereby obtained the right to choose freely the best blocks in the whole territorial waters. With the production agreement from PGS as its only asset, in December 2004, Equator Exploration was soon after the transfer reg-

---

88   Memorandum: Oil Business Between DRSTP and Nigeria, ERHC, Exxon-Mobil and PGS, Washington, 12 April 2002.

istered at the Alternative Investment Market (AIM) in London. In this operation, Cherwayko's company gained $100 million in share capital, but the only thing STP was left with was $2 million in signature bonus from when PGS entered into its production agreement in 2001. So far, much money has been made as a result of the transaction in oil rights—but the country itself has received limited earnings.

STP tried to renegotiate the contracts, but only two small adjustments were made. After President Menezes had fallen out with Patrice Trovoada, who had been his counselor for petroleum affairs, de Menezes had no interest in preserving such contracts which only brought profits to PGS and Patrice Trovoada. Renegotiation of contracts had more to do with personal revenge than a matter of state interest. The number of blocks was reduced from three to two, and the signature bonus which PGS was under obligation to pay the day the final contract was to be signed was unbelievably reduced from $5 million to $2 million. Furthermore, although PGS lost an oil block, they negotiated an agreement which constituted less risk for the company than the previous one. If the future oil wells prove empty, the company would not lose as much as it otherwise would have done. In the seismic services agreement, STP got a better deal. PGS was supposed to receive 10% of all signature bonuses. However, during the renegotiations, this was reduced to 10% of the signature bonus from the first licensing round. The amount was intended to constitute $4.92 million. PGS has nevertheless retained most of the rights in the seismic services agreement. Up to 2011, the company has, in practice, monopoly with regards to seismic surveys in the country.

In 2001, STP and Nigeria reached an agreement regarding the joint exploration for petroleum in waters claimed by the two countries. After a lengthy series of negotiations, in April, 2003, the Joint Development Zone (JDZ)[89] was opened for bids by international oil firms. The JDZ was divided into 9 blocks; the winning bids for Block One—Chevron Texaco, Exxon Mobil, and the Norwegian firm, Equity Energy—were announced in April, 2004, with STP taking 40% of the $123 million bid, and Nigeria taking the other 60%. In 2006, the auction process of the JDZ blocks finished and only six of the nine blocks auctioned were

---

89   http://www.nigeriasaotomejda.com/

granted. STP and Nigeria agreed to withdraw the auction of three of the nine JDZ oil blocks, which had not prompted the interest of companies. The lack of interest from the market was due to the fact that the three blocks are located in very deep water, which technically is a great investment. Of the six blocks auctioned, only one block was awarded to U.S. company Chevron Texaco which, in partnership with Exxon-Mobil, began drilling in the same year, whilst five other blocks have production-sharing contracts. The joint exploration agreement with Nigeria gave STP entitlement to 40% revenue, but the money received so far does not correspond to 40% due to the agreement signed in 1997 and renovated in 2001 with ERHC, which invested in the research of the blocks and is now delivering the dividends of that investment, and has preferential right to purchase the blocks. The agreement signed with ERHC has led the country to lose approximately 50 million U.S. dollars up until now. STP stands to gain significant revenue from both the bidding process and the follow-on production; however, this only remains intact should reserves in the area match expectations. In mid-2009, the Joint Development Authority (JDA) announced that four new blocks in the JDZ would be auctioned from 2011. At that time, they had spent almost three years in which activities in this area were virtually halted. Field work in Blocks 2, 3, and 4 were continued by the hand of Sinopec and Addax Petroleum; these three blocks in the JDZ were drilled from November, 2009 through to January, 2010, and these companies ensure that there is oil and gas in all blocks. Block 1 had been drilled in 2006 by the American oil Chevron, without the detection of reserves with commercial potential.

Aside from the JDZ, the Government decided to start the exploration activities in the Exclusive Economic Zone (EEZ). The first auction for oil exploration in the EEZ of the country was launched on March 2, 2010, in London and, according to press reports, has received much interest from international oil companies. The launch took place on the side-lines of a conference on oil and gas, "APPEX 2010," which took place from March 2 to 4, 2010 in the British capital, organized by the American Association of Petroleum Geologists (APG). In this first round, the National Oil Agency auctioned seven of the 19 existing blocks in the area. This is process was considered to be historical for having been entirely organized by STP.

"New Friends" Out There

STP is under the crossfire of interests of foreign companies and governments. International partners (ERHC, PGS, Nigerian government, etc.) have taken advantage of ignorance, greed and carelessness of national public officials, signing contracts highly damaging to the country. This shows the lack of honesty of foreign partners in this business. There is a lot of money, resources and opportunities at stake, and so all parties involved seem to be transformed into true predatory beasts, devoid of solidarity. Nigeria, for example, disputed the maritime border with STP, and forced it to accept an agreement to form a Joint Development Zone (JDZ) in which 40% of revenues from oil production would go to STP, and 60% to Nigeria, despite the fact that JDZ is located entirely within the EEZ of STP.

There is also much oil near the maritime border between STP and Equatorial Guinea, but the Equatorial Guineans were not interested in joint exploitation. Many rumors abound that they also exploit (steal) oil within the EEZ of STP. This is why they do not like to talk about it. Angola similarly has interests in exploring STP's oil. Moreover, there is unofficial information that Angola is funding the MLSTP/PSD to make things easier on their side. Interestingly, Prime Minister Rafael Branco and the Minister of Foreign Affairs and Cooperation, Carlos Tiny, visited Angola several times recently. From the Angolan side also, STP received visits from the senior representatives of public and private companies. In early 2010, Africa Monitor Intelligence reported that the MLSTP/PSD received "financial and other" support from the People's Movement for the Liberation of Angola (MPLA), which is the ruling party in Angola. Although the São Toméan law prohibits foreign funding of political parties, the Government did nothing to prevent such an offense.

In recent years, dozens of countries have intensified their diplomatic efforts and forged close links with STP. On October 7, 2002, John Lee Anderson published in *The New Yorker* a very interesting article entitled "Our New Best Friend: Who needs Saudi Arabia when you've got São Tomé?" The first image was of a half-white, fat man, probably living alone in an island. It looked like a caricature of President de Menezes. There was a young rising sun shining behind the fat man; a new light's hope. Did that image mean prosperity? The author gave a long history of his stay in STP, his curious approaches to de Menezes, having lunched and dined with the President on several occasions at his home in Quinta da Favorita, and the experience of walking around, relaxing and eating at the same table with high public figures, former presidents, families of presidents and other dignitaries.

From the title, Anderson suggests that São Toméans are the "new best friends" of the Americans. Besides, he reports that President Bongo and President Obiang were friends of President de Menezes. As latter represents the people of STP in the article, and the former two presidents cited represent their respective nations, then São Toméans, Equatorial Guineans and Gabonese are mutual friends. However, a friend of my friend is my friend, and so the President Bongo and the President Obiang are friends of the American people! This is a contradiction, since Americans have moved international campaigns against these corrupt leaders. Still from the content of the article, the Americans want to cooperate with the Nigerians—or to be their friends. By the way, the São Toméan people consider Nigeria a hostile nation, despite the JDA. This is another contradiction, because if my friend's friend is my friend, and the enemy of my friend is my enemy, then the Americans would be, at the same time, friends and enemies of the São Toméans. What suddenly turned the São Toméans into beloved friends of the Americans? Oil.

What Can "Friends" Do to Help?

Anderson's article exposes the new intentions of the Americans: building a naval base in STP to protect the São Toméan (or American?) interests in the Gulf of Guinea. The article also states the intention expressed by President de Menezes that that would happen soon. Another article published by *Petroleum Africa* in July, 2007, entitled "The United States and Maritime Security in the Gulf of Guinea," authored by Mark J. Sorbara, confirms this view, stressing that the US is interested in establishing an effective military presence in the Gulf of Guinea. Moreover, a unit of the US Navy was scheduled to be installed in the Gulf of Guinea by September, 2008. However, to date, there is no evidence of such a unit having already been established. Quoting the article:

> In late 2006 the US announced that the military's new Africa Command (Africom) will be up and running by September 2008 and is actively looking for a location for its headquarters which is mostly likely going to be in the Gulf of Guinea. The US undertook a feasibility study for the construction of a deep-water port in 2003 and donated maritime surveillance equipment to São Tomé in 2006, hence many people believe São Tomé, which is well positioned off Nigeria's coast and insulated from onshore troubles, will mostly likely house Africom (Sorbara 2007, 57).

Another country which is interested in establishing military presence in the archipelago is Nigeria. In December, 2009, President de Menezes and his Nigerian counterpart met in Abuja and announced they would create a Joint Military Commission of Defense in order to maintain safe conditions in the Gulf of Guinea, where the JDZ is located. Again, due to the ignorance of state officers, such as de Menezes, the country seems to be falling into yet another "tale of a vicar"—and is likely to make the same mistakes he made with the agreements previously signed with oil companies and foreign governments. What would be the interest of Nigeria in creating a joint military commission with STP—a country that not even a navy or coast guard has? Where would the bases of the joint commission be installed, and who would command them? Could it be that the interest of Nigeria would be only to create dependencies and militarily dominance or to control the defense of STP? Could it be that Nigeria intends to do what it did with the case of joint exploration agreement, resulting in delays and damage to STP?

As incredible and ironic as it sounds, the STP's predatory political class only survives thanks to the relationships it has with other political forces and foreign governments, including international organizations, such as the United Nations, the World Bank, International Monetary Fund, the African Development Bank, and so forth. These organizations have followed the way that foreign aids have been used in the country: to support networks of corruption and finance the partisan activities of the political class. However, they have closed their eyes to the allegations of flagrant corruption, and continue to assist by giving development assistance, even knowing beforehand that such aid does not arrive within reach of the ones who need them. International partners do not make any kind of pressure and continue to sign papers to accept as ambassadors and representatives in their national institutions individuals with curricula tainted by corruption, such as former public officials.

PART THREE: RISING FROM THE DEAD

Chapter 5: Understanding the Political Class

The nature of those who have been governing STP to date is close to that of predatory beasts; the São Toméan people are their prey. They behave as if they were computer with software, which was developed for a specific purpose and cannot go beyond what it is programmed for. And, no matter whether the actions their physical machines undertake are good or bad, they cannot do the opposite—only ever what their ingrained software dictates for them to do. There is no evidence that they can learn from past experiences, adjust their attitudes to reality, love their own country, think about prosperity of the whole with a lack of interest to prosperity of only a few, or believe in democracy and observe its main principles. They have lost all the opportunities offered to them, wasting all chances given for them to repair their pasts.

People entrusted upon them the management of the country, but being awful managers, they led all to bankruptcy and instilled chaos and insecurity into their grounds, leading whole families into poverty and suffering. The injured parties often try to get explanations from those responsible, but the latter, versed in the art of deceiving, hide behind all sorts of excuses. They live quietly, unconcerned and confident that there is no justice for all these failures, ignorance, passing of the book and neglect of taking responsibility. As a way to ensure public veneration they need to perpetuate on the throne, they exasperatedly spend the time claiming qualifications of bachelor's, master's and doctor's, and do little to deserve, or at least obtain them, in fact.

The public administration is nothing but misappropriation of the common good. Officers cast their orders on the population as if each demand and commend were a cry of war. The harmful public management has left only ashes, and their move through the throne is like a hurricane: everything which it is unable to carry, it simply chooses to destroy, leaving a path of devastation in its wake. How many public leaders have left power after destroying all that is good, all that was put at their disposal, so that their successors cannot reap the benefit and bathe in the same opportunities? For example, if a car was delivered to a minister or ministry director and, for some reason, the individual had to leave office, as an angry and selfish individual, he destroys the car or cuts it into some relevant parts, making it impassable. Thus, when a substitute is inaugurated, he or she automatically demands a new car. Thus, the problems of the people are kept in the drawer and the parliamentarians spend the time discussing the release of funds for the maintenance of their private and semi-private lives. Where do the São Toméan people benefit from the lavish expense of two cars? And that's two for the sake of this example; how many extravagant outlays have really been made, and to what cost?

The ordinary citizen, emulating their leaders, does everything to trick the system he or she is part of, without realizing that the main victims is him- or herself and those who are close to him or her. What the people are trying to do, in this circumstance, is to recover what should be given to them by law, but, unfortunately, this is not the right way to go about justice or regaining what is rightfully theirs; this way makes thieves out of the innocent, and the citizen is thus labeled "little thief," something shameful, like the famous "chicken thieves" in the villages.

Children and adolescents are more of the innocent victims, who will grow up to become men and women with serious problems of socialization; problems which have been inflicted upon them by their leaders and supposed role models. Currently, they are all too often harassed and forced to enter the world of malice, serving as objects of sexual fantasies of public figures, who demonstrate nothing deeper than a fake love. They are quickly taught the art of cheating, which they learn with ease and no delays in putting into practice and, when they reach adulthood, they will then experience the difficulties in being honest—either with themselves or with others. What blame can we assign to those men and women in the future when they will show lack of decorum and nurture a profound social parasitism? All that will be the result of what is being taught to them by the masters of corruption, and the blame sits heavily on the teachers' shoulders.

Understanding People's Drivers

People aspire to reach or build a *welfare state*, which implies turning *liberty, equality, justice* and *welfare* into something available for everyone—this is their goal, where the state ought to go and what the nation needs to strive towards. But, in order to move towards that goal, one needs *drivers*. A nation has basically two types of *drivers*: 1) *Primary drivers*, which mainly comprise people's instincts, and 2) *secondary drivers*, which basically comprise people's sets of beliefs.

One example of primary drivers is hunger. This physiological need, being instinctive, drives people towards looking for food. It is a primary driver not only because everyone is influenced by it, but also because everyone is driven by it in almost the same way. One example of secondary drivers is religion. For many people, religion is the only moral authority, the only guide, the only reason to do good and avoid evil. It is a secondary driver because although being important to people's lives, it is not a vital necessity; its legitimacy and need can be interpreted in different ways and be dependent on rational arguments.

Although primary drivers are capable of exhaustively driving everyone in similar ways, they are often adjusted to one's subjectivity, that is, for instance, in the above example, whilst every man impelled by hunger will certainly look for food, not every man prefers the same kind of food. Therefore, not every man will look for the same type of food whilst driven by this primary driver. In this case, it is a subjective primary driver. But if we take thirst for water as an example, it will be an objective primary driver.

The set of a nation's primary drivers is the collection of all individual primary drivers of its integrants. Even if, individually, a person doesn't have certain physiological needs, collectively, he or she should assume them as being his or her own, if there is an integrant of the society he or she pertains who so does. This leads the entire society to the desirable state of harmony among its elements, promoting peaceful coexistence and stimulating the collective pursuit of common good. And because both subjective and objective primary drivers are instinctive and universal, they depend only on the physiological constraints and determinations of human nature. There is little or nothing man can do to change these drivers, keeping the slave motivations generated by them, which results in a permanent search for their respective satisfaction. So, being inherent to human desires, we can conclude that primary drivers are implicitly present in all phases of any social struggle. There is no need to make any comprehensive approach on them. We will concentrate on those which are less instinctive, whose strength as drivers of man depends on the mode and the intensity with which they are grown up—the secondary drivers.

In their most primitive or rudimentary status, people's beliefs are shaped by everything that is induced by habit, environmental condition, past experience, and so forth. In their most evolved status, they are shaped by ideologies of the societal system they belong to; for example, religious systems, political systems, cultural systems, and the like. Such drivers are not born human attributes; they are learned. The learning process begins with the exposure of man to the society. Firstly, his subjective primary drivers are put into action: Driven by physiological needs, in the "new" society, the individual identifies needs and opportunities of meeting them. However, he or she has to be restricted to the offers available. He or she must decide between the possibilities offered by society, and determine which of those best meet those needs. Thus, the human constructs habits shaped by societal and environmental conditions, and becomes experienced. At this point, the individual has achieved the first status in the development process of secondary drivers.

Secondly, then, due to the permanent exhibition, the person identifies repetitive signals and phenomena in society and, with reference to past experiences, he or she reacts in a similar manner each time he or she faces the same situation. This is because the person expects that by acting in a similar way, he or she will obtain similar results. This way, because of the particular frequency and likelihood of environmental or social phenomena, human builds solid—sometimes incorrigible—beliefs. And, through the use of mental faculties, he or she goes to a far more advanced stage of the learning process: Interpretation, generalization, and synthesis of past experiences and habits for the construction of the ideological model he or she will later transfer to the society. Therefore, human has developed formal high-status secondary drivers, which will now lead him or her to the pursuit of ultimate goals.

However, although the elements of a given society may cultivate many common values and beliefs, being secondary drivers they depend on the subjectivity of each, i.e. the views, feelings or subjective perceptions of each human being. Thus, secondary drivers can hardly be seen as objective but subjective in that the intensity with which each drives someone is an assigned subjective value. For instance, the São Toméan people may identify usual signals of their society or environment and have similar reactions to them. With few exceptions, every man and woman in this country has a set of values he or she cultivates regarding local music, dance, food and sports preferences, etc. Those values may be common in most aspects, but when talking about the intensity with which each one expresses his or her preferences, we are getting into the field of subjective secondary drivers. Indeed, some people prefer music more or less slow than another, or food more or less salty.

In their most advanced status, the drivers a nation needs should be described by an ideology carefully planned for the required purpose. What purposeful rational set of ideas, values, and beliefs should comprise the real drivers of a nation, i.e., what should be imprinted in the nation's souls and minds? Which are necessary feelings, needs, and rationales capable of leading people towards a democratic welfare state? It is not difficult to determine. We can identify four key drivers, which are: First, the "desire to live a welfare state," which brings liberty, equality, justice and welfare; second, the "love of the homeland and the nation"; third, the "need to achieve supreme well-being"; and fourth, the "need to survive to eternity." Therefore, an ideology that considers all these key drivers and explains how either each one or all of them together should lead people to the achievement of the welfare state is the one which fits. Such an ideology should also explain precisely how these drivers should be created, maintained and enforced within the people's heart. For instance, one particular skill that a good ideology should have is the ability to cultivate living heroes, role models, inspiring individuals, examples of courage, determination and competence, all of whom serve as guides or drivers. One must understand the ideological essence of the abstract thoughts and set interpretation for each situation, each social group, each entity, and so on.

An Invincible Force

It is crucial that people recognize their forces, their capabilities, their talents, and thereby acknowledge that the Government has a force infinitely small compared to theirs. The recognition of people's strength encompasses understanding in their role, their numbers, their duties and rights. How can a force as small as that of a government be able to dominate a force infinitely greater than itself, which is the people? This happens when the people naively assign ruling responsibilities to a small group of people and do not call them for accountability. There are basically two forms of behavior which determine, respectively, the total usurpation of power by the ruler and the absolute control of power by the people. They are: a) *Action from the inside out*, causing the decline of people's power and consequent concentration of power in the hands of rulers; and b) *Action from the outside in*, causing the increase of people's power and consequent reduction of power in the hands of rulers.

People can always choose the path to their happiness and determine who should be their guide along the way, but the guide—the Government—in possession of the whole administration, all of the power, and all of the resources, can always do the reforms and institutions it deems necessary. In this vein, so that people can lead the Government as the Government can control people. These two are the only entities truly sovereign and truly powerful. In practice, people only command the Government during a very short period of time, when they are allowed to choose. People play a fair game without hypocrisy or diplomatic tricks. This is because, despite being powerful, they are naïve, and often do not know how much power they possess. They allow the rulers to govern them and make them submissive.

The nation is a set of forces that exercise power only when all of its components act from the outside in, focusing on a single point, which is the Government. All institutions are actually governed if all national forces converge at the necessary point. When people's forces take action disorderly, cancelling each other out, there is no convergence of forces into a single point. This fact allows any other force, even lower than theirs, to easily rule them. In this case, the people do not govern but are rather governed by a force lower than their strength—the Government. In STP, there is no convergence of people's forces; therefore, people do not rule the Government. The nation has an influence almost nil over the state, for their forces act from the inside out; their political actions are completely void, allowing the ruler to become all-powerful and authoritarian. The ruler thereby strengthens his hegemony, since he has the space to act. The action from the inside out is a situation where all national eyes are turned to emigration as a means of prosperity, which means refraining from a participative intervention, or collaborating with an inefficient government. To emigrate is to allow the country, its resources and opportunities to drop like flies or to be under the damaging management of a hegemonic power.

Emigration is not just an attitude in favor of moving out of the country, but it also is reflected in the change of beliefs and behaviors in relation to the economy. Different types of emigration can be classified into "territorial emigration," "political emigration," "labor emigration," "social emigration," and so on. All forms of emigration—when committed on a large scale and are not careful—are detrimental to the advance of a nation. Instability is an extreme situation, where there is widespread emigration on a large scale. Politically and socially, there is only an optimized model of solution to the problems of economy and development; such a model must be found by experts suited for this purpose and, once found, it must be implemented. The current instability means a lack of unique solutions, i.e., there are several competing non-efficient solutions. This lack of efficiency can lead to a solution becoming economically very costly or even disastrous. A society which is able to find its ideal solution is a stable society, because the solution is unique and is the one which best serves everyone according to unique needs.

The action from the outside in means the return of workforces into the country, promoting active participation in policy-making and rejecting any behavior which can be seen as harmful to good governance. When standing under public pressure, the Government has little room for maneuver, and it is smothered by the overwhelming power of the masses and, under such a permanent, demanding and disciplinary pressure, it looks for the best possible solutions, i.e., transparent, fair, democratic and effective solutions. In short, the power of the Government shall be multiplied by cancelling the people's power, and shall be reduced under action of popular forces, turning its actions inside and seeking to respond to problems. Therefore, the power of the people increases with the limitation of the Government's power.

The people of STP have not yet realized how important their land, resources and opportunities are; yet, so they seem very distracted and unconnected to the political reality that precedes the situation into which the country was conducted. In fact, people still retain the dream of travelling to other countries and then find means of subsistence. However, the whole world is experiencing a period of great crisis and, therefore, almost all countries are closing doors to immigration. This has explained the dramatic situation in which migrants live in the world today. Why people would abandon their land, resources and opportunities, and migrate to another country where they would live in conditions more deplorable than the ones in which they live in their home country? This happens when they are not yet aware of how much worth lays within their lands, their resources and their people. Each one of these things is worth everything they need to survive. Their happiness depends on the success they reap during the task of rehabilitation of their things, which have been deteriorating over time. Their pride and collective self-esteem depends on the success of this task.

CHAPTER 6: THE ULTIMATE ASSIGNMENT

Our journey to this point has been an ordeal. We have visited a country which, although it played an important role in the global economy, nevertheless remains virtually unknown to the outside world. We have met its people and observed how they have lived and how they have been governed since 1975. We have witnessed the misery and despair in which these people are still submerged—and we draw conclusions: there is no doubt; the country needs to be reborn.

In order to foster a healthy population with a healthy and productive attitude, conditions must exist that foster the development of strong and healthy bodies and minds. Abject poverty and destitution have to be alleviated, and education has to be provided. Until conditions are improved, the individual will not be able to help society to solve its basic problems. The problem of food supply must be resolved first and foremost. It is not possible to secure any form of development with malnourished bodies, minds and spirits.

When addressing the issue of the satisfaction of basic needs, food supply or self-sufficiency—or even eradication of poverty and its derivatives—the question of wages automatically arises. A salary is by definition a monetary compensation made to employees for a specified number of hours worked and is intended to defray the purchase of products and services necessary for the employees' and their families' survival in modern societies. Primarily, we must consider the National Minimum Wage (NMW)—a minimum wage stipulated by the Government for a certain number of hours worked. In STP, when determining the NMW, successive governments have not been concerned about the real satisfaction of the minimum needs of citizens, and the wages thus have not been set so as to represent the minimum amount of goods and services—i.e. the "minimum shopping basket"—necessary to meet the needs of a worker.

It is common sense that the "minimum shopping basket" for an adult should be enough to defray the cost of an average family. If the minimum wage does not meet the needs of the individual, the individual will need to seek ways outside of his or her workplace to meet the remaining needs; indeed, the individual may feel forced to perform illegal acts, which undermine his or her productivity and efficiency and contribute to the destabilization of the state apparatus. In STP, there is a perception that an individual spends more than 10 times the salary he or she receives, which means that over 90% of the needs of a person are paid by extra work and, consequently, most of an individual's work efforts are intended to implement secondary or parallel activities. Accordingly, an individual has low productivity at work. Collectively, this has resulted in disastrous productivity of the national productive apparatus, creating the image that, statistically, the people are lazy and do not really produce anything of any real value.

Under the conditions associated with poverty, such as malnutrition and a lack of decent material conditions, the individual does not have appropriate tools to develop his mind or to plan and implement projects successfully; this, in turn, does not allow neither the qualitative accumulation of experiences nor the development of mechanisms of cultural transmission, either to contribute to improving the lives of his or her contemporaries or for future generations. Furthermore, in this situation, a person's social existence incurs costs upon society, directly, and through to the negative influences he or she prints into social actions and projects, acting as a friction force, reducing the collective efficiency.

The ineffectiveness of the Courts, the lightness of the penalties, and the relative comfort of prison conditions enjoyed by prisoners have provided a fertile ground for the commission of crimes. There are three main reasons for this:

- When the crime is intended to obtain some benefit, the light penalties and the relatively cozy prison services, as opposed to discouraging the practice of crime, develop into genuine incentives for offenders. Whatever happens, the offender comes out a winner.

- For many, the living conditions offered in prisons are higher than those they knew outside, living in the streets, in the open air, in tents or in slums. Much of this population receives less than $1 per day, which is not even sufficient to deliver a daily meal. In prison, they are guaranteed the minimum conditions of housing, food, hygiene, health, and even entertainment, which costs public funds tens of dollars a day per prisoner.

- The lack of speed of the Courts and the inefficiency of criminal investigation services, trafficking of influence, etc., have left many offenders unpunished and free to commit new crimes. The high number of cases awaiting trial in the Courts has fuelled the belief in judicial impunity among offenders and victims alike.

Raising a New Nation

A nation comprises people of usually the same ethnic group, who speak the same language and have similar customs. Subjective conditions for evidence of a nation rest on the bonds that unites individuals, which determine the collective will to live—the essence of man as a gregarious animal. These bonds comprise the individual consciousness, and germinate and develop the "collective affinity consciousness" from which nationality derives, and whereby individuals feel attached to a body or a group, distinct from any other, with own life, special interests and unique needs.

Thus, a nation dies or becomes another when the affinities between their constituents cease, or when they become other affinities. If elements of a nation are replaced with individuals with new habits, new collective consciousness, new interests, new needs, new language, new religion, etc., then that nation becomes a different nation. Similarly, if you change the habits, language, needs, interests, religion, etc., of a given nation, then you will also get a different nation. Hence, in order to raise a New Nation, it is required to populate an area with "new men" or those who are "reborn" and unlinked to the current nation. By simply changing the consciousness, the habits, needs, interests of people etc., one creates new affinities among them.

STP demands a nation that is capable of correcting the defects of the existing one. Hence, the country needs to be "populated" with people shaped in the "new style" and possessing new virtues. It is not intended—nor is it feasible—to proceed to the physical replacement of existing members of the nation with others fulfilling the desired requirements. "Replacement" must be carried out at political, spiritual and philosophical levels, leading to the worship of appropriate virtues. Since integration into society requires that individuals fit standards, patterns and relationships between its various members, a "collective future" must be constructed by the aggregation of individual contributions. It is similar to the construction of a giant building in which thousands of workers are involved. Each worker is responsible for a particular task, depending on his responsibilities and powers, and so each will add details to the building, within a pre-defined standard, little by little, until the completion of the work. However, in order for the construction to match the building plan and the desired quality, it is necessary that all individual contributions are acceptable and approved by the project superintendent. The same goes for the construction of the collective future of a nation. In addition to the necessary skills, there are principles, rules and standards that must be respected by individuals, and any individual contribution must be approved by the regulatory body of society. Society, then, must be prepared to recognize and reward values, proven capabilities, and the like.

What is done, however, to merit? The recognition of merit applies not only to individuals but also to legal persons. Individually, merit grants rights to enjoy a certain status in society, on the one hand, but, on the other hand, it enforces high responsibility and greater commitment, given that, whilst recognizing, rewarding and compensating someone for his or her merit or "ability to perform," society requires and expects of that person greater commitment, greater responsibility and greater contributions, i.e., it hopes that the person concerned will bring more benefits to the community. Collectively, the merit, on the one hand, gives a group of individuals, organizations, sectors, or institutions, better positioning in relation to competition, higher credibility compared to similar entities, and greater confidence of users; on the other hand, however, it demands and expects of that person goods or services of better quality, more guarantees, more added value and lower costs.

A socio-political system based on merit brings benefits to all parties as follows:

- Individually, the entity to which merit is conferred proves through competitions, examinations, tests, results in projects, experiments, etc., that it has the skills that distinguish it from all others;

- Collectively, certification and public recognition of the individual and collective merit guarantees credibility and trust, giving to stakeholders—either quantitatively or qualitatively—an indication of what to expect from organizations, individuals or institutions;

- The existence of a system of merit leads entities to continuously seek improvement of skills, which also means that those at the top of the "league table" will continue to develop and improve for not running the risk of being exceeded by their competitors. This works as a race with several ultimate goals. An individual can reach the first goal in the first place and win this stage, but there is no guarantee that he or she will be the winner in the second and subsequent goals. A person must continue to give evidence, and to overcome and surpass others permanently, because if he or she fails, he or she may consequently be left behind.

- Merit enforces competition that turn out to be permanent, continuous and thorough. Persons must always ensure high performance so as to remain well-positioned. They must not simply keep the level of performance that has allowed them to reach their current position, but must continually improve that performance, since the opponents are always improving themselves and can overcome them at any time.

When a collective future is not realized, individual aspirations and fantasies are similarly not realized. For example, at the time of the São Toméan state formation in 1975, setting up a democratic welfare state was the collective dream, in which all individuals were to be considered "welfare citizens." However, citizens have not experienced the status of "welfare citizen," although the political circumstances in which they are living suggest that this is what should be. It is a collective dream that did not become reality, leading to the non-realization of individual aspirations and fantasies. The inability to achieve that collective dream quickly translated into disbelief concerning the legitimacy, rationality or fairness of the "collective life," which lead to disappointment and anger. Subsequently, faith in collectivism converted into faith in individualism. Lately, it has been practiced throughout the country a kind of social conduct, commonly denoted by "arm-breaking"[90], whereby people study and implement various methods in order to creatively scam third parties.

Today, in STP, the ruling class spends its time antagonizing each other, particularly the disadvantaged folks. This only contributes to the lack of social cohesion, disinterest in collective achievements, disregard of collective needs and interests. There are clearly situations in which only actions of selfish natures are promoted, enhanced and carried out. For example, in the act of "arm-breaking," the actor does not seek to establish a permanent trust relationship with the target of his action; there is no desire to comply with an undertaking to preserve the interests of both parties; one is not concerned with safeguarding any kind of relationship that seeks a collective view. Given that all this tends to be practiced on a national scale, affinities between individuals cease. Not existing affinities, the ambitions and achievements of collective projects are stopped. Quickly, the social organization was replaced by promiscuity and chaos.

In order to participate in the rehabilitation process of a society, it is necessary to conceive the respective territory as being a homeland, and then love and stay in that homeland. Landless, an individual is nomadic and does not create links to, respect or reverence for any land; rather, he or she becomes a "believer" in emigration. That person therefore contributes to brain drain and capital flight, simply because of the high degree of disorientation and nomadism. As an immigrant in any

---

90   Lit. "partir o braço".

foreign country, a person does not contribute to the progress of his or her homeland.

A group of individuals is only able to accomplish the mission that it is destined to succeed if it has a good leadership. The leader must be someone who has exceptional skills and qualities that are suitable to mobilize, motivate and lead a group of individuals toward certain goals. Any leader must possess a given set of skills and qualities; how-ever, since different groups are made up of different entities, the lead-ers of different groups must have other skills and qualities appropriate for the group they lead; one cannot speak of "universal leader." Thus, a leader for a New Nation must possess, indeed, very different abilities and qualities comparing to a leader for a current or extinct nation.

The leader's role in the New Nation is of the utmost importance, and hence his or her presence, representativeness or influence must ex-press that importance. From the moral point of view, the leader must be a cultivator of virtues, a model for emulation. From the political point of view, the leader must represent the interests of everyone and not just of a simple elite or majority. Moreover, he or she must inspire confidence and provide a glance of the future, simply because humans have inertia in their behavior and are antagonistic to change. However, humans usually only accept and undertake the challenge of change by the inspiration of a visionary leader or emulation of the heroic deeds of that leader. Often, we see in our country behaviors, procedures and practices that are as old—often inappropriate to the system at stake or any other that existed then—as the beginnings of colonization of the country. These behaviors, methods and practices have neither followed the evolution of mankind, the scientific-technological development, modernization nor innovation; rather, they are implemented blindly as they were originally learned or taken. Besides being old, they are very expensive and, worse still, they negatively contribute to the country's image. People and institutions do not seek new methods, new knowl-edge or practices—not because they have no capacity to do so, but for the lack of motivation and inspiration of an appropriate leader.

The lack of leadership is a huge obstacle to the development of the country. Leadership is not only something merely emblematic or sym-bolic, but something which affects the efficiency of people and institutions; something that both qualitatively and quantitatively affects the return to investments and can represent heaven or hell, depending on whether it is a good or poor leadership. If the leader is less educated than the followers, then, owing to the emulation of the personality and deeds of the former, the society will then tend to retreat in the process of development. It is like printing on the consciousness of people the feeling that it is unnecessary to progress beyond the limits that the leader represents so that "going further" is the same as adding one cent to one billion.

In STP, the leaders are known to be corrupt, delinquent, and irresponsible individuals, with few skills and with no heroic deeds. It has thus recorded in people's consciousness the idea that it is unnecessary to live a virtuous life; that virtues do not add anything to the individual and collective performance. How much will it cost to change this mentality?

Any leader must be brave or at least not be cowardly. A coward is someone lacking any ability to face problems. But a coward is a potentially reckless, faithless, and treacherous. He or she defends him- or herself at any cost, and most likely will defend him- or herself at the expense of sacrificing innocent lives, such as those of children, the elderly, the poor or, more generally, helpless people.

The cowardice can manifest itself in different ways from one person to another, from one culture to another. There are cowardly people who reveal the fear they have towards others without any complex or shame, but there are people who hide behind masks, making themselves look brave, especially when they are in the presence of others. Some avoid discussing such feelings, afraid to reveal their true selves; some are still rushing to talk about cowardice, defining it in their own way by providing examples of cowardly people, and presenting numerous lists in which they themselves do not belong. All of these forms of cowardice can be considered harmless, given that the cowards either officially display their characters and are ignored or helped, or use inoffensive masks which only distract attention from others.

However, there are forms of cowardice which can be considered dangerous, threatening or offensive. These are forms of cowardice in which one takes refuge in defensive behaviors which are highly harmful to others. We have, for example, the case in which an entity uses innocent or vulnerable people, or even people who are under its purview, as shields or "decoys of war," distracting attention from potential enemy or potential threat and fleeing looking for a safe haven to settle, leaving its administration orphaned. Such cowardice is a characteristic of the current São Toméan political class. Often, given the slightest threat, public officers put themselves on the run or resign early, thereby leaving the nation adrift. When the situation becomes unavoidable and even the leaders are not likely able to escape, they loosen up, running in panic, seeking aid for themselves, ending up laying down their arms to the enemy, surrendering. Sometimes, when the situation can be circumvented by the side of the rulers, they make pacts with the enemy— even if that requires delivering as hostage everything that is under their tutelage: people, opportunities, resources, and so forth.

The other form of hurtful cowardice is when a leader throws innocent and defenseless people on to the fighting fronts without any preparation or prior notice. One by one, that population becomes easily "food for guns" and, whilst this "food" exists, it fuels the war, quenching the thirst for blood of the enemy, whilst the one who threw them there runs like hell. Like blind and deaf sheep, all these people are sent to death. Examples of what is widely practiced in the country cover frequent mass layoffs, persecution or demotions of employees who do not support the ruling party. Successive Government changes have caused crisis of layoffs, ranging from Government officials and civil servants to employees of state and private enterprises. For members of successive governments, people who do not belong to their political party pose threats to their political projects. Consequently, every year, many people are wrongfully dismissed, unemployed or transferred from one function to another. Political quarrels always result in replacements of staff, structure and programs. Defeated parties usually flee abroad, feeling that, out of power, they are vulnerable.

A New Nation must be capable of generating synergy. People are interested in a society that rewards and maximizes the collective performance, seeking ways to efficiently bring together the efforts of everyone in favor of the overall development. Often, maximization of individual performance, when not coordinated with the efforts of others, becomes harmful to the collective performance. Being integrated into the system, an individual sees his individual effort multiplying. If the social system is efficient and able to synergy, individual efforts are multiplied and, consequently, collective performance and yield are higher.

Because it comprises living organisms, the New Nation itself must be regarded as a living organism. Living organisms are sets of structural and functional entities. The smallest of these entities is the cell, which is the structural and functional unit of any organism. For a nation, the cell is the family. This means that, both structurally and functionally, the constitution and performance of a nation depends on how families are formed and maintained. If families work in a stable manner, the nation is similarly functionally stable; if the families are self-sufficient, balanced, harmonious and rich, also the whole nation is. Thus, it is imperative to cultivate virtues that contribute to the good of families. For instance, ethically and legally, society must censor or ban polygamy or adultery. Polygamy and adultery are widespread in STP, and have brought harmful influences upon society, such as parental irresponsibility, school dropouts, proliferation of single-parent families, poverty, child prostitution, child labor, child and juvenile delinquency, the loss of values, etc. Generally, polygamy means fewer resources available for each family and less time devoted to children education and monitoring, resulting in lower school and social performances.

Because family is the structural and functional unit of society—just as a participant of a single family—the individual can benefit from the advantages which this entity provides. Family helps to gather resources and wealth. Family unity provides greater safety, comfort, confidence, self-esteem and social responsibility for individuals, and further contributes to social cohesion, order, harmony and progress. Polygamy, contributes to social disintegration and underdevelopment.

As discussed above, a nation is born with the emergence of affinities and links amongst individuals, and remains alive as long as such affinities and links are maintained. One of the main links is the mother tongue, which allows effective communication amongst members of a given nation. It is also the primary vehicle of mother culture, allowing individuals to understand and express facts, ideas and feelings in a peculiar way. It is the only language in which a person is truly fluent.

In STP, it is just up the Portuguese the official language and the main language of communication. None of the national languages holds similar status and importance. As a result, the national languages remain in the state of informality, tending to disappear: they are not taught in schools; they lack systematic studies, grammatical studies, and the like. This has brought enormous disadvantages for society; for example, the current high rate of illiteracy and difficulties of communication.

When a person speaks a foreign language, he or she gives native speakers of that language the opportunity to be understood, but does little to be understood by them. Thus, the speaker of a foreign language is in a vulnerable situation, with lots of disadvantages, namely:

- In personal terms, the individual has a low self-esteem and poor communication performance because, even if he or she so desires, it is difficult for the person to be as fluent in a foreign language as a native speaker of that language;

- The person makes a double the effort to communicate, whilst the native invests only a small effort for the same purpose, and reserves most of his or her energies to invest in other projects designed for his or her wellbeing and progress;

- The individual runs the risk of poor performance and, in terms of returns, the native will always come out winner;

- The individual will not develop skills in his or her mother tongue, which will be neglected and maintained as secondary or even unimportant;

- When the person makes any "production" in his or her mother tongue, the fact that it is not understood by foreign people causes the market for absorption of that "production" to be limited only to his or her homeland. In contrast, when the foreign people "produce" in their language, they have a large market for exhibition and sale of their work.

Accordingly, we conclude that speaking a foreign language is investing in the welfare of native speakers of that language; it is the same as making an investment without return. Mother tongue is closely linked to the ability to reason and communicate of a people; therefore, these people must develop skills in it at the highest level.

Affinities and links based on a common mother culture are important for national development. When a person loves his or her culture of origin, he or she invests in it and works to develop and disseminate it. This all helps to create jobs, make money and improve the living condition of his or her countrymen. If people from a given place love local products, they have less need to import goods from abroad. This avoids troubles such as the export of currency, travel and transportation costs, taxes, and competition to local products. In this case, the spotlight is turned over to the local products, services and opportunities, which contribute to reduction of cost and improvement of quality, due to proximity to the centers of production and expertise.

How much does STP lose when importing foreign culture or products? The state has exported a lot of currency and inflicted losses upon local producers due to their distinct disadvantages compared with foreign competition. On the other hand, there is the ominous import of consciousness, which is expressed through the idea that, if the nation imports products from abroad, this is owing to it not producing them or otherwise because what it produces is of poor quality or deficient. Importing foreign culture or products has been the same as devaluing the local currency and domestic production.

There are objective factors that express affinities between individuals and classify them as members of a particular nation, and subjective factors that are shared or transmitted. If spread across a large community, these factors assert themselves as common characteristics and subsequently become affinities. Examples of these subjective elements are experiences, discoveries, talents or abilities, habits and customs of individuals. The sharing or transmission of these subjective elements may only be made through frequent exhibitions in schemes of social interaction, the media and education. When certain experiences, habits, talents and individual skills are considered exceptional and useful, they must be transmitted or broadcast by all. The most efficient mechanism used is the system of national education, which is directed to the education of the local folks for national progress. For the São Toméan nation, for example, national education must teach an individual how to be São Toméan, how to love STP, and how to think about the development of this country. The country must have its independent, self-sufficient and complete educational system, because otherwise it would not be able to promote its own development.

It is currently not possible to speak of mother culture without paying special attention to the roles of the National Television (NT) and National Radio (NR) in its transfer, dissemination, protection and development. Both NT and NR must be designed so that the development of the individual is perfect. If we want the NT to contribute to the raising of a New Nation, the stereotypes of the former must represent the later. This means that the NT cannot contain any image, information, or symbol—anything—that might directly or indirectly divert the New Nation's attention from this purpose. For example, if the NT deliberately introduces programs from foreign television stations without any purpose other than the promotion of foreign culture which, instead of promoting the "local" nationality, promote a foreign nationality, drawing people's attention to realities which are large distances away from theirs, and accordingly does nothing to improve their local conditions, then that television is not fulfilling its role.

In STP today, a child sees only images of foreign children in both public television and in foreign channels; he or she only hears foreign languages or accents; only sees stereotypes, examples, realities, dreams, tastes, manners, events affection, prejudices, opinions, beliefs, doubts, stories, experiences, and related, linked to the cultures and ideal models of other peoples. As a result, that child learns that it is only worth respecting, valuing, venerating or mimicking what he or she watches on television. For that child, the right is to do as others do; similarly, to live well, be civilized or to succeed is to be like the others; however, he or she is not around anything that looks like what he or she watches on television, and so the child creates and feeds in his or her mind the idea that the land from whence come the images and people that television show is the "promised land."

Similarly, an adult only has the opportunity to see television programs bearing images, values, aspirations, opinions, beliefs, addictions, doubts, stereotypes, etc., from other people. As a result, he or she links these virtual reality models of perfection to the idea of what is right, perfect and ideal. That person develops a belief centered on the fact that it is what television shows that is what is to be proper, civilized, successful, ideal, or the like. Furthermore, like the child in the previous example, the adult sees nothing similar around him or her, and once the virtual reality that television shows is a place, a people and a culture far from his or her own, the person simply decides to live that reality and to hold that distant place materially and spiritually, getting close to those people and drinking that culture. This is the source of the widespread spirit of emigration which invades the São Toméan people. Why would NT and NR freely contribute to the promotion of other nations and other cultures? If the NT and NR have the function of promoting local citizenship, why would they then act to the contrary of this objective?

Additionally, for the national education system to meet its objectives of standardizing education and training of the nation, it is necessary that the following conditions are fulfilled:

- It must be planned, funded, implemented and supervised by the state alone;

- It must be free and geared to excellence, according to international standards, in order to contribute to local and the world's development; and

- It must study and disseminate knowledge about the local reality and inspire national development.

Foreign financiers want to invest in the country to maximize their return in the country, and this cannot be effectively done only with the knowledge acquired elsewhere. The national education and local manpower must be prepared to galvanize local development. Accordingly, if the national education does not promote local development, it will not contribute to maximizing the return on investments made on-site, and will similarly not contribute to the development of the world.

It is through the process of training that an individual achieves awareness of what his or her role is in society. It is important to note that people's education is not only done through the national education system; indeed, there is a fundamental component of training, say, the informal part of that training, which begins before the insertion of the individual in the system of national education. The way this component is developed ultimately determines the level of the individual's sense of quality. This is responsible for the quality level of a product, service, or task, which an individual requires. If people are born in precarious conditions—i.e. poor housing, poor nutrition, poor clothing, poor health, poor social services, poor education, etc.—then they adapt to those conditions and consider them to be acceptable standards; in fact, they have never seen well. They do not develop levels of demand for quality standards far exceeding the limits with which they were provided, and therefore they think "further" is not essential for survival or for a healthy, comfortable life. These people, when adults, have levels of awareness and performance which are not unlike the patterns in which they lived or learned thus far. In STP, work performance, social performance, and the like, are very poor and well below the standards internationally considered normal. It is not necessary to be a genius to realize that those performances derive from the degrading quality of life, poor health systems, degrading education system, quality of the media, and forth. Services is poor at all levels. The concept of competition does not exist or is primitive. People consume anything they can get. Often, a person who raises questions about the quality of a product or service is frowned upon by the supplier—or even by other consumers.

To change this status quo, it is deemed necessary that the education of new generations is devised under high-quality standards. It must not consist only of formal education in schools, but must involve all aspects of human life. The encouragement and development of the sense of quality must occupy a central position in the process. Services in schools must be of excellent quality in order to allow the individual to learn, demand and provide quality. If materials are not of better quality, if food offered in cafeterias is not accurately rich and high-quality, if the hygiene and health care facilities are not excellent, if teachers, classrooms, the school enclosure do not respect good standards of quality, then what will be expected of the trainees throughout their education process and when they complete their studies and join society? In such cases, they will perform below reasonable standards, providing products and services with low quality; therefore, a quality global education is the forerunner of a quality society, adds value to the domestic industry, and helps to achieve competitive advantage in international markets. The national currency thus acquires weight and strength, and galvanizes the economy.

Affinities and links are established, maintained and strengthened through relationships based on commitment and trust. In a state which does not respect the commitments, there are no joint projects operating; no agreements or contracts are met. And because no individual can develop in isolation; there is always the need to cooperate with other individuals, to sign contracts and to accordingly establish agreements. All of this is guaranteed if there is respect for commitments made, and the confidence that the expected results will be obtained.

In a contractual relationship, the disrespect of commitments between two parties may result in the violation of commitments made to third parties which, in turn, can lead to a chain of losses. Trust ensures commitment and the expectations of meeting the objectives agreed between the parties. Trust determines the expected degree of compliance with the commitment made to one party by another; it provides an indication that the other party has capacity, credibility, substance, etc. suitable for achieving the commitments. The loss of trust leads to the lack of credibility in the break-up of relationships and low expectations that the commitment will be fulfilled by the other party, thereby resulting in poor collective performance.

In order to better understand this, imagine the following scenario: A society comprises only two elements: a farmer (PF), and a producer of grain (PG). In order to survive, in addition to producing meat, PF also needs grain, and PG, in addition to the grain he produces, he also needs meat. Accordingly, a mutual commitment was established between them whereby, out of a certain number of days, PF produces M amount of meat and PG produces G quantity of grain. The amount M of meat is the minimum necessary to meet the needs of the two elements of this society; likewise, the amount G of grain is the minimum necessary to meet the needs of both. In order for those involved to respect the commitments undertaken, it is necessary that PF has the confidence that PG is capable of producing the necessary quantity of grain, and PG similarly has the confidence that PF is capable of producing the required amount of meat. As the survival of both fundamentally depends on this relationship, each party gave the other the necessary guarantees. As always, at the beginning of any contractual relationship, mutual confidence is at its higher limit. However, this confidence is maintained only whilst respecting the commitments undertaken;

otherwise, the trust declines until it reaches the minimum threshold, which results in the breakdown of the relationship.

Summary of commitments established between PF and PG: Within one period of time, say, monthly, PF is expected to produce M amount of meat and PG should produce G amount grain. M and G are the required minimum amounts, respectively, of meat and grain to meet the needs of PF and PG together.

However, either situation can occur: (A) Both producers fully comply with the Commitments; (B) One of the producers produces, but not all, the agreed quantity of product, but the other fulfils his part; (C) One of producers produces a surplus and the other just the agreed quantity; (D) One of the producers does not produce anything, and the other fulfils his part; (E) Both satisfy, but none at all; (F) Neither respects the Commitment.

- If both producers fully respect the commitments undertaken, then there is a balance and all needs are met; there is no crisis, excesses or deficiencies. In this situation, the society remains economically stable and develops harmoniously. Trust between stakeholders remains high. There are neither inequalities nor injustices, and apparently there is no reason for the emergence of internal conflicts for possession of resources or seizure of power. It is a closed economy, self-sufficient, not dependent on the outside. It does not export, but also doesn't import; therefore, the trade balance is fair.

- If one of the producers produces a quantity smaller than agreed and the other complies with his part, the following happens:

- Lack of a product and the consequent increase in the price of that product due to its shortage: this results in that the needs of the one who complied with his compromise will not be satisfied. As this man produced the agreed proportion, the one who has not met his part will have most of his needs met, but will pay less for them, because he can only pay with what he produced, which is little. In addition, since each producer can only consume, say, half of each of the quantities of M and G, half of what the producer whom has complied with his commitment has available must be "disposed" to "market"; otherwise, it deteriorates. There is only one consumer in the market, who cannot pay a fair price because he has no resources to pay. Result: the one who does not respect commitment, puts in the market an amount of product inferior to the demand and charges the price he wants, or sells more expensive than the cost of production, whilst the producer who has complied with his commitment, brings to market the exact amount but, due to weak purchasing power of the one who did not fulfill his commitment, is forced to sell at a price lower than the production cost. The one who produces less satisfies all his needs, whilst the one who fully produces has not available in the market enough products to meet his needs.

- The producer who has complied with his commitment will make a greater effort to meet his needs; for example, he will have to find alternative ways of getting what he needs. Given that society has no more providers, he must rely on imports which, due to transport costs, customs, trading, etc., decrease his purchasing power.

- Social injustice and inequality: the wealth of the one who produces less increases and of the one who produces more decreases.

- "Social parasitism": to a large extent, who does not meet the commitments takes advantage of the effort made by the person who fulfils the commitments.

- Economic imbalance: the shortage of one of the products requires more efforts to supply the product at stake through imports, which in turn generates export of currency.

- The purchasing power of the one who produces less increases because he does not consume the imported product and sells more expensive than the costs of production; the purchasing power of the one who produces more decreases, because he sells cheaper than the costs of production, and needs to consume imported product.

- Trust of the one who fully respects the commitment made in the one who does not respect the commitment declines up.

- If one of the producers offers a quantity exceeding the demand, and the other provides only the agreed quantity, there is abundance of one of the products on the market. After fulfilling the market, the surplus can be exported, earning foreign exchange. The purchasing powers of both producers increase, because either one or the other can pay a fair price for the products he buys. this generates:

- Plenty of products on the market

- Increase of the collective wealth: both producers have all their needs met; there are surpluses that can be exported to generate surplus revenue

- Reduction of inequalities and injustices: in this situation, there is neither parasitism of the one nor of the other.

- There is a great level of mutual trust between the social partners.

- If one of the producers (thereafter "non-doer") does not produce anything and the other (the "doer") complies with his share, then there is no domestic supply to meet the demand of a needed product. It is only guaranteed the fulfillment of the demand of society for the other product. Being available only one of the expected products, there cannot be "exchange," and since the "doer" can consume, say, only half of what he produces, there will be one of the following circumstances: (1) the "non-doer" will receive part of the doer's product on credit, (2) the "non-doer" will receive from the "doer" products for free, or (3) the "non-doer" will not receive any product.

If condition 1 occurs and there is no assurance that the non-doer's debt will be paid to the doer, or an independent arbitration that would force the non-doer to do so, a conflict between the only two elements of society will quickly arise owing to the non-payment of the debt. As there is no regulatory body, the strength of the fittest (or the most cunning or the smartest) prevails. If the non-doer wins the fight, he ultimately will not pay the debt and will turn the doer into his slave. In this case, he will install a system of injustice and extreme social inequalities, where the doer fully comes out to lose. If the doer wins the fight, he may force the non-doer to pay the debt or otherwise turn him into a slave. In this case, the doer can easily recover the debt and relieve the non-doer or the former can force the latter to pay the debt and take advantage of his weakness, turning him into a free labor force—a slave—in his favor.

If condition 2 occurs, the non-doer will unduly stress the doer—parasitism. However, that situation is untenable, simply because society cannot survive the lack of the good whose production is dependent on the non-doer. Consequently, not being there beforehand anything that forces non-doer to comply with his part, quickly, there will be a conflict between both the doer and non-doer. The strongest between the two wins. Furthermore, as has been seen in condition 1, if the non-doer wins the conflict, this one will ultimately not compensate the doer but will turn him into a slave. He will install a system of injustice and extreme social inequalities, where the observant element will be totally disadvantaged. If the doer wins the fight, he may force the non-doer to observe his commitment or may rather opt to turn him into his slave. In this case, the doer may just want the non-doer to contribute to the economy of the society or may transform him into a free labor force—a slave—in his favor.

If condition 3 occurs, the non-doer may wither and die for a lack of livelihood (which is unlikely) or may immediately install a struggle for possession of the product that is in the hands of the doer. If the non-doer dies, society will have only one element—the doer. So, in order to survive, this one will have to produce everything he needs—or simply live with only one type of product, or even produce enough to export surpluses and import the product that he has missed. If it happens that there is a struggle for possession of product that is held by the doer (the most likely case), then, as in other situations, the strongest will win. If the winner is the non-doer, he will take possession of the goods; the doer will be turned into the non-doer's slave, and the non-doer would establish a system of injustices and inequalities, where the doer will be totally disadvantaged. If the doer wins, he could force the non-doer to work for compensation (a wage or something alike) or the former may abuse the latter's weakness and turn him into his slave.

From what can be seen in circumstances 1, 2 and 3, the probability of situation D giving rise to a system of social injustices and inequalities is almost certain. Trust between social partners declines. At this point, since the likelihood that the administration of the society going to be borne by a despot is also almost certain, the question of supplying the product which is missing can then be resolved in one of three ways: (1) the dictator opts to keep things as they are (which is unlikely); (2) the dictator will opt for accelerated domestic production at the expense of slave labor (which is more economically feasible for society); or (3) the dictator will choose to import them (economically most expensive).

If case 1 occurs, there will be a society in crisis of food supply. The society will suffer from serious food-borne diseases, and if the missing product is essential for life—for example, water—this situation will become untenable in the short-term and will consequently lead to the choice of case 2 or 3. If case 2 occurs, society will not depend on the outside and, therefore, its trade balance will be fair. As slavery, in general, generates huge profits and surpluses, it is likely that the society will become a great export economy. If case 3 occurs and if another product for exchange is required—being there absence of surplus for export—the import can only be made on credit or for free. As there is no such thing as free lunch, the hypothesis that there would be free import is excluded. It remains then, the hypothesis of the society to incur debts and thus pay high cost for debts, and the hypothesis of the society to get in a food supply crisis. Foreign creditors just "spin" their products to whomever offers counterparts or any other type of guarantee. If a society has valuable resources which could be awarded as compensation, then, okay! Accordingly, it will have a chance to import by credit or benefit of what is commonly referred to as "food aid"; otherwise, it will suffer the crisis.

In the event that the society is able to import on credit, we will face an economy dependent on the outside, with severe trade deficit and a high external debt—an import economy. The imported product will be distributed to the elements on credit or for free. If the distribution is to be done on credit, it will generate domestic debt. If it is for free, it will generate a hole in the accounts of the society—money lost—which will seriously affect the economic health of society. If neither credit nor society can import the product it needs, then it will have to opt for case 2, which is—at least economically—the most viable.

Whatever happens—whether he would become a despot or a slave—the non-doer will be in debt both to his internal partner and to the society itself; he gets both the products he needs without offering anything in return. It is the non-doer who is responsible for the economic and social degradation of the community.

- If both producers comply, but none at all, a situation where parts of both required products are to be imported is born, which generates the export of currency, thereby consequently leading to external debt and trade imbalances. We are facing a poor economy but no notable social inequalities—poverty is collective, as is underdevelopment. It may happen that, in order to increase production, to balance trade, to pay external debt and to subsequently eliminate foreign dependence, con-

flict arises between the two elements for the establishment
of a "power" or "government." In this case, the winner will
become a tyrant, and the loser a slave. In this case, economic
problems may be resolved quickly, but the regime to be introduced is based on a system of extreme inequalities and injustices. Trust between social partners, of course, will decline.

• If none of the members of society respect the commitment, the
crisis is total, hunger is widespread, and the hatred is real.
There may be attempts to 'clean the hood', i.e., attempts
to blame the other for the crisis. Trust between management and labor will decline. This is a situation very close to
Situation D; however, since there are no products available in
society, there is no reason for infighting for the possession of
such, and certainly cases 1 and 2 of Situation D will not occur.
Of course, case 3 will, and none of the non-doers will receive
any product; therefore, the non-doers will wither up and die
for lack of livelihood (which is unlikely) or opt for the importation of the goods they need. If the non-doers die, society
will become extinct. In order for them to survive, someone
has to work, but none of them is willing to do so voluntarily.
It is then very likely that they will trigger a struggle for possession of 'power', whereby the winner will become a despot
and the loser will be made a slave. It will be introduced—as
in the other cases discussed above—a system of extreme inequalities and injustices. In this case, the despot may solve
the problem of food supply by: (i) always importing or (ii)
importing in a first stage and then opting for accelerated domestic production, using slave labor. If the first scenario (i)
is confirmed, then there will be no surplus in the society to
be exported; thus, imports can only be made on credit or for
free. This situation corresponds to case 3 of the previously
discussed Situation D. If (ii) is confirmed in a first stage, the
performance of society will then be one that was described in
option (i) above. However, soon after, with domestic production based on slave labor, the society will produce surpluses
for export—which promotes the entry of foreign currency—
and will get high profits for the stabilization of its economy.
Subsequently, the external debt will be paid, resulting in the
end of external dependence. The society will quickly move
from an import-economy-state to an export-economy-state,
with positive trade balance. However, it will not cease to be
a morally undesirable system based on social injustices and
inequalities of the worst kind—a slave regime.

- Although the analyses made above are based on the case of a society with only two elements, they can be generalized so as to encompass any other society. Respect for commitments generates trust in social relationships and promotes economic development, freedom, equality and social justice. The reverse—i.e., the disregard for commitments—is responsible for the breakdown of trust between the different elements of society and is the source of internal conflicts, despotism, slavery (or exploitation of man by man), poor economic performance, external debt and dependence on external donors, as well as the trade imbalance and other problems. To raise a New Nation based on equality, freedom, justice and social welfare, it is moral condition that individuals meet the commitments established amongst them and commitments inherent to social existence.

Now suppose that the above considered society is the Democratic Republic of STP and the only two elements are, respectively, the São Toméan government (hereinafter the Government) and the São Toméan Nation (hereinafter Nation). Given that, in order to survive so as to govern the country, the Government needs the work and the participation of people, and the nation, beyond the work and participation in Government programs, requires good governance, i.e. a governance that results in its development and progress, it was established between these two entities, a mutual commitment that, in each term, the Government formulates and implements effective governance and rules with mastery and transparency, and the Nation, in turn, actively and honestly works and participates in the implementation of these programs, and oversees the Government operations.

A Government program is said to be effective if, and only if, it competes for protection of national territory and preservation of peace within the borders of the country, and ensures that all national households have the space to reside and means of livelihood within the national territory. Similarly, Government has mastery and transparency when it diligently obeys the constitution, administers the laws enacted therein, maintains the Nation informed, ensures that the latter's confidence remains high, protects the rights of persons, and adheres to democratic and moral principles. the Nation, in turn, actively and honestly works and participates in Government programs, or programs that actively support the society, when its constituents offer all that is required from them to support themselves; when individuals contribute in all appropriate ways to their development. For example, qualified people to public office should feel obliged to contribute to its good performance; otherwise, the civil service will be relegated to people with fewer qualifications, and governance can more easily become corrupt. Additionally, it is said that the Nation oversees the Government when, on the one hand, it critically observes the terms and behaviors of rulers and, on the other hand, it evaluates the programs implemented, comparing obtained results with the expected ones, the amount of time spent with the expected one, benefits with damages obtained, and so forth.

The obligations outlined above are the minimum necessary to meet the needs of society, both on sides of the Government and of the Nation. In order for those involved to respect the commitments undertaken, it is necessary that the Government has confidence that the Nation is able to actively and honestly work and participate in its programs, and that the Nation has confidence that the Government is able to develop effective programs and govern with transparency and mastery. As the survival of both depends on this relationship, it is necessary that each party involved—the Government and the Nation—gives assurances, as always, at the beginning of their contractual relationship; for example, through referendums or elections. When the Nation elects a person or group to govern, it shows confidence in that group or person; also, when a group or person offers itself to govern the Nation, it is implied that that group or person will get the job with active and honest participation of persons. At the beginning of these contractual relationships, mutual confidence is at its highest level. However, confidence only remains alive whilst commitments undertaken are respected; otherwise, it declines until reaching the lowest point, which is the breakup of the relationship.

Summary of Commitments between Government and Nation: In each term, Government is committed to develop and implement programs of governance and rule with mastery and transparency, whilst Nation is committed to work and to participate actively and honestly in the execution of those programs, and supervise the actions of Government.

If neither Government nor Nation respects the commitments undertaken in each term, the country will face Situation F, i.e. a total crisis. This is what happens in STP today: there is a Government that does not fulfill its obligations, i.e., is unable to develop and implement programs or rule with mastery and transparency; there is a Nation that neither works or participates in the implementation of Government programs nor supervises the actions of the latter. For these reasons, widespread poverty—a sort of widespread hunger—affects more than half the population. The differences between the various political forces and the discontentment of the population have generated a situation of real hatred between the sons of the Nation. There have been lots of attempts to "clean up the hood" of each other, i.e., attempts to blame others for the crisis. Trust between the Government and the Nation has reached the lowest possible level. There is neither remarkable "democratic production" nor "economic output" in the country; therefore, neither the Government nor the Nation has benefited economically and democratically. As a result, as the whole country cannot wither up and die economically and democratically for a lack of "livelihood," all eyes are then instead focused on the importation of goods. Since in order to survive they must "work," and neither the Government nor the Nation are willing to do so voluntarily, they have triggered a struggle for possession of "power" in which the winner—the Government—became a despot, and the loser—the Nation—became the slave—a system of extreme inequalities and injustices. The despot has two options to solve economic and democratic development problems: (1) always import; and (2) import initially but soon after opt for accelerated domestic production, using the Nation's (slave's) labor. Option 2 is the most viable, but the despot has chosen the worst option—1.

In this case, there is no surplus in the society to be exported; the import can only be made on credit or for free. As discussed earlier, "there is no such thing as free lunch," and so the hypothesis of free importation is put out. Consequently, the country has incurred debts, and thus paid high costs for debts. As foreign creditors just "spin" their products to who offer counterparts or any other type of guarantee, STP has only managed to import on credit and benefit of what is commonly known as "food aid" because it has valuable resources that have been granted as compensation. This is an economy dependent on the outside, with severe trade deficit and high external debt—an import economy. The imported product is often distributed free or on credit. Distribution on credit has generated internal debt, and the one which has been made free has created a huge hole in the public accounts—funds lost—which has further aggravated the economic health of the country.

If the despot opted for solution (2), initially the performance of the society would be the same as described in (1). However, soon after, with domestic production based on slave labor, the society would produce surpluses for export—which would promote the entry of currency— and obtain high profits which could be used to stabilize the economy. Subsequently, foreign debt would be paid off, resulting in the cessation of external dependence. The country would quickly move from the status of import economy to the status of export economy, with a positive trade balance. Soon after winning the economic battle, a democratic struggle to end social injustices and inequalities would be won. In this situation, if the despot does not pay the off debt—amassing fortunes at the expense of the Nation—a doubly plagued society would result: internally damaged by slave labor and the consequent injustice and extreme social inequality, and externally by the international dependency that would lead to economic sanctions. It would be a situation close to the one in which Cuba lives today.

Now, on to the other possible situations:

I.   One of the entities does not respect the commitments undertaken, but the other fully complies with;

II.   Both entities comply with the commitments undertaken, but neither does it in its entirety;

III. Both entities comply fully with the commitments.

Situation I involves both Situation B, where one producer offers a quantity less than the agreed quantity and the other fulfils his part, and Situation D, where one of the producers (the non-doer) does not produce anything and the other (the doer) fully complies with his part. In light of Situation B, let's consider, first, that the Nation does not respect commitments, that is, people do not work or participate enough in the implementation of Government programs and do not properly supervise the actions of the latter.

Due to limited participation of people in the tasks of development control, human resource cost increases due to its low return—both in terms of production volume and in terms of the quality of products and services offered. The amount of products and services offered does not fully supply the market. Adding this to the high prices and the low quality of offers, the result is an economy which is both uncompetitive and deficient. Moreover, the limited contribution of people (or higher demand for labor and participation) results in that part of the latter's objectives cannot be met only with the domestic products, services, resources and opportunities. In order to enforce its programs, the Government resorts to the "international aid," which means importing goods, services, supports, opportunities, partnerships, etc., from the outside, which in turn contributes to the increase in external debt and trade imbalances. Assuming that the Government honors its commitments to develop effective development programs and governs with transparency and mastery in the agreed proportion, then the Nation has all its governance needs met, but pays less for them, because it can only pay with what it produces, which is little. In addition, since it is assumed that both the Government and the Nation benefits in equal proportions from good governance, it will be installed a situation of generalized social parasitism—a source of inequality and social injustice.

As the country is the only market where the Government sets out its product (good governance), then there is only one consumer, the Nation, which cannot pay a fair price, because it does not produce enough for that. Result: The Nation, by setting in the market an offer lower than the demand, exchanges it for another of greater value offered by the Government, i.e., the Nation sells more expensive than the cost of production, whilst the Government, placing in market its product in the right proportion of the demand, it exchanges it for another of lesser value, or sells it at a price below the cost of production, due to weak purchasing power of the Nation. The Nation meets all its needs for good governance, but the Government does not receive in return the assistance it needs for the success of its programs.

The Government must make a greater effort to meet its needs, bearing additional costs that decrease its performance. The economic imbalance caused by the weak national contribution leads to an increased effort of Government, paying for "foreign aid," which, in turn, generates export of currency, dependence and trade imbalances. Thus, the Government's share decreases and that of the Nation increases—accordingly generating social injustice and inequality. The purchasing power of the Nation increases, because it does not consume "imported government" and sells more expensive than the costs it has with the production; the Government's purchasing power decreases, because it sells cheaper than the costs it has with production, and it needs to consume imported products. "Social parasitism" of the Nation is thus fed off. Hence, the confidence of the Government in the Nation declines.

Since the Nation does not cooperate with the Government, it is the tendency of individuals to act outside the laws and standards. People will pay little attention to public speeches and give little value to national symbols as a way to express contempt and defiance of authorities and public institutions. The moral authority of the Government will be almost nil. It is very likely that people feel more comfortable practicing illegal activities, engaging in prohibited economic activities and developing methods to cheat the system installed. Once the bond of national unity—the Government—is not valued, individuals will hardly believe in or bet a common ideal; people most certainly will choose selfishness and individualism and deny the existence of absolute truths: "What things look like for me, so they are to me" will be the motto applicable. The likelihood that the country moves very quickly to anarchy is almost certain. In turn, the Government, in charge of small elite, seeing the prevailing state of "save yourself if you can," will make every effort to safeguard the interests of that elite, using trafficking in influence, corruption and nepotism as weapons. Without pressure from the people, power and hegemony of the Government increase to a compelling level—the country will be appropriated by a handful of individuals. Afraid of losing power and hegemony, those people soon will become despots and make the Nation a slave. The establishment of a system of social injustices and inequalities will be inevitable, thought undesirable.

Now suppose that who does not respect commitments is the Government, but the Nation so does; that is, the Government is unable to establish effective development programs or govern with transparency and mastery, but the Nation eagerly works, participates in Government programs, and oversees the actions of the rulers. Consequently, the Nation suffers from a lack of good governance and the cost of inefficiency of services, the slowness of public institutions and agencies in the implementation of projects and laws, corruption due to poor supervision, a lack of national cohesion, a lack of good leadership, a lack of synergies, and more. All of this will ultimately result in the situation where, no matter how much effort the people unleash, their cooperation and participation in the implementation of Government programs will nevertheless fail to generate positive returns. With Government programs poorly designed and their management poorly carried out, the result can only be disastrous in terms of effectiveness and return on investment. That weak economic performance will lead to poverty, injustice and social inequalities.

Given that the Nation produces in the agreed proportion, the Government has all its needs met, but ultimately pays little for them because it can only pay with what it produces, which is little. In addition, since the Government has the monopoly of resources, power and coercion in the whole, public funds from national production will remain in control of rulers who, due to corruption installed, make a bad use of them, in particular, relying upon them to fatten their bank accounts—both inside and outside of the country—to finance illegal activities and actions that contribute to the support and expansion of their collective hegemony. Obviously, the Government will assume to be the sole consumer of labor and popular participation, but cannot pay a fair price, because it does not produce enough for that. The result: the Government markets a quantity of product lower than the demand, providing a weak governance, and exchanges it for a huge popular production, i.e., it sells more expensive than the cost of production, whilst the Nation, setting in the market the right amount of effort required for implementation of Government programs, receives in exchange a Government that does not create value to the work done; that is, the Nation is forced to sell at a price below the cost of production. The Government meets all its needs, whilst the Nation gets not sufficient supply to meet its.

The Nation must make a greater effort to meet its needs, finding alternatives. Given that, internally, there is no alternative, it will have to resort to importing, say, "good governance." However, as "good governance" abroad is strictly linked to the respective foreign government, and the government concerned only can exercise sovereignty over the territory it governs, importation of "good governance" implies displacement of elements of the Nation to foreign territory—that is emigration. This phenomenon entails immense social and economic costs, including the export of currency and the brain drain, which further reduces the "purchasing power" of the Nation. The wealth of the Government (who produces less) increases and the Nation (who produces more) falls—which generates, clearly, social injustice and inequality. Thus, "social parasitism" of who does not meet commitments—the Government—is fed off. The "purchasing power" of Government increases, because it is not forced to consume imported product and sells more expensive than the costs it has with the production. The "purchasing power" of the Nation decreases, because it sells cheaper than the costs it has with the production and needs to consume imported product.

The Nation withdraws trust and support to the Government and, therefore, the former discredits the programs drawn up by the latter. The Government loses its moral authority over the Nation; laws, rules, decisions, ideas, etc., from the Government are not obeyed by citizens. The number of people acting on the margins of society increases. In an unsuccessful attempt to restore order and legality, the Government may resort to coercion, yet the Nation, feeling harassed, challenges the Governmental authorities. Thus, an internal conflict between the Government and the Nation is born, and that can end in two possible ways: (1) there is a national revolution, causing the downfall of the Government and change of the current regime to a regime of popular inspiration or (2) the Government brings a massacre or a violent crackdown on the people, which will culminate in the establishment of a despotic dictatorship. Case 1 is desirable because it can lead to a system based on liberty, equality, justice and welfare. The remnants of the outgoing regime could be eliminated, promoting balance and cooperation between the Government and the Nation. To avoid past mistakes, the new Government seeks to better meet the commitments made to the

Nation, and vice versa. Case (2) is undesirable because it will perpetuate the corrupt Government along with all its vices; even more, with the establishment of a repressive dictatorship, led by a despot, the vices of the past will worsen and new undesirable defects arise. Inequalities and social injustices could reach levels never seen before. Having the Government become a despot, the Nation will become a slave.

In light of Situation D, let's assume that the non-doer is the Nation and the Government is the doer. In this case, there is no job offer or popular participation in implementing Government programs in the country. The Nation does not supervise the actions of the Government as if it had no responsibility to do so or had nothing to do with the performance of society and the economy. Only good governance is guaranteed. In this system, there is no "currency" properly, and the transactions are made through barter, i.e., the "currencies" are the commitments undertaken by the parties. Since only the Government respects the commitments, there can be no return, and since both the doer and the non-doer benefit on a fair level from the product the former offers, one of the following circumstances occur: (1) The Nation benefits from good governance but the due compensation is to be paid by "credit," i.e. the Nation is indebted to the Government; (2) the Nation benefits from free good governance, i.e., the financing of governance from the state is done at no cost; or (3) it shall not be permitted to the Nation benefit of good governance at all.

If the condition (1) occurs and there is no assurance that the Nation will pay the debt to the Government, or if there is no independent arbitration that would oblige the first to do so, then quickly conflict between these two entities rises because of the non-payment of the debt. Not being there any single regulatory body, because these two entities are sovereign, the strength of the strongest will prevail. If the Nation wins the fight, it will not ultimately pay the debt and will make the Government hostage. It follows the collapse of the Government and regime, giving rise to a new Government and a new regime inspired by the popular will. In this case, the new Government will be made in the image of the Nation that inspires it, a Government of non-doers. As seen above, this will generate a system of injustice and extreme social inequalities, based on slavery or exploitation of man by man. If the

Government wins the fight, it can force the Nation to pay the debt or make it a slave. In this case, the Government can simply recover the debt and free the Nation or may force the Nation to pay the debt and take advantage of its weakness, making it a free labor force—a slave—in its favor.

If the condition (2) occurs, the Nation will benefit unduly from the Government's effort—parasitism of the Nation. However, this situation is untenable, because society cannot survive the scarcity of work and participation in the implementation of Government programs, nor can there be wise and transparent governance without the supervision of the Nation. Consequently, not being there, beforehand, anything that forces the Nation to fulfill its part, then, quickly, a conflict between the Nation and the Government will be born. The strongest between the two wins. And, as has been seen in the condition (1), if the Nation wins the conflict, this will not ultimately compensate for the effort undertaken by the Government and will oust it and overthrow the regime installed. a system of injustice and extreme social inequalities, based on the exploitation of man by man will be installed. If the Government wins the conflict, it could force the Nation to honor its commitment, or the former can turn the latter into a slave. In this case, the Government may only want Nation just to help the economy of the society or may transform it into a free labor force—a slave—in its favor.

If the condition (3) occurs, a connecting link between individuals will cease and no human rights will be respected, because there will be no mediation by the Government in resolving conflicts; the judiciary will be dead, indeed, no public institution will run. As it was discussed earlier, the Nation may languish and die for lack of livelihood (which is unlikely) or it may immediately install a struggle for possession of the "product" (i.e., power, support, regulation, authority, diplomacy, the monopoly of coercion, etc.) that is in the hands of the Government. If the Nation wither up and die, society will have only one element—the Government. So to survive, it will have to produce or import whatever it needs. If a struggle for possession of the "product" that is held by the Government happens (the most likely case), then, as in other situations, the strongest will win. If the winner is the Nation, it will take possession of that "product," overthrow the Government and the current regime, and establish a system of injustices and inequalities, based on the exploitation of man by man. If the Government wins, it could only force the Nation to work through compensation or abuse its weakness and make it a slave.

In conclusion, in the presence of the Situation I, the probability of raising a system of social injustices and inequalities is almost certain. Trust between the Nation and the Government declines. It is very likely that the leaders of the society will become despots, and problem of providing the "product" that is missing can be resolved in one of three ways: (Ia) the dictator chooses to keep things as they are (which is irrational), (Ib) the dictator will opt for accelerated domestic production at the expense of slave labor (which is more economically feasible for society), or (Ic) the dictator will choose to import the missing product (economically most expensive).

If the case (Ia) occurs, it will be a society in crisis of performance—either the Nation does not support the Government or the Government does not support the Nation. Given that both good governance and popular support is essential to the existence and performance of the society, either of these two situations will cause society to suffer serious "social and economic illnesses." Soon, these diseases will become unsustainable and will lead to the choice of (Ib) or (Ic). If the case (Ib) occurs, society will not depend on the outside and, therefore, its trade will be balanced. As slavery, in general, generates huge profits and surpluses, it is likely that the country becomes a major export economy. If the case (Ic) occurs, there is no surplus for export; the country can only import by credit or benefit from what is commonly known as "food aid," entailing great counterparts. Consequently, the society will incur debts and dependence on international donors—an economy dependent on the outside, with severe trade deficit and high external debt—an import economy. The imported product must be distributed to the elements free of charge or by credit. Distribution by credit will generate internal debt. If it is done free of charge, it will generate a hole in the accounts of the state—lost money—which will seriously affect the economic health of the country. If not even by credit the society can import, then it will have to opt for case (Ib), which is economically the most viable. Whatever happens, whether it becomes a despot or a slave, the non-doer will be in debt both to its internal partner and society itself—"social parasitism".

Situation II: Both parties, Government and Nation, respect the commitments made, but neither does it in its entirety.

This case can be analyzed in light of the Situation E discussed above: "If both producers comply, but none at all, then a situation where parts of both products are required to be imported appears, which leads to currency exportation, external debt and trade imbalances." Since the Nation does not give full support to the Government, it is likely that the latter will import human resources, counseling, technology, knowledge, etc., from the outside. If Government programs are too ambitious in terms of timing, size, responsibility and funding, then the imported manpower, advice, technology, and knowledge must be highly qualified. Then, part of the national offers that do not meet the requirements provided by external offers will be ignored. Thus, in addition to the export of currency, there may increase unemployment and, consequently, dissatisfaction, unrest, and protests by those affected.

Clashes between national factions and the Government can be solved in two ways: (a) The Government gives in to popular pressure, uses the less labor-skilled local workers, and jeopardizes the success of ambitious projects that are underway, making foreign manpower return to their country of origin, or (b) the Government uses coercion and represses popular pressures. In (a), everything can return to square one, i.e., the country might return to the state of poor economic and social performance and stagnate; the cycle may repeat itself. In (b), a conflict between the Nation and the Government for the possession of absolute power can arise. In this case, if the winner is the Government, it will become a despot and the loser, the Nation, a slave of the Government. It is very likely that legitimacy for the Nation to supervise or participate in Government decisions will be withdrawn and that the latter uses too drastic social, political and economic measures to promote the development of the country. In this case, economic problems may be resolved quickly but the scheme introduced will be based on a system of extreme inequality and injustice. Trust between the Government and the Nation certainly will decline. However, it will keep social tensions that could trigger conflict at any time; the cycle will repeat itself. If the Nation wins the stakes, both the Government and the political regime will be overthrown; a new regime and Government shall be established. At this point, nothing can ensure improvement of the situation neither on the part of the Nation nor on the part of the new Government; the cycle it can repeat itself indefinitely.

Situation III: Both entities, Nation and Government, comply fully with the commitments.

This is the ideal situation and may be examined in light of the Situation A: "If both producers fully respect the commitments undertaken, then there is a balance; all needs are met; there is no crisis, excesses or deficiencies. In this situation, the society remains economically stable and develops harmoniously." On the side of Government, fully respecting the commitments undertaken means being able to develop and implement effective development and govern with transparency and mastery. This is all an economic system can expect from its administration. However, for programs to be implemented and the Government to have the opportunity to govern with transparency and mastery, it is necessary that the Nation works and participates actively in the implementation of Government programs and oversees the activities of this one. Since, on the side of the Nation, all this is guaranteed, then, with available resources—as is the case of STP—there is apparently no reasons for failures, inequality, injustice, conflict or attempt to seize power. Trust between social partners remains high. The economy develops smoothly and there will be little or no external dependencies.

In a society—and thus in an economic system—the cult of respect for commitments and preservation of trust between individuals is a basic condition for development, progress and social justice. Respect of commitments makes each one contribute with a great amount of effort to meet the demands of society in terms of products, services, affinities, etc., which in turn ensures the maintenance of trust and close ties amongst individuals. In these situations, the waste is minimal; the yield is higher, leading toward full development.

In other words, an underdeveloped society is one in which there is no respect for commitments and no trust between entities. Consequently, injustices and inequities are extreme, and the production or acquisition of products to meet the vital needs has a high cost for indi-

vidual financial capabilities; therefore, having no respect for commitments or trust between entities, there can be no cooperation; thus, the
more likely it is that the entities operate individually. Otherwise, if in
a society, people have to strive to achieve, individually, all things they
need, there will be no culture of exchange; there will be no conception
of market.

For example, in the event that the purchase of a product requires
travelling long distances, if the distances are long and the quantities
that each one needs are few, then the total product cost will be high, for
it will include efforts invested in its acquisition plus the cost of travel
to and from home. If the products are perishable, then whenever one
needs them, one has to return to the source, travelling the same distances. Since there is no "market" or the ability to carry out any exchange,
there will be no possibility to exchange the surplus with other products one needs—the surplus will deteriorate; therefore, there will be
much waste and little income. In addition, each one must be an expert
on everything he or she needs; consequently, there will be no efficiency,
for no-one will be able to devote sufficient time to a specific profession
or art in order to master it. Moreover, if an individual is unable or does
not have enough knowledge to manufacture a good for satisfaction of
certain basic needs, then that individual may suffer shortages of that
good to the point he or she can die or easily become a slave of another,
who has in its possession the good at stake and is looking to abuse the
weakness of the other to achieve his or her ends.

With no cooperation, there are no organized groups or teams;
therefore, individuals will be subject to easy exposure to the threats of
wild animals, natural disasters and other men. In the absence of social
organization, there will be no civilization or standards or measures. Accordingly, it is unlikely that the community has human institutions,
assessment systems or authority capable of imposing laws and orders.
There will be little or no common values to defend. Nothing that relates to civilized communities—for example, the objective knowledge,
rights and obligations, procurement and transmission of knowledge,
feelings of heroism, patriotism, lasting relationships, collective projects, exchange of experiences, leadership, and the like; none of these—
will find fertile ground to develop and bear good fruits. Two funda-

mental concepts for development—the concept of "investment" and "medium- or long-term project"—will also not be observed: People will eat all available seeds without throwing some of them to the ground in order to give rise to new plants and, therefore, new seeds, for they will ignore that the seeds, when thrown to land, they multiply.

All that will be developed will be based on feelings of greed, jealousy, selfishness, and derivatives thereof. The proliferation of conflicts will find room to maneuver, especially the struggle for possession or control of resources and opportunities. Once the defeated or unsuccessful people will probably freely leave the community or be forced to do so, there will be frequent waves of nomadism or emigration.

Here's an example that illustrates how the cult of respect for commitments and preservation of trust between elements of society, which foster cooperation, contribute to the reduction of costs in a society. Suppose that, to meet the needs of the product P, elements of society S have to import it from the region R. The cost of P in the source is X and the cost of transportation from S to R is Y, regardless of the amount transported. If there is no cooperation amongst individuals, each one will have to buy P at the origin, R, and carry it thence to S individually; therefore, the total cost of P per person, IC, will be $IC = X + Y$. If there is cooperation, it will happen that, to minimize travel costs, individuals will get together an amount that meets the needs of the entire society and will carry it at once. Suppose that society is composed of N elements $(N > 1)$; then, they would have to buy N times the amount of product P. As the cost of transport does not vary with the amount, the total cost of buying, TC, will be $TC = N \times X + Y$. If we divide TC by the number of elements that make up society, N, we get new individual cost, NIC, which is: $NIC = (N \times X + Y)/N = X + Y/N < X + Y = IC$. As you can see, easily, the cost could be drastically reduced if persons cultivate respect for commitments and maintain confidence amongst themselves.

To illustrate this view, let's discuss what happens every day in STP in the process of acquisition of food in production sites, its transportation to the urban centers, and its commercialization or delivery to final consumers. As there is no industrial production of goods and services in this country, the entire domestic production of goods and services is done by hand. Every day, hundreds of vendors are moving individually from inside the country to, for example, the São Tomé City, carrying small amounts of food for sale. In the same transportation vehicle, many people travel along with the products for sale in city markets. Accordingly, the values of individual transport ticket from origin to destination and the individual cost of subsistence of the people involved in the process are added to the acquisition costs. Suppose that the price of a particular product, for example, banana, from the origin is P, the cost of an individual transport ticket is T, the cost of transport of Q amount of product is C, and the subsistence cost per person during the process is S. Suppose further that in a given car, N people travel, carrying equal amounts of load, say, Q. Then the final product price, FP, when shipped individually from source to destination is FP = (Q × P + T + C + S)/Q + profit = P + (T + C + S)/Q + profit. Since, in the same car, N traders travel (N ≥ 2) with equal amounts of load, Q, we have that the total cost is TC = N × Q × [P + (T + C + S)/Q] = N × Q × P + N ×Q × (T + C + S)/Q = N × Q × P + N × (T + C + S). Suppose now that traders, after ensuring the necessary trust between themselves and assume a commitment to that end, agree to cooperate amongst themselves to efficiently carry out the process, reducing costs and increasing profits. Instead of moving N traders, the task is entrusted to only one of them (for example, the more experienced or more successful), which allows the remaining N-1 traders to engage in other economic activities. Since the amount of product being transported is N × Q (Q amount of load for each of the N traders) and only one trader travels along with it, the new final price of the product, NFP, will be *NFP = (N × Q × P + T + N × C + S)/(N × Q) + profit = P + (T + C + S)/(N × Q) + [(N-1) × C]/(N × Q) + Profit ⟨P +2 × (T + C + S)/(N × Q) + profit ≤ FP*. In this case, the new total cost, NTC, will be *NTC = N×Q×P+T+N×C+S= N×Q×P+N× (T+C+S) - (N-1) × (T+S) = TC - (N-1) ×(T+S)*, which means that, collectively, they save *(N-1) × (T + S)* STD (national currency), or save (N-1)/N × 100% of the costs of travel tickets and livelihood! As *lim N → ∞ [(N - 1)/N × 100%] = 100%*, these savings increase as the number N of traders increases. For example, if N = 10, then the savings will be 90%; if N = 100, the savings will be 99%; if N = 1000, the savings will be 99.9%, and so on. In other words, if the number of traders involved is too large, the cost of travel and subsistence will be diluted almost completely.

A third example which illustrates the damage that a lack of respect for commitments and non-preservation of trust between entities causes to society is the issue of strikes. A strike is a social phenomenon, protected by law, which is a collective and temporary stoppage of work activities, decided by the workers as a means of pressuring the employer or the Government to meet their demands, which in general are: increased wages, improved working conditions, guaranteed entitlements, etc. That is, a strike implies a claim of rights and, at the same time, the exercise of a right of workers. This only happens when workers are dissatisfied with the employer or the Government, say, workers allege or feel that certain commitments of the employer or the Government are not being met, or they have no confidence in that the latter are up to voluntarily meet the needs felt by the former. When it comes to the enforcement of rights, prima facie, the morality of their actions is not questioned. However, the strike is a form of pressure that manifests itself through suspension of work activities. But it is not just a form of pressure. Viewed with other eyes, it is a kind of legal blackmail aimed at, through the threat of damage, forcing employers or the Government to cede to the demands of workers, who, under the law, can self-importantly use it whenever they so wish. So the strike is counterproductive and, because he has no predefined deadline, it can occur endlessly, obeying only a collective and radical decision of workers, seeking only to satisfy their interests and without worrying about the society, the Government or the employer. This is not a dispute that either party can win; therefore, its morality is compromised.

Since the strikes occur in industrial environments and profoundly affect the economic activities related to these environments, they should be safeguarded so as to bring benefits to all parties involved and not just one party. One must establish and maintain, in Government, a competent body to assess workers' needs, balancing them with the economic performance of the employer, and producing a formula that determines the manner in which the needs of workers—working conditions, wages, and the like—should be automatically updated over time. For example, in a production environment on the rise, the formula would determine the way in which gradually the wage adjustments and improved working conditions should be made, or the way in which legal and temporary suspensions (or strikes) must occur in order to the occurrence of a strike to aim solely at eliminating unnecessary or negative work[91], contribute to business performance and optimize the production of wealth. Similarly, in a production environment poor or moderate, the formula would prevent the suspension of work activities from occurring in circumstances that harm the required or positive work[92].

If the work environment is deficient and has serious economic problems, i.e. it does not produce enough to cover expenses and to profit, then it lacks the necessary or positive work. In this situation, society cannot afford the luxury of allowing the suspension of labor activity, because that further reduces the production and productivity and the economy can be led to bankruptcy. If at the outset there is not enough wealth production, then with the advent of the strike, there is a delay, which further reduces production and leads to other charges. If, furthermore, the workers' demands require a large financial outlay by the employer, then, this inability to meet the demands of workers may lead to the undue extension of the suspension of work activities, which is counterproductive. This is one of the situations in which the authorities must intervene to end the strike, considering it prohibitive, impractical and unsustainable.

Suppose we are in a universe full of resources, our economic wealth is extensive and there are too many surplus productions. The market is saturated and there is no outlet for surplus production or how to use them for useful purposes. The more one works, the more production will increase, generating even more surplus, more attrition on the production system, more burden on the employer, more depletion of resources and, ultimately, more waste and no return. Any production effort will be unnecessary or negative work. In this situation, a solution to the economic problem may be, first, the collective and tempo-

---

91   Unnecessary or negative work is any type of work, say, a surplus, counterproductive, wasteful, that increases production but not productivity, or do not contribute to business performance. This type of work does neither contribute to organizational efficiency nor to the economic health of the organization..

92   Required or positive work is any kind of work that contributes to the increase of economic wealth; contributes to increased production and productivity. Such work is vital to the survival of the employer and compliance with pre-established commitment between it and the Government.

rary suspension of work activities until the stock is reduced to levels supportable by the market. Thereafter, power would gradually resume production, reducing working hours for each employee in order to keep supply and demand in balance. This collective and temporary suspension of work properly negotiated between employers and workers associated with the subsequent gradual resumption of work activities would be called a strike. The strike would be a positive factor of production, a factor of efficiency control; it would aim to eliminate waste and optimize production.

However, if people live in a poor or moderate economic environment, requiring constant maintenance of work activities to produce the wealth needed for self-subsistence, then the daily work would be as vital as the air one breathes. In this case, if they stop working, they cannot keep up the economic system and, thus, they will produce no surplus or the surplus produced will not be significant to both suffice the needs of the market and generate substantial returns. In this situation, any suspension of work activities will not be welcome; it will be a negative factor of production, a vector of inefficiency, instability, loss and crisis.

In STP today—a precarious economic system—there is an immature law in force—the Strike Law. The country does not produce even for self-subsistence. However, the proliferation of strikes has been a plague to the national economy, causing stoppages of work activities, which can last half a year! Since the claims of workers have been, basically, wage increases—often to around 200-500%—and improved working conditions, through acquisitions of equipment and machines extremely expensive for economic capacities of employers and Government itself, most of the workers' demands have not been met, which, besides causing more breakdowns, have discouraged the working class and dramatically reduced the local production. The São Toméan man learned that the humanity once won the right to strike and that he could make use of that right when and how he wished. This was enough to lead him to create a law that has allowed the occurrence of strikes with no brakes and no rules in the country, increasingly sinking the economy into a ditch. Each time that workers think, dream or imagine they have a problem—and sometimes the problem really arises—

they do not think twice, triggering a strike. During that period, they produce nothing. Nobody makes a balance between damage and the benefits obtained from the strike. After countless days or months of negotiation, they reach an agreement that apparently satisfies both parties. However, in reality, it creates more burdens for the state charges, which then drown the country into a major crisis, which in turn leads workers to return to strike, incessantly, endlessly...

If someone tells us that the strike is an indispensable civilization tool to guarantee certain human rights, we must ask him or her about what to do with the economic and social decay that the strike has caused. Arguments that the strikes have contributed to solve problems are inconsistent with the results obtained in practice, resulting from weak economic performance and degrading living conditions of workers in STP, which are derived from the stoppages of work activities. In an underdeveloped country, one must devise other forms of pressure to solve the problems of workers, and these forms of pressure should not affect the economy, but they must give to the productive system the opportunity to continue production without disruption, without unbalance, seeking optimization. Just, for example, cultivate respect for commitments and preserve the trust between the entities, so that the new system works and meets its objectives.

In a degrading economic environment, the strike as a form of pressure acts as a narcotic in the body of an addict: The individual has a temporary feeling that his or her problems are resolved—or very well resolve—but hours later, the backwater comes and causes him or her excruciating pain. This obliges the person to consume, repetitively, a given dose of the drug, creating addiction. As usually, the drug has a high price for the possessions of the addict, which will gradually degrade his or her economic situation, whilst the person's problems are experienced every day, without exception. In addition, as the drug has side effects too harmful to health, the physical condition of the individual also becomes debilitated. Conclusion: Instead of solving the problems of the individual, the narcotic complicates it and degrades his or her economy, physical and mental health (including consequences to elements of the society surrounding him or her). The same goes for strikes in a country like STP: it just downgrades the economy and leads the country into a vicious cycle of instability and socio-political and economic delays.

In a developed society, entities and institutions cooperate to re-duce efforts and increase profits. And all this is done at the expense of respect for commitments and preservation of trust between these entities and institutions. For a given commitment to be met and for there to be trust between two or more entities, there must be compat-ibility between functions that constitute the commitment and exper-tise of the entity to which such functions have been assigned. Usually, for a given task, there are several individuals who meet the require-ments of compatibility. As the need for manpower to perform certain tasks is limited, if there are more applicants than the required number, then they must select the most promising. This generates competition, which in turn causes the candidates to strive to surpass each other, improving both individual and collective skills.

On behalf of the commitment, confidence and progress, as well as in an effort to improve the Nation, the society must excel itself by establishing:

- Compatibility of individuals to the roles they play in the system in which they live;

- Competition to select the best amongst the candidates, ensur-ing the maximization of individual performance which, in turn, guarantees better collective performance, in circum-stances where there are more individuals compatible with the function than the number of places available. Competition requires that, individually, persons strive to obtain the best possible performance (to beat the personal record) and out-perform other candidates, which in turn leads to better per-formance, both individually and collectively.

A society that underestimates compatibility, competition and com-mitment or does not promote these things, forbids its elements the path to progress, both of themselves and of all mankind; that is, society does not activate the spontaneous functions of development or has a performance that is incompatible with evolution itself. The exercise of instinctive human reproductive functions may help us to understand this. To procreate, a person must prove to have compatibilities for that purpose. Everything starts with sexual attraction, which means that instinctively an individual of a certain species found another of the op-posite sex of the same species, whose attributes are compatible with its and those attributes are capable of, combined, enabling procreation in order to create a new individual of the same species capable of continu-ing the generations. However, since this is a team work, procreation as the act which results from the combination and compatibility between two individuals, requires that from the side of the opposite sex, there is also a favorable response to begin to trigger functions, the project or instinctive reproductive tasks.

Competition is a natural proof and expresses a relationship of struggle between two living beings, where the fittest is the least affect-ed. The experiences and inter-relationships between people naturally express the competition—it is present at all sites and in everything one does. For example, walking in the streets of the São Tomé City, two beautiful ladies talked about the daily challenges of womanizing, ini-tiated by their respective suitors. They spoke about the methods and techniques they use to defend themselves from "attacks of the males" and the need they have to protect themselves against the immorality that threatens the process. Often they struggle to forgo satisfaction of desires to remain socially well-respected. They seemed to be well-respected. The individual effort they make every day to meet the social and moral condition of keeping a good reputation has to do with the competition factor. Having a good reputation is an indication that they are potentially good wives, companions, mothers, or even good profes-sionals. Good reputation of those misses increases their social value. In addition to a social function, they serve an instinctive function linked to procreation. They strive to ensure and improve their compatibility with the largest possible number of male suitors. By "defending them-selves" from "attacks" of the males, they were instinctively running the criteria of a selection process, which is competitive by nature and in-cludes checking the compatibility. Each of them ends up selecting the man who offers better guarantees.

The very nature establishes and administers a thorough process of competition, which includes selection of individuals for natural func-tions and goes through the determination of compatibility, which, in turn, leads to efforts towards continuous improvement of the capacity to overcome obstacles and ensure the survival of species, produce the best possible individuals for the respective species and select the most suitable for their intended functions. However, the natural system not only benefits from the improving skills of the fittest, but also the improvement of individual capacities of all parties involved, which leads to collective improvement.

Compatibility is enough to trigger reproductive functions, but nevertheless, in situations where there are more than one compatible suitor, the selection process requires competition—The target of conquest selects from amongst the candidates the one who offers the best compatibility. This fact is then translated into better performance for the reproduction process, which will generate individuals with higher capacities. Thus, the selection process requires that, individually, each candidate struggles to persuade or show that it is capable of better performance. The reproduction process gains from competition.

The same is true for a human society. Having ensured the compatibility of the candidates for a particular post, and grouped those who satisfy the requirements in a smaller universe, competition must be initiated in order to select the most skilled. Candidates shortlisted on the basis of their compatibility might undergo specific training or guidance in order for them to better themselves both individually and collectively. Even if the potential winner is known beforehand, competition is still necessary because it helps to improve qualitatively both the potential winner and the other candidates. Even if the latter are not selected for the jobs at stake, they may be better used by society for other purposes. Through competition, individually, each candidate strives to excel and overcome his or her opponents, which is very advantageous to the whole society. In terms of performance, it is possible for the initially considered less able candidate to overcome who better matched requirements. Collectively, the competition generates increased skills, i.e., all parties gain something more from competition between the candidates, and the system itself is enriched in terms of individual and collective skills.

Commitment in a social system implicitly involves collaboration amongst social elements. This takes many forms, for instance, it is (1) cooperation between individuals to complete a given task, (2) a team work, (3) participation of someone in a collective project. When there is no need for collaboration, it must be avoided, because it can lead to waste or injury. Since living in a society requires, necessarily, belonging to one or more teams, when the ingredient "collaboration" is included into speech, it reinforces the idea that the work is inherent to social life, which in turn is the antonym of parasitism.

There are humans in STP who are proud of being sustained at the expense of others' efforts. These people are, by definition, parasites. Being a member of a society means to agree with social reality, its rules and standards and to have a reasonable level of sanity, self-censorship, social conscience and good morals. But these attributes are closely linked to the sense of justice, which must guide the social existence of an individual. And this is inconsistent with parasitism. Thus there is no support for the social existence of someone who survives at the expense of others. However, there are many individuals in STP whose social existence boils down to complete leisure, supported by the institutional neglect of the state apparatus. The social existence of the leaders of this Nation, from the highest to the lowest, is entirely parasitic. Besides not conceiving or implementing effective development programs or management of public affairs, they spend their time plundering the goods and services to which they are responsible, diverting public funds for private purposes, and making catastrophic expenses trifles such as trips, parties and events that contribute nothing to the country's development. They are not actually interested in solving practical problems, so they do not go to the bottom of things, seeking the causes and most appropriate solutions. They are concerned only with the aesthetic aspect of discussions in which they can show their fake intellectualities and the superficiality of their ideas that do not go beyond a mere narcissism, custom, aestheticism and banality of public discourse, based on catch phrases and flashes of genius without any real rationale or framework. That is the essence of their state of consciousness and provides the motivation they need to live an everlastingly parasitic life.

Following this principle of existence, they convert the act of forming opinions into a masquerade, where they amuse themselves lavishly and leading public opinion is treated as a game—and those who seem more humorous—clowns in formal attire, carrying big books under their arms—stand to gain. Their everyday masses take place at the Congressional Palace, and sometimes discussions are so time-consuming and futile that they become stressful and overwhelming. In 2004, the National Assembly spent a whole term (4 years) discussing the viability of funds for the purchase of vehicles for deputies whilst the urgent problems were left pending! Most people, albeit disgruntled, sell their votes to political candidates in return for a "little fish." Thus, they contribute to the legitimacy, strengthening and perpetuation of corruption and are themselves victims of the pitfalls they help to create.

Another widespread form of parasitism in the public has to do with the mismanagement of public assets. Often, rulers who have led huge public projects or investments to bankruptcy, exhibit exuberant personal fortunes—stuffed bank accounts, property of great value, etc. Their fortunes must have come from some form of delinquency or criminality, because, if they led to failure the projects whence their income derived, certainly, they could not have had enough wealth to buy properties or become rich. For them to be able to build personal fortunes, they apply their intelligence, knowledge and efforts in the practice of illegal activities—including corruption scandals.

Parasitism of public administrators is not only detrimental to the country for harboring corruption, incompetence, neglect, and delinquency, but also and more serious still, for inspiring and nurturing the parasitism of a very significant part of the workforce. In 2008, the National Statistics Institute (INE) estimated the rate of unemployment in the country in more than 40%. Since then the official number of unemployed people rose by about 3.5%. Now let's look at the facts to understand what unemployment means for the São Toméan man, so we can better interpret the statistics and understand the reality. Most of the economy of this country is small-scale and informal. People not only survive with what they officially receive as salary; almost all of them have more than one source of income, and this is what guarantees their survival. Indeed, the INE's estimates only reflect the situation of people formally employed, i.e., people whose economic and professional activities are linked to legal persons. Because much of the population does not have a job recognized by the state, their employment situation is not considered for statistical analysis, because the state has no control over their activities. It is that group of people which supplies the market with products manufactured in the country. But they pay no taxes; they do not report income to the state; they do not pass bills and hardly deposit money in banks. The actual volume of production is unknown and the qualities of the products are not guaranteed because they are not inspected by the competent authorities.

Once those people are not officially recognized as producers or professionals, their earnings are not declared and they do not pay taxes. It is that group of people that forms the bulk of what is considered unemployment, which is estimated at more than 40%. This is paradoxical, precisely because that population group is the one which earns more income, thought that income does not match the contribution they give, because the prices are arbitrary and unreasonable. Informal traders, for example, buy at a given price and sell several times more expensive than they bought; the laborers or craftsmen charge several times the official salary for a few hours of work, i.e., something one must take several months to earn in an official job, they earn in a few hours of casual work.

However, by charging exorbitant and arbitrary prices for the products or services they offer, not paying taxes, working just a few hours a day and earning several times more than their compatriots who work officially, they are in a sense living at the expense of others—this is, by definition, parasitism. Every day throngs of people line up along the roadsides, talking, drinking or just watching the movements of cars and people who go to jobs. This cluster of people often complains of lack of work or unemployment. If they are unemployed, then whence the money they squander every day with drinks and trivia comes from? Answer—one of two things: either they subtract the resources they squander and offer nothing in return or they have some unofficial source of income. What is perceived as "officially unemployed" or "living idly" means, in practice, dedication to a harmful work activity, on the fringes of society; that is, in the formal point of view, these people are unemployed, because they do not have a formal job, but in the real point of view, they live in delinquency or criminality, which is a parasitic activity. Those people, basically, live on the money of others. So one must give utility to the idle hours, skills and qualifications these people afford, and place them in the official circuits of the economy.

In the raising of a New Nation, each individual must have an acute awareness of the self within society. Replacement of current elements of the Nation by others is required. However, no physical replacement is required; just political and moral, allowing each man to cultivate appropriate virtues.

Raising a New State

The purpose of raising a New State is that of correcting the defects in the current one. Such defects are restricted to the structure of the state apparatus, its management and operation. The New State must be able to avoid instabilities, corruption, mismanagement and poor socioeconomic development in its unit, and all this must be run at the highest level by its political regime. And in the present context, the political regime in STP is semi-presidential democracy. Public authorities have emphasized the strengthening of democratic institutions at the expense of large public investments but, overall, there is increasing degradation of public institutions, loss of state authority, enormous instability in the state apparatus, and rapid socioeconomic degradation. For these reasons and common sense, if we want that past mistakes are not repeated in the future, it is necessary to conceive a political system suitable for the new state.

Key Questions

The New State project must be designed the same way one conceives a plan to build a new system. It is necessary to define the state's personality, destination, structure, and performance rule. That is answering to the following questions:

(1) What is the target system (the New State's definition)?

(2) What is expected as a result of system operation (the goals of the New State)?

(3) What are the system's structure and actors (structure, organs and members for the New State)?

(4) What functions each must play? And

(5) How they must relate to each other (ethics for the New State)?

Defining the New State

The desired state is a political system that can maintain its stability, ensure sufficient continuity and completion of projects and development policies, and promote the social, economic and cultural development; that is, to correct the defects of the current system (semi-presidential democracy). Thus, it must not only depend on the popular vote for decision-making or the so called people's self-determination; however, it must not be dictatorial or authoritarian nor be led by a hereditary ruler. The power must be centralized, although retaining the characteristics of a state of law; the economic system must be decentralized. As a welfare state, it must guarantee respect for civil liberties, namely respect for human rights and fundamental freedoms through the establishment of a legal protection. The national political authorities must respect the rule of law.

The Goals of the New State

As is enshrined in the current state constitution—and universally accepted as being the ideal of a state of law—the goals of the New State must be: (1) to build a free, fair and caring society; (2) to ensure national development; (3) to eradicate poverty and marginalization, and reduce social and regional inequalities; and (4) to promote the good for everyone, without prejudice of origin, race, sex, color, age and any other form of discrimination.

A New Political System for the New State

The New State must be regarded as an assembly of institutions that functions as a stable whole and holds the property of life—a living body; that is, it must be capable of *responding to stimuli, reproduction, growth* and *development*, as well as *maintenance of homeostasis as a stable whole*. Like any living organism, it must have a management organ—its brain; its government—and such an organ must be unique, indivisible and central; otherwise, internal conflicts of instructions, ambiguities, contradictions and chaos can arise, which is incompatible with the vital functions.

The capacity of response to stimuli calls for the New State's ability to detect changes in its internal and external environments, and produce the adequate response. Those changes are cyclical phenomena that affect the country's politics, such as climate change, natural disasters, institutional crises, international relations, etc. *The capacity of reproduction, growth and development* is the ability to grow in terms of population, economy, maturity, complexity, and so forth, adapting to epochs, and crossing generations. This ability allows the state to reorganize, multiply, create or eliminate its institutions. *The capacity of maintenance of homeostasis as a stable whole* is the ability to regulate its internal environment so as to maintain stable, constant conditions (stability of the state apparatus), which are appropriate for the implementation of medium- and long-term development projects.

Accordingly, the democratic system installed is not able to meet these expectations, for it has led the country to a complete chaos; therefore, it is required to resize and restructure the states' apparatus deeply and devise a new political system capable of correcting the defects of the current one. The new system must be able to eliminate the widespread anarchy in the country, reintegrate the state apparatus, take the country's economy out of the cave in which it now resides, reinstate the state's authority, and improve the country's image before the international community. For successful planning and implementation of the state's long-term and medium-term projects, a stable government is required. The state cannot develop without producing and absorbing adequate and sufficient knowledge. In this sense, the new regime must also be able to promote the production and dissemination of knowledge, as well as ensure the quality of the scientific and educational apparatus.

The changes to be made must result in a new constitution, defining state organs and laws capable of driving the state machine and preventing deviations to the established rules and standards. It must also be devised in order to maintain close control and supervision over state's activities so that it can guarantee that delegates are faithful and goals are being effectively achieved. The new structure must conform to an optimal political and administrative structure, devised to be capable of promoting 'collective intelligence', ensuring that the available resources are put to the best use, whilst fighting economic recession. This is absolutely possible, although it does, of course, require efforts, dedication and commitment from all stakeholders.

Because collective projects cannot be successful without people's engagement, reducing the existing political illiteracy will improve people's understanding of the state's projects, programs, and ideology, and will subsequently improve their participation in the execution of public tasks. They must be educated regarding their role in the socio-economic life, raising their awareness on issues relating to the actions they must undertake in order to claim their rights, fulfill their duties and actively partake in the state's business. A successful people's participation is only achieved if they are properly educated, informed and aware of the state's affairs. It is imperative to reflect upon the way in which society will be structured based on legislation, which must assure that social inequalities do not arise from the legislated model; the model must legitimize a fair life for everybody, without the prevalence of the strongest on the weakest.

Thus, the New State System (NSS) should be composed of four interdependent organs of sovereignty: The Office of the State (OS), so as to ensure that holders of public office have the knowledge and skills necessary for the exercise of power; the Electoral Subsystem (ES), so as to ensure that the selection of projects and individuals is made within strict standards and engage the collective will; the Government Subsystem (GS), in order to ensure that programming and implementation of projects and public policies happen in ways that result in positive returns and ensure continuity of Government functions; and the Judiciary Subsystem (JS), in order to ensure that the system operates within legal and constitutional standards.

The OS must be a permanent collegial body, responsible for the analysis, evaluation and training of state organs, statesmen, academics and organizational leaders. The ES must be responsible for registration, identification and verification of eligibility of candidates for Government positions. This body must also be collegial and permanent. The GS must be responsible for planning and implementing programs of governance. The JS must be responsible for implementation of justice and enforcement of law; it must also be a permanent body.

The Configuration of the Bodies

OS and ES must be composed of, say, persons of good reputation, sages only, i.e. those with the highest academic and scientific recognition and demonstrated experience in the country. There should be at least one scholar for each science or discipline that is necessary for the efficient performance of the state. Each scholar must be possessed of good morals, good human relationships, good physical and psychological condition, and have been approved in tests of intelligence and competence up to their responsibilities. The recruitment of each new scholar must be done individually by participating and passing a series of public trials, under criteria set out beforehand. Such tests must be performed and evaluated by the already existing collective of scholars and supervised or followed by the other three bodies of the NSS. OS will not have, say, local agencies or regional bodies; it must be unitary and indivisible by its nature and responsibility. Due to its peculiarities, ES must have an agency in each local or regional government, and each local agency should possess a certain degree of autonomy but must be accountable or subordinate to the central ES.

Although the recruitment of elements of the JS will be done similarly to the OS and the ES, in hierarchical terms, the JS must adopt a structure compatible with the functions of the judiciary. Also like the ES, the JS will have a representative or agency in each local or regional government, paying bills or being subordinate to the central JS, although possessing some autonomy.

The GS should fundamentally comprise a leader, at least two deputy leaders and an executive for each agency or department of the state (ministry, secretary of state, or similar). The number and names of the various departments or agencies shall be defined by the constitution, and that number and their names should not be amended except by revision of the constitution. There must be an agency or department of the state for each area of economic activity and social policy. The identification of individual agencies or departments will be subject to a previous study to determine their need, function and composition.

Thus, it is guaranteed the centralization of political power and decentralization of economic power, which in principle is a basic condition for solving the fundamental problems of collective development of STP, which is the governing instability, widespread corruption and poverty, and socioeconomic backwardness. The four NSS agencies listed above advocate for the establishment of a central political power with rotating leadership, responsible for generation and distribution of wealth and knowledge in a stable, transparent and fair framework.

Admission to the NSS

Each individual who apply for a body in the NSS must have a general advanced education. With a fragile economy, a population so young, and such a huge lack of knowledge and experience, in addition to a state apparatus so inefficient, and so many resources to explore, opportunities to take advantage of and dreams unfulfilled, the nation should never put the power in the hands of anyone without first having ensured that the person concerned has the right profile and is likely to perform well.

STP lacks infrastructure and people with the relevant knowledge, skills and experience. Therefore, the state must ensure that its agents have the capacity and skills necessary for the role they will play; it must ensure that public leaders study and plan projects properly.

Because OS, ES and JS shall obey recruitment processes executed by their individual agencies and supervised or observed by the other three, the selection process is explained in those organs. However, the selection for GS must require further attention. Social groups should be responsible for the formation of full Government teams (lists) and submission of applications to the ES. Legalization of a political group is not relevant, because any group of citizens could apply for the GS, provided they meet the requirements described above.

There should not be a fixed deadline for the mandate of a government, neither at the central nor at local levels. The duration of each term of the Government depends on the time required or proposed for the project that formed the basis of its candidacy and is expected to draft a medium or long term (nationwide). The term of a government must never be less than five years, and projects submitted must be considered to be consistent with this minimum period, in addition to meeting all other highlighted criteria. The terms of the GS should be continuously supervised by three other agencies: JS, ES and OS. Elec-tions for the GS could be scheduled to be held just before the end of the current mandate so that, before the end of that period, a new team is already formed and ready to take office, ensuring the continuity of governmental operations. There is no need to coordinate with the local election headquarters. Every election at local, regional or central level should be held at the convenience of their bodies.

Once a list is submitted, the ES should record, verify the eligibility conditions and check the respective projects of governance for com-pleteness, both at general and specific levels. Then, the projects could be submitted to the OS and JS which, much like ES, could make a pre-liminary assessment, resulting in acceptance or rejection of projects. After preliminary approval by ES, JS, and OS, the elements of the se-lected teams should participate in a public examination for defense and justification of their proposed projects. In such examinations, each of the involved agencies should assign a grade to each project. The move to next stage would depend on the grades obtained.

After this phase, ES could hold a ballot in which all citizens of the country would vote. That could include minors and disabled people. The concept of vote here does not merely consist in a conscious choice of people with legal maturity, but represents the existence of someone belonging to a certain group that is supposed to depend on the policies proposed by political groups. Another reason is the fact that our popu-lation is mostly comprised of people under eighteen. Until now, most of their fates have been determined by people older than eighteen years old—a minority—which does not seem consistent with the very idea of democracy. For example, currently, a family with five people—two parents and three young children—and another family with only one man and one woman have the same weight in political choices. If we put these people on a scale, there is imbalance: the side of the family of five will weigh more. The same is true in society: There will be greater social responsibility and higher financial needs and opportunities in a family of five people than in a family of just two. As such, the side of five people will have greater weight in the choices of public policies.

In the NSS, all persons (single and legal) should have the right to vote. The voting of an organization could be conducted by its legal representative and comply with a ballot internal to the organization. This makes sense because both people and organizations have legal personality and must pay taxes to the state. Organizations have social responsibilities as citizens do (sometimes even more), why don't they have the right to vote?

The vote of individuals should have less weight than that of organizations because individuals do not have tools, resources, expertise, availability, or even permission, to rigorously assess and determine feasibility of governing projects. Such projects are often complex and extensive, requiring very detailed technical and feasibility analysis, which must be the responsibility of technically savvy people. The consistency, viability or legitimacy of a Government team cannot be determined only by the vote of the people and organizations. It is necessary to consider the technical accuracy, legality and governance framework of projects with development strategies and objectives of the state. The state must be governed by capable persons and not by persons chosen by people based on superficial information obtained through electoral advertisements, conversations on the street, rumors, personal sympathies, patronage, as has been recorded in the STP.

For a list to be complete and properly produced, it must submit a candidate for each position open in the GS. At the head of the lists should be three persons who will lead all the projects of the executive, namely, a president of republic and two vice-presidents. The role of the vice-presidents is to advise the president in his duties and replace him in his impairments. This ensures the continuity of the elected executive, even in extreme situations such as physical disappearance. This trio should be called "presidential candidates." Each application must contain a general political project for the trio of presidential candidates, and a specialized project for each of the elements of their squad. All these projects should be linked and integrated into the collective project. Both as a whole and in particular, each of these projects will be evaluated and graded by three bodies (ES, OS and JS).

However, in addition to the marks obtained in the assessments made by the three agencies mentioned above, it is necessary to include consideration of people and organizations, a classification based on the opinions of these entities, to demonstrate the public participation, awareness, and consent, because any government—democratic or dictatorial—that does not have popular support is a bankrupt government at birth. However, the contribution of the popular and organizations vote may never be able to determine alone the choice of representatives of the nation; moreover, it should be only the minimum necessary to symbolize popular support. Thus, there are defined five different types of classification, which are: classification of the electoral subsystem (CES), classification of the Office of the State (COS), classification of the judiciary subsystem (CJS), percentage of individuals voting (SV), and the percentage of votes from legal persons (LV). Each type of classifications has an associated weight, which ranges between 0 and 1: WES, WOS, WSJ, WLP and WSP, which are, respectively, "Weight of the Electoral Subsystem," "Weight of the Office of the State," "Weight of the Judiciary Subsystem," "Weight of Legal Persons Voting," and "Weight of Single People Voting". These "weights" determine the liability and the relevance of each of these entities in the selection of members of the state government. They assume values between 0 and 1, and the sum of them should be equal to 1, i.e., WES + WOS + WSJ+ LPV + SPV = 1. The WOS must take a value greater than that of each of the other variables, given the central role that OS has in the analysis of technical accuracy, appropriateness to the national development strategy, coherence, relevance for the country as well as continuity with projects of previous governments.

Fig. 1 General formula for calculating the final ranking of candidate lists to the GS.

$$C = (WES) \cdot \frac{1}{N-2} \sum_{p=1}^{N-2} (CES)_p + (WOS) \cdot \frac{1}{N-2} \sum_{p=1}^{N-2} (COS)_p + (WJS) \cdot \frac{1}{N-2} \sum_{p=1}^{N-2} (CJS)_p + (WLP) \cdot LV + (WSP) \cdot SV$$

Table 2: Table-Summary of Variables, Indicative Values and Meanings

Variable	Meaning	Domain	Acceptance Value	Remarks
N	Number of elements of the governmental staff	-	-	This number must be provided by the constitution
p	Index of governmental project.	Varies from 1 to N-2	-	1 is the index of the project of the three candidates for the presidency (the president and two vice-presidents), the other indices correspond to the remaining projects.
CES	Score awarded by the ES	From 0 to 100	85 minimum (indicative)	Satisfactory (from 85 to 89); Very Satisfactory (from 90 to 94); Full Satisfactory (from 95 to 100) —indicative values only.
	Score assigned by the ES to the project of index p.	From 0 to 100	Idem	Idem
COS	Score awarded by the OS	From 0 to 100	Idem	Idem
CJS	Score awarded by the JS	From 0 to 100	Idem	Idem
WES	Weight of the ES	Between 0 and 1	0.2	Indicative. WES + WOS + WSJ+ WLP + WSP=1
WOS	Weight of the OS	Between 0 and 1	0.3	Indicative. The WOS must have a value greater than each of the other variables.
WJS	Weight of the JS	Between 0 and 1	0.2	Indicative.

WLP	Weight of the Legal Persons Voting	Between 0 and 1	0.2	Indicative.
WSP	Weight of the Single Persons Voting	Between 0 and 1	0.1	Indicative.
LV	Percentage of Legal Persons Voting	Between 0 and 100	0	
SV	Percentage of Single Persons Voting	Between 0 and 100	0	

Finally, for a given list to be approved, each one of its projects (general and specialized) should obtain a minimum average grade of "Satisfactory." Such a grade, C, could be determined by the formula specified in Fig.1 below, where N is the total number of members of the GS provided by the constitution; is the grade assigned to the joint project of the three presidential candidates (the president and two vice presidents) by the ES, and , p = 2, ..., N-2 are, respectively, the scores assigned by the ES to the N-3 projects relating to each of the remaining team members; is the grade assigned to the joint project of the three presidential candidates by the OS, and , p = 2, ..., N-2 are, respectively, the scores awarded by the OS to the N-3 projects relating to each of the remaining team members; is the grade assigned to the joint project of the three presidential candidates by the JS, and , p = 2, ..., N-2 are, respectively, the scores awarded by the JS to the N -3 projects relating to each of the remaining team members.

The Transition Period

Because any new system to be installed must comply with a probationary period, the establishment of the NSS must respect a "transitional period" (minimum necessary for the arrangement of the first leaders, managers and public administrators) in which the state organs must be formed and the institutions subsequently created and duly installed. The coordination of these tasks of "installation" of the New State should be in charge of a body, i.e. the Council for Installation of the New State (CINS). The elements of the CINS should be responsible for the training and setting up of elements of the ES, JS and GS. Following the transition period, the CINS could become the Office of the State (OS).

Ethics for a New State

Now that we have the raw material needed to build a new society, it becomes essential to reflect on how different elements of the society should relate to each other and how they should behave with their peers and with the authorities, the organizations, culture, nature, the collective heritage, etc. As an ideal society, the New State cannot survive without relying on virtues such as truth, merit, justice, liberty, equality, and the like. Successful political regimes are usually supported by strong ideologies, which are all based on great virtues. Therefore, every effort should be made to bring the man to the great virtues. In the New State there will be no room to grow hatred between factions, social classes, ethnic groups or individuals. The word "enmity" or "enemy" should be banished from the dictionary. There will be, of course, space for the free confrontation of ideas, but only in terms that lead to a tangible result, a viable solution. Any divergence of ideas or opinions that lead to conflicts of indefinite duration should be cancelled. Well, it sounds very good to the ears of citizens, the following sentence: "This great man is my friend on the left" or "this great man is my friend on the right," referring to someone defending an idea, respectively, against or in favor of the idea of the interlocutor. Friends, this is the best a nation can receive as a gift; citizens will never make personal attacks, but they will only in an intellectually honest way discuss different viewpoints. Any kind of violence is unjustifiable; all parties are required only to use mental resources, such as mental, ideological and factual tools, and to take advantage of these. Brute force and violence should not, and need not, be tools for overcoming disagreement. We can start now making our kick-off: "The great men and women of the São Toméan political class are our friends on the left!" Of course, without any irony. They are but friends always on the left side, for they will forever defend ideas diametrically opposed to ours.

The word "victory" is to be reclassified. Victory should always mean—without exception—"a best possible balance of the good over evil, of the conscientiousness over the lack of conscientiousness, of the wisdom over the ignorance, of intelligence over stupidity, and so on. The opposite is not victory, but "cheating".

In the New State, society is the extended individual life; the nation is the extended family; the state is the assurance of citizens' rights, obligations, and relating issues regarding the "extended family"—the nation; and the country is the extended private property. Also, the New State is the nation's belief in a government for the people's good—the way it thinks it should be better ruled and managed.

It is not possible to speak of society, nation and state without talking about culture. Culture is the extended individual soul, that is, people's collective sense. The nation owns a culture, but that culture did not rise from nothing. It had to have been carried or forwarded from past generations onto the next generations. One must know how that culture originated, when, where and how it developed. One must appreciate what it represented and what it stands for now. The nation exists only if its culture so does; thus, culture is the cradle of the nation, and should be protected and passed on.

In the New State, the nation is considered to have life only if people are able to dream, love, plan, build relationships with others, have strong feelings, and perpetuate generations. The nation's life is the composite of each individual life which interacts and dreams together of the same goal: Surviving to the eternity. This is the sum of all individual dreams and, consequently, the greatest dream; ultimately, it is the only dream that needs and deserves preservation. The nation's dream is the idea of full common realization, which comprises self-sufficiency and satisfaction of everybody's needs, say, political, social and cultural stability, internal and external security, and the ability to allow generations to continue life.

For Marx, it is not the conscience of man which determines his social being, but rather it is his social being that determines his consciousness. This thought reflects the idea that it is just society that makes man, not otherwise. This postulate is not entirely correct: Both is the life in society that determines the conscience of man and is the man itself, with his multiple form of social intervention, his vices and virtues, who leads the society to adjust to his needs, that is, causing social change, reinventing society in such a way that he can fit. Thus, the man tries to avoid any society's evolutionary trends which seem to be in opposition to the standards he established. If this were not the case, the man would still be in his primitive state, and there would not be human civilization.

Who causes social evolution? Who leads it to the stage of adapting to the man's evolutionary trend? It is not the society that reinvents itself; it is the man, not as a social element but as its agent who reinvents the society. In this perspective, the man has two natures as a social being: First, he is an element or constituent of the society and, two, an agent or monitor of the society. Society, in turn, also acts in two roles before the man: On the one hand, society is the man's "servant" and protector, providing place and meta-human conditions of existence, and on the other hand, it is "interpreter" of the man's actions, "reading" and "writing" the charges of man, derived from its evolutionary process. Thus, society is the complement of the individual life. The former adds new capacities and potentialities to the latter, and provides, if necessary, means to the continuation of life. The man is the agent or monitor of social reality. This means that at any moment man can, if he desires, shape society in its own way to meet his needs. And this is what is required of the individual in the new society: To be able to shape society in a positive way.

But this complementary status between man and society is not an automatic process: It requires commitment from both the man towards society and then returned from society towards the man, and vice versa. However, there are situations in which the charges and trends of the society prevail, leading the man to trigger an enormous effort to find the necessary balance, such as when the man is prevented from exercising his power and influence on a regular basis. As this only involves short breaks in human history, there is always a generation which must decide whether to suffer in order to give the generations that follows happiness and prosperity. In the case of STP, that is the current generation: The entire nation's conquest should be the result of a collective endeavor. Nothing falls from the sky; major achievements—such as independence, development, and prosperity—must be achieved at the expense of huge collective efforts, in the spirit of sacrifice, prudence, determination, cunning, and the like.

An underdeveloped, envied and coveted nation like this one can only reach the stage of development and control of its territory, its resources and trades, if the current generation is able to accept the conditions in which it lives and consent work towards future generations' development. Nothing happens overnight: Living beings are born and need significant time to grow; things need time to rise and come to fruition; patience is a quality so important that it is used by major predators when hunting large prey or those with cunning intelligent.

The idea of emigrating to achieve prosperity in other countries is out of the hypothesis. Therefore, emigration should be considered treason to the homeland, since the problem must be resolved internally, and nothing is gained by citizens running away.

The use of existing resources should be optimized. In a country where there is no bread but there is fertile land and a suitable climate, why not sow the wheat and make the bread with that? In a place where there is no paper but there are forests with enough trees, why not cut trees to make paper? In a country where there are no books but there is enough paper, why not use paper to make books? In a land where there is no money in cash but there are so many resources, workforce, and so on... what does "money" mean after all?

In the New State, humanity should be the central point. It stresses the role of the existing human resources, shaping the human character in order to fit the spirit of ideal citizen and ruler, which focuses on objectivity, transparency, merit, competence, honesty, and accountability. An ideal citizen or ruler should be able to: (1) Recognize the nation as supreme authority; (2) identify the greatest sins and fight them; and (3) be obedient and loyal to the state.

Recognizing the nation as the supreme authority teaches that the nation is the source of inspiration of the state and its constitution. This cannot be disassociated from the fact that neither the state nor the law that governs it is above national unity, which justifies the need to pool all the will in pursuit of national consensus for the resolution of problems. The state is nothing but a legal institution which is representative of the nation and which acts in light of this; the constitution is merely the setup of the state at a given time; therefore, both state and constitution are the nation's subordinates at any one time.

Identifying the major sins and fighting them means, for instance, that one should neither take ownership of the state's belongings nor take advantage of the exercise of public office. A person must be able to recognize his or her own mistakes or any kind of infringement to the state's rules, and take responsibility for them, accepting the appropriate punishment for the sins committed without complaint. Similarly, rather than simply accepting reprimanding, he or she must also cooperate with the state in order to ensure that the punishment is as effective as possible and fully implemented. This person must also be able to denounce any act or behavior that is considered or believed to be immoral, illegal or detrimental to the interests of the nation.

Being loyal and obedient to the state as the legitimate agent of the nation means to be guided by the constitution whilst carrying out the duties or whilst in the exercise of rights, even whilst providing a patriotic voluntary contribution to the nation. A person must be accountable for his or her own actions and those that have been committed in accordance with his or her orders. He or she also must ensure respect for individual and collective responsibilities.

As an agent of social change, the ideal citizen or ruler must be competent. High levels of competence in a person is determined by the ability to carry out, i.e., the ability to perform a task, from start to finish, successfully and on time. As the state feeds off citizens' souls, its competence is measured not only by the sum of powers of its more capable elements, but also by the intersection of individual skills of all of its varying elements. It is crucial that this intersection maximizes the strength and results in the minimization of cancelling forces. The ability to carry out a task depends on several issues: Quality of individual qualifications (education level, specialization and the context), individual intelligence, collective intelligence, individual motivation, social motivation, national motivation, patience, ruse, spirit of sacrifice, perseverance, work, compromise, rigor, and the like. Thus, deciding on delegating functions or political jurisdiction should not play the game of political sympathy, as is often manifested by a misinformed public; it is a matter of administration and management of resources, an economic issue, a social issue, and a matter of citizenship, which should be secured. Thus, the political and administrative division of the country—far from being subject to the whims of the rulers—must be optimized in order to better enable management of the available natural resources and manpower. Rather than the actual short-term ministries, the state's departments should be permanent, optimally designed and stable in order to optimize management and guarantee accumulating experiences, allowing for quick adaptation and improvements, and resulting in the most possible powerful state administration.

Local authorities should also not be short-term, for this promotes irresponsibility, unaccountability, lack of seriousness and volatility; local authorities should therefore be permanent and long-term oriented. Their objectives, goals, and efficiency must be frequently monitored and evaluated, and, rather than being subjected to a simple moral or political punishment, the liable persons must be criminally punished for mistakes, irresponsibility, immorality, and the like, in accordance with the law. Successful achievements, good initiatives, efforts, and the like, should similarly be rewarded.

In the New State, it is the citizens' moral obligation to improve their intellectual, professional, and cultural conditions for the sake of the collective improvement. Studying must be considered to be a moral duty rather than an individual choice; it must be a national obligation; the process of understanding the world. How is it possible to live and prosper in a world we didn't build without ensuring we have a deep and thorough understanding of it? To understand it is to understand its origin, its evolution, and its state of affairs, as well as its future trends and its philosophy. A citizen can afford an equilibrated and productive life in society only if he or she strives to get the most out of studying, researching, and working hard. A state which fails to invest in educational excellence for its people is a state which is in the process of denying opportunity to win the battle of life, and removing from the people the advantage of affording an enjoyable and prosperous life; such a state closes all doors to happiness and perpetuation of people's generations. Moreover, a state which does not have a properly educated population is unable to feed off their souls, because they are unsafe for consumption; therefore, in this condition, a state starves.

Every citizen whose performance causes harm to the nation has the moral obligation to repair his or her faults, paying back his or her debts to the state, either with work or goods, services, money, and so on. For example, a Government official who caused huge losses to the nation should have his bank accounts and properties confiscated; he ought to prove the origins of his properties, money, and the like before the relevant court. If he cannot give plausible justifications, all of his money should revert to the state.

So far, the national despotic regimes have expressed conspiracy against the people's masses, especially towards the poor people and those considered to have a low status in the hierarchy of the society. This fact promotes a permanent cold hate among people rather than pacific coexistence.

The New State is the belief in that the São Toméan people must have the opportunity to remedy their pasts, correct their errors, guarantee their present and plan their future with confidence, determination and courage. It is the understanding that a state is an entity that lacks feelings whilst a nation is an entity full of feelings. A state "feels" with its brain whilst a nation "thinks" with its heart; thus the New State should exploit the nation's feelings and lead this one on to the envisioned goals. The nation must be able to perpetuate life through successive generations. This means winning the fight against the adversities of nature, through the establishment of a powerful society with a high economic and civilization's status. That society must occupy a privileged position amongst other nations. If the nation is unable to comply with these requirements, it will be doomed to a hell of trouble, and will always run the risk of disappearing from the Earth's surface completely. Otherwise, with some understanding, time, passion and commitment, this beautiful people will be a happy nation, and they will have a lot to offer the world.

CONCLUSION

At this point we can breathe a sigh of relief, having confronted reality, filled as it is with beasts of prey. But the beasts still walk free.

There is no description that can be as true to life in this country as the one that combines the idea of spatial and temporal co-existence of hell and heaven. STP is just this: it is a paradise, which can be seen if one looks at its immense wealth, natural beauty, and cultural and historical heritage; however, it is also a hell, when one looks at the social, political and economic degradation, as well as the degradation of the human qualities of the men, women and children who inhabit this place.

Since independence was established in 1975, the country has been governed in the way a flock of sheep would be guided by negligent shepherds—lacking orientation. In such conditions, the sheep graze wherever they want, and the shepherds cannot gather the animals in to an orderly flock. For the flock to graze in an orderly and convenient fashion and in order to ensure that they are protected from wild beasts, furtive hunters and/or thieves, the shepherds must be competent, skilled and experienced. In this view, the competence of a shepherd is related to the fact that he has a correct or accurate understanding of the flock, the grazing fields, imminent dangers, etc.; moreover, it is not enough that shepherds simply have mere ideas in their minds; rather, it is fundamental that they know precisely how to implement those ideas; that is, they ought to know how to apply the knowledge they possess in the correct orientation of the flock, keeping them within their sight, never leaving or allowing them to graze outside of the ideal order.

In short, precision, skill and experience are not only required but fundamental attributes.

Analyzing this people and those who govern them was not an easy process; it was necessary to look at a multitude of factors, namely, history, culture, motivations, aspirations, people's beliefs, and the like. Rulers rule and are driven by a destructive creed which they follow blindly. Amidst all this, there is something that nobody can deny: people are left for grabs and suffer for the sins of their leaders and, in addition to no longer believing that one must change things, they are afraid to act not to suffer reprisals. Public officials feel like landlords: they are so used to failing and not being punished for committing crimes that they never imagine that, one day, they will be expelled from the throne where they rest comfortably on a huge fortune at the expense of the sweat, blood and tears of thousands of people.

For decades several development strategies, plans, and projects have been implemented, but few—or none—have achieved the expected results. Despite their consistency in terms of economic concepts, policies and practices, they did not meet the country's expectations—in part due to the existing lack of supervision and inadequacy to or incompatibility with the existing infrastructure, human resources, and legislation. Most development solutions were based on, proposed and developed by external entities, such as international organizations and foreign governments, through mechanisms of cooperation and development frameworks.

As incredible and ironic as it sounds, the predatory political class who rules this country only survives thanks to the relationships and connections it has with other political forces and foreign governments, including international organizations such as the United Nations, the World Bank, International Monetary Fund, and the African Development Bank. All these institutions say they are friends of the people of STP and that they are willing to help. However, these organizations have followed the way foreign aids have been used in the country: to support networks of corruption and finance the partisan activities of the political class. However, these international organizations and governments have closed their eyes to the allegations of flagrant corruption, and continue to assist with, for example, giving development assistance—even knowing beforehand—that such aid does not arrive within reach of the poor. They do not make any kind of pressure and continue to sign papers to accept as ambassadors and representatives in their national institutions individuals with curricula tainted by corruption, such as former public officials. They could act in a different way, limiting the support they give to the country's political class, thus weakening their network and discouraging acts of corruption. But this is not the case: these entities continue to smile with the political class, getting close to them to take pictures of family, eating with them at the same table—and all at the expense of the misery of a people who at least has been martyred since it became aware of its existence.

From the experience we have obtained from the raid we have carried out thus far, we have learned that if things go wrong today, everything is due to proceed in the way the country is organized as a system, the level of skills it has, the determination with which people seek to realize their dreams, the tools they use to assist them in these tasks, the level of respect for commitments and preservation of trust between partners that they cultivate, the symbols and heroes they worship and the "gods" in which they trust. In order to restore this country and to give it legs to, once again, walk alone toward the goal set, it is necessary to reform the institutions, to re-qualify this people, and to accordingly provide leadership to match national expectations. If a magic recipe for curing the ills affecting this country can be given, then we have no doubt that it would cover essentially the following ingredients:

- Complete removal of the current political class, and the destroying of their bases of support: dismantling their networks of influence, their lobbies, their beliefs, etc.

- Redefining the national identity: deeply reflecting upon what identifies someone as São Toméan.

- Rethinking the ideological system and the system of beliefs of the nation

- Reclassifying the mechanism of ideological "instrumentalization": choosing the right tools to properly achieve the objectives of the nation.

- Rethinking the constitution and the political regime.

- Rethinking institutions and the economic system.

- Reorganizing the country's administration.

- Rethinking the education system and cultural system.

- Rethinking the national defense system

Having learned this, we come to the conclusion that it is necessary to reform the country by implementing what we refer to as the *New State System* (NSS) capable of reversing the course of things. We propose the raising of a New State by claiming the country's rebirth, based on four main pillars: 1) a redefining of the state which will shape the state's personality; 2) a redefining of the state's goals, to determine the state's destination; 3) a determination the structure of the state's apparatus; and 4) a suggestion for the state's performance rule.

The changes to be made must result in a new constitution, new state organs and a public administration capable of reducing expenditure and encouraging efficiency, which will ensure that the available resources are put to the best use, whilst actively fighting economic recession. This proposal is based on the following principles: simplicity & clarity (of the state system, actions and plans), objectivity (of the state system, actions and plans), transparency (of the state system, actions and plans; includes accountability of those involved), continuity (of the state system, actions and plans), efficiency (of the state system, actions and plans; includes reduced costs and conclusiveness of projects), stability (of the state system), and merit (including justice and skills assessment).

Such changes are the best hope for rebuilding a country that has been destroyed by the bad faith of a handful of men and women—members of a sect that only preaches corruption, despotism, and nepotism, crimes mankind commits against itself and against nature.

Acknowledgments

We pay tribute to all those who collaborated in this project—real heroes; the friends of our cause—and express our gratitude for all their help and the confidence they have placed in us, without which our voices would not be audible to the world:

To our editorial team, in particular, Mr. Martin DeMers and Mrs. Andrea Sengstacken, for plucking us from anonymity and making possible the realization of this humanitarian project;

To Ms. Hayley Brierley-Roberts, who has been with us from the completion of the first edition of *Exorcising Devils from the Throne* in 2009, helping to overcome language barriers that would be insurmountable without the assistance of a person as dedicated and competent as she;

To Mr. Geisel de Menezes, a sociologist and an official of the Ministry of Finance of STP, and Mr. James Neves (petroleum engineer from the JDA), who provided us with important references and documentation for the enrichment of this work;

Our thanks are also extended to Dr. Karl Gerhard Seibert, the author of one of our essential reference books, *Comrades, Clients and Cousins, Colonialism, Socialism and Democratization in São Tomé and Príncipe*, who promptly volunteered to read and comment on various aspects and suggested improvements;

Furthermore, we express our thanks to all who responded to the first edition (published personally by the authors), above all Mrs. Maimouna Jallow (BBC correspondent in STP), Dr. Paul Adams (Director of Community Networking, University of Illinois at Urbana-Champaign), participants in the São Tomé Yahoo Groups Forum such as Mr. Abílio Neto (RDP Africa's journalist and commentator), Mr. Xavier Muñoz (geographer), and many more who cannot be mentioned here, for no other reason than lack of space.

Given the contributions of the people to whom we express public gratitude here, this work is no longer the sole intellectual property of the authors; it is a collective heritage belonging to humanity.

CITED WORKS

AbsoluteAstronomy.com. "List of countries by percentage of population living in poverty." AbsoluteAstronomy.com. 2010. http://www.absoluteastronomy.com/topics/List_of_countries_by_percentage_of_population_living_in_poverty (accessed 04 03, 2010).

Africa's Eden. *São Tomé & Príncipe, 2010.* http://www.africas-eden.com/Sao-Tome—Principe.asp (accessed 03 31, 2010).

BBC News. "Oil key to Sao Tome." 07 16, 2003. http://news.bbc.co.uk/2/hi/africa/3070813.stm (accessed 03 30, 2010).

CST (Companhia Santomense de Telecomunicações). "SERVIÇO INTERNET-Dial up e ADSL(Imposto s/ consumo de 5% incluido)." CST(Companhia Santomense de Telecomunicações). 2010. http://www.cstome.net/tarif/default_inter.htm (accessed 04 12, 2010).

Frynas, Jdrzej George, Geoffrey Wood, e Ricardo M. S. Soares de Oliveira. "Business and politics in São Tomé e Príncipe: from cocoa monoculture to petro-state." *African Affairs*, 2003: 51-80.

Index Mundi. *Sao Tome and Principe.* 12 18, 2008. http://www.indexmundi.com/sao_tome_and_principe/ (accessed 04 1, 2010).

IPAD (Instituto Português de Apoio ao Desenvolvimento). "PIC e PAC." 2010. http://www.ipad.mne.gov.pt/index.php?option=com_content&task=view&id=281&Itemid=251 (accessed 04 03, 2010).

Kataria, Anuradha. *Democracy on Trial, All Rise!* New York: Algora Publishing, 2010.

The Obo National Park. *National Parks.* 2010. http://www.obopark.com/en/saotomeprincipe/nationalparks.html (accessed 03 30, 2010).

PNN Portuguese News Network. "Descontentamento na ilha do Príncipe por causa do petróleo." *Jornal de São Tomé e Príncipe.* 11 10, 2003. http://www.jornal.st/noticias.php?noticia=19 (accessed 04 02, 2010).

Seibert, Gerhard. "A Ilha de São Tomé (1961), de Francisco Tenreiro – uma releitura contextualizada." *Revista Economia & Sociologia* (Universidade de Évora), 2008: 69-88.

Seibert, Gerhard. "A política num micro-Estado : São Tomé e Príncipe, ou os conflitos pessoais e políticos na génese dos partidos políticos." *Lusotopie,* 1995: 239-250.

Seibert, Gerhard. "saotome * SÃO TOMÉ E PRÍNCIPE." Yahoo! UK & Ireland Groups. 03 31, 2008. http://uk.groups.yahoo.com/group/saotome/message/20346 (accessed 04 13, 2010).

Seibert, Gerhard. Camaradas, Clientes e Compadres. Colonialismo, Socialismo e Democratização em São Tomé e Príncipe. Vega, Limitada, 2001.

Shaxson, Nicholas. *Poisoned Wells The Dirty Politics of African Oil.* New York: Palgrave Macmillan, 2008.

Sorbara, Mark J. "The United States and Maritime Security in the Gulf of Guinea." *Petroleum Africa,* 2007: 56-58.

United Nations Statistics Division. "Sao Tome and Principe." UNdata. 2010. http://data.un.org/CountryProfile.aspx?crName=Sao%20Tome%20and%20Principe (acedido em 01 de 05 de 2010)

The Washington Post. "Corruption in Nigeria." *The Washington Post,* 01 de 06 de 2005: A.18.

INDEX